*Vilna
on the
Seine*

Vilna on the Seine

Judith Friedlander

JEWISH

INTELLECTUALS

IN FRANCE

SINCE

1968

Yale University Press

New Haven & London

Grateful acknowledgment is made for permission to reprint from the following: Richard Burgin, "Isaac Bashevis Singer Talks . . . about Everything," *New York Times Magazine,* November 26, 1978. Copyright 1978 by Richard Burgin. Reprinted by permission of Curtis Brown; Stuart Charmé, "From Maoism to the Talmud (With Sartre along the Way): An Interview with Benny Lévy," *Commentary,* vol. 78, no. 6, December 1984. Copyright 1984 by *Commentary.* Reprinted by permission of *Commentary;* Alain Garric, "Une Génération de Mao à Moïse," *Libération,* December 22–23, 1984. Copyright 1984 by *Libération.* Reprinted by permission of *Libération;* Benjamin Harshav, *The Meaning of Yiddish.* Copyright 1990 by the Regents of the University of California. Reprinted by permission of the University of California Press; Salomon Malka, *Lire Lévinas.* Copyright 1984 by Editions du Cerf. Reprinted by permission of Editions du Cerf; Thomas Mann, *Doctor Faustus,* trans. H. T. Lowe-Porter. Copyright 1948 by Alfred A. Knopf. Reprinted by permission of Alfred A. Knopf; Richard Marienstras, *Etre un peuple en Diaspora.* Copyright 1975 by Editions Maspéro. Reprinted by permission of Richard Marienstras; François Poirié, *Emmanuel Lévinas: Qui êtes-vous?* Copyright 1987 by La Manufacture. Reprinted by permission of La Manufacture; Philippe Ganier Raymond, "L'Express Document," October 28–November 4, 1978. Copyright 1978 by L'Express. Reprinted by permission of The New York Times Syndication Sales; Edward W. Said, "Representing the Colonized: Anthropology's Interlocuters," *Critical Inquiry,* vol. 15 (Winter 1989). Copyright 1984 by University of Chicago Press. Reprinted by permission of University of Chicago Press; E. Amado Lévy-Valensi and Jean Halpérin, eds., *La Conscience juive, données et débats.* Copyright 1963 by Presses Universitaires de France. Reprinted by permission of Presses Universitaires de France.

Designed by James J. Johnson. Set in Galliard type by The Composing Room of Michigan, Inc. Printed in the United States of America by BookCrafters, Inc., Chelsea, Michigan.

Library of Congress Cataloging-in-Publication Data

Friedlander, Judith, 1944–
  Vilna on the Seine : Jewish intellectuals in France since 1968 / Judith Friedlander.
    p. cm.
  Includes bibliographical references (p.).
  ISBN 0–300–04703–7 (alk. paper)
    1. Jews—France—Intellectual life.   2. Intellectuals—France.   3. France—Intellectual life.   4. Jewish learning and scholarship—France.   5. France—Civilization—Jewish influences.   6. Judaism—Europe, Eastern influence.   I. Title.
DS135.F83F75   1990
944'.004924—dc20
                                                                                  90–31502
                                                                                  CIP

The paper in this book meets the guidelines for permanence and durability of the Committee on Production Guidelines for Book Longevity of the Council on Library Resources.

10   9   8   7   6   5   4   3   2   1

For My Mother,
Silvia B. Paulson
Scholar, Teacher,
Lover of Life

Contents

A Note on Citations and Orthography

Most of the works cited in this book were written in French. Unless I indicate otherwise, I quote from the original, making my own translation. If the passage in question has already been translated into English, I provide a full reference, giving the page number in the American edition. When I paraphrase the ideas of a particular author, I note only the pages from the French, but do indicate if the work has been translated into English. In the case of books written in German, Russian, Yiddish, and Hebrew, I rely on the English translations alone.

When it comes to the spelling of non-English words, I have made the following compromises:

1. For Yiddish, I follow the conventions set out by the YIVO Institute for Jewish Research, except when the word in question has already entered the English language in another form.

2. For Hebrew, I follow the spellings used by the *Encyclopaedia Judaica*, except when the word has entered the English language in another form. This means that I have accepted the Sephardic pronunciation, in almost every case, instead of the Ashkenazic one used by the Jews of Vilna. While I would have preferred to maintain the Hebrew of Eastern Europe, to do so would have made recognizable words and concepts unnecessarily exotic.

3. For French, I leave the spellings of words in French, with no explanation if the form resembles the English. When I refer to a French institution that has a Hebrew or Yiddish name, I preserve the French rendition of the name. La Yéchiva des Etudiants, for example, remains *Yéchiva* and not *Yeshiva,* as we spell it in English. When I am not using the proper name, however, I do refer to this school as the yeshiva, using the English spelling.

A Note on Place Names in Eastern Europe

During the eighteenth, nineteenth, and twentieth centuries, the boundaries dividing Russia and its European neighbors shifted several times and may shift again in the 1990s as the Baltic republics of the USSR demand their independence. Depending on the period, Vilna, for example, was Russian, Polish, or part of the Union of Soviet Socialist Republics. And the name of the city changed accordingly: Vilna in Russian, Wilno in Polish, and Vilnius in Lithuanian. I use the Russian form in the text because the people I interviewed identified with the Russian Vilna. On the maps, however, I use the contemporary Lithuanian name of the city. I do the same with the other towns and cities, calling them by the names commonly used by Jews at the turn of the century, but identifying them on the maps with their present-day names: in Lithuanian, Byelorussian, Russian, or Polish. While in some cases place names have remained the same, they usually have changed, at least by a vowel:

Name in Text	*Name on Map*
Dvinsk	Daugavipils
Kovno	Kaunas
Libau	Liepaja
Mariampol	Mariajampole
Memel	Klaipeda
Ponevezh	Panevezys
Pren	Prienlai
Radin	Radun
St. Petersburg	Leningrad
Shavli	Šiauliai
Subocz	Subačius
Tarnopol	Ternopol
Vilna	Vilnius
Žetl	Zdzieciol

Acknowledgments

I began doing research for *Vilna on the Seine* in the late 1970s and have received help from many people and institutions over the years, in the United States, France, Switzerland, England, Germany, and the Soviet Socialist Republic of Lithuania. While I wish I could thank everybody at length, describing the role each person has played, I must ask my family, friends, and colleagues to accept this short, but heartfelt expression of gratitude. The names included in the lists below all gave me invaluable advice and encouragement as I worked my way through the various stages of the project. I regret to add that some of these people have since passed away.

In the United States I wish to thank Dina Abramowicz, Lisa Adler, Roberta Barkan, Joel Beck, Marshall Berman, Jonathan Boyarin, Bell Chevigny and the other members of our study group, Lucy Dawidowicz, Walter Einhorn, Stuart Fiedel, Nancy Foner, Stanley Freed, Paul Friedrich, Charles Grench, Benjamin Harshav, Naomi Holoch, Barbara Kirschenblatt-Gimblett, Hadassa Kosak, Myra Jehlen, Claudia Koonz, Stacey Mandelbaum, Marysa Navarro, Silvia Paulson, Catharine Stimpson, Peter Swerdloff, Gaye Tuchman, Rabbi Mordecai Waxman, Ruth Waxman, Elizabeth Wood, and Marilyn Young. I also acknowledge the National Endowment for the Humanities, the State University of New York Research Foundation, and the Wenner-Gren Foundation for Anthropological Research for their willingness to fund the research, and SUNY, College at Purchase, and the YIVO Institute for Jewish Research for their academic support.

Let me express my deep appreciation for the continuing help I received in France from Françoise Basch, Rachel Ertel, Elisabeth de Fontenay, Nancy Green, Olga Katunal, Mordecai Litvine, Marie-Claire Pasquier, and Luc Rosenzweig. I thank as well Rav Eliahou Abitbol, Marianne Basch, Jean Baumgarten, Martine Cohen, Monique-Lise Cohen, Alexandre Derczansky, Alain Finkielkraut, Aaron Fraenckel, Françoise Gail, Rachel Gordin, Joseph Gottfarstein, Sam Gottfarstein, Francis Gribe, Sonia Grinberg, Jacques Hassoun, Alain Kleinmann, Dvorah Kosman, Emmanuel Lévinas, Rav Alain and Claudine Lévy, Benny Lévy, Yvonne Lévyne, Richard and Elise Marienstras, Henri Minczeles, Itzhok Niborski, Rabbi Marc-Alain Ouaknin, Emmanuel Pasquier, Françoise Pasquier, Jean Pasquier, Julian Pitt-Rivers, Laurence Podselver, Freddy Raphaël, Dominque Schnapper, Adolphe and Gilberte Steg, Jacques Tarnero, Shmuel Trigano, Kiwa Vaïsbrot, Jean-Jacques Wahl, André Wormser, and Jean Zacklad. I also acknowledge the following institutions: La Bibliothèque Medem, l'Ecole des Hautes Etudes en Sciences Sociales, and l'Alliance Israélite Universelle.

In Switzerland, I thank Jean Halpérin; in England, Simon Guttmann, Nicholas Jacobs, Kate Young, and Helen Warby; in Germany, Claus-David Luschnat, Gudrun Schwarz, Jacob Taubes, Annemarie Tröger, and Manfred Voigts; in Lithuania, Dalia Epsteinayte, Grigori Kanowitsch, Jonas Mardosa, and Lyuta Zhabinskaya.

Finally, despite my resolve to thank people collectively, I must make one exception. For if anybody inspired me to write this book, it was Catherine Lévy Lawton, whom I have known since the late 1940s, when I was four and she was in her midtwenties. We met soon after she arrived in the United States, where she had come to work as a simultaneous interpreter at the United Nations (U.N.). Perhaps by chance, perhaps by Divine intervention, this young French woman of Alsatian and Swiss Jewish origins ended up living with my family for a little more than a year, during which time she and my parents had the mutual shock of discovering how differently they identified with their Jewish heritage.

In the late 1940s the newly created U.N. set up offices in Lake Success, a suburb of New York, while it waited to move to its permanent headquarters in Manhattan. Lake Success was only a small community at the time and did not have the facilities to house the organization's large staff. Given the problem, the U.N. advertised locally, asking residents in the area to open their homes. My mother responded, and Catherine Lévy came to us in Great Neck, to a family of left-wing Jewish intellectuals who still observed some of the traditions of practicing Jews. While my mother and father had a great deal in common with Catherine Lévy, they, unlike her, had maintained religious ties to Judaism, to rituals inherited from their immigrant parents whose families had fled czarist Russia in the 1880s and settled in New York.

Catherine Lévy soon married and returned to Europe, where she continued working at the U.N. for many years. We never lost touch, however, and she went on to play a major role in my life, introducing me to French culture when I was a teenager and to the multitude of historical circumstances that separate assimilated French Jews from their counterparts in the United States.

Introduction

When anthropologists do research in urban settings, they usually choose to study the poor, recent immigrants, for example, or members of
other ethnic minorities who inhabit the edges of
society. I have decided to work with the privileged, highly educated people who participate in
a culture where scholarly achievements are val-
ued. Literary critics, writers, and philosophers,
some of the people I interviewed for this book
have international reputations. Famous or not,
they have all taken part in the major intellectual
and political movements of their time. Many of
them have also endured racial persecution and
tragic personal losses.

Vilna on the Seine tells the story of a group of
Jews who live in contemporary France. While
some of them were born there, most came originally from Eastern Europe, North Africa, and the
Middle East. Raised in different places, they also
belong to different generations.

The older members of the group were born
in czarist Russia at the turn of the century. Growing up in enlightened middle-class homes, they
were schooled in both Jewish and European traditions. After World War I and the Bolshevik Rev-

*Exile, immigration, and the
crossing of boundaries are
experiences that can . . .
provide us with new
narrative forms.*
—EDWARD SAID

I

olution, they went to university in Germany and France to study philosophy and literature in some of the most outstanding institutions of higher learning in Europe. But when Hitler came to power in 1933, those living in Germany quickly fled the country and joined their compatriots who had moved to France. Recognizing the dangers that lay ahead, these Jewish immigrants of Eastern European origin responded politically, and all risked their lives to fight National Socialism, joining the French army and participating in the Resistance.

Among the younger members of the group, many came of age in the shadow of the Shoah, their childhood years filled with a longing for relatives who would never return. Others suffered less, as they grew up on the southern shores of the Mediterannean Sea. Their families, too, lived through difficult times, but the problems they faced rarely compared to the misfortunes of Jews caught in Europe during the Second World War.

Despite differences in age, education and historical experiences, the people described in this book have much in common. They are all intellectuals who have chosen to work on matters concerned with being Jewish in the modern world. Writers and scholars, they identify themselves as diaspora Jews, a choice some of them made after seeing themselves first as universal men marked by neither ethnic nor gender specifity. They now take an interest in the heritage of their people and in the many traditions that separate Jews from their Gentile neighbors.

When they decided to dedicate themselves to Jewish scholarship and letters, those in the older generation had vast resources to draw on. But those in the younger generation did not. Looking for help, the young turned to the works of historians and philosophers of Eastern European origin, to books written by people raised in a time and a place very different from their own. And as they read about a world they knew little about, these younger Jews, who identified with the generation of 1968, stumbled upon cultural and political models that suggested new ways for them to live as Jews in present-day France. More often than not, the ideas that inspired them emanated from the Lithuanian city of Vilna (Vilnius), previously one of the greatest centers of Jewish culture in the world.

But why should Jewish intellectuals in contemporary France turn to Eastern Europe and back to the past to find answers for themselves from a Jewish community that no longer exists? One reason, clearly, has to do with the Shoah, with the obligations many feel to preserve the culture of Eastern European Jews, the main victims of the Final Solution. In France, the fate of these people remains newsworthy and the subject of heated debates. Still burdened with the shame of Vichy's collaboration during the Second World War, the French have recently been forced to defend the memory of the millions murdered in death camps, from claims made in France by revisionist historians that gas chambers never existed. They have also had to protect the living from new acts of violence directed against Jews.

Still, the Shoah alone cannot fully explain why intellectuals in France have expressed a particular interest in Vilna and Lithuanian Jewry. We must acknowledge as well the influence of a handful of scholars who have used the ideas of Lithuanian thinkers in debates going on in contemporary France. Some of these people are themselves from Lithuania, among them the eminent philosopher Emmanuel Lévinas.

Born in Kovno (Kaunas), the sister-city of Vilna, Lévinas writes about ethical questions confronting Jews in the Diaspora, frequently building his arguments out of the teachings of both European philosophy and Jewish thought. In recent years, former radicals of the generation of 1968 have begun reading Lévinas with devotion, finding ways through his work to move beyond the limitations of their earlier political assumptions and into a world of ideas open only to those familiar with Europe's philosophical heritage and the analytic tradition associated with Lithuania's Talmudic scholars.

Lévinas and others of Lithuanian origin have introduced the French public to a style of learning developed by the legendary Gaon of Vilna in the late eighteenth century and passed down for generations by rabbis trained rigorously in the scholarly tradition established by this brilliant Talmudist. Still others have presented the French with programs created by secular Jews from Vilna who dedicated their lives to building a national culture for Jews in the Diaspora. Recognizing the way Jews with ties to Lithuania have influenced the thinking of intellectuals in France, I trace the life histories of several individuals, all of whom were born at the turn of the century and describe the circumstances that led them to play important roles in the intellectual development of members of the generation of 1968. In doing so, however, I do not mean to imply that there exists today on the shores of the Seine a thriving community of Lithuanian Jews. Vilna-in-Paris is a cultural symbol, not a part of town, an evocation of a place where Jewish traditions once flourished in more than one language and in a variety of secular and religious forms.

I have organized *Vilna on the Seine* around issues concerning Jews of the generation of 1968 who have recently returned to Judaism in several different ways. The life histories I present of members of the older generation are personal links to the world that has influenced the young. Educated in both the Jewish and European traditions, these intellectuals of Eastern European origin tower above those identified with 1968 both in learning and experience, providing models that inspire and humble.

In anthropology today, many have expressed concern about the ethnographer's voice. Who do we think we represent? With what authority do we describe the cultures of others? I myself struggled with the issue while doing research in a Mexican Indian village[1] and decided to try to resolve the problem by working next with people I could call my own—A naive notion I quickly rejected as I began my new project.

I do not presume to speak for the people I have written about, as if I were one of them. The story I tell is clearly my own, not in the autobiographical sense, but in the conceptual. I have chosen the plot, presented the characters, and put the narrative together for my own purposes, among them, to look for new ways to describe and understand the transmission of culture by people who have chosen to remain in exile.

Still, I have tried to be faithful to the individuals who appear on these pages, basing my account on observations they kindly shared with me and on information published by or about them. Many of these people have written extensively about Jewish philosophy, history, and letters. Some have given interviews to others. What follows, then, is my version of their lives and their intellectual and political contributions, which I have woven together out of material I have read and conversations I have had, with them or with members of their families.

1

Vilna on the Seine: The Setting

For Jews who knew Vilna before the Second World War, the city's name evokes images of Talmud and revolution, of rigid orthodoxy and cosmopolitanism. Some elevate it to sacred heights, calling it "the Jerusalem of Lithuania." Others poke fun at it. But everyone agrees that Vilna played a critical role in the history of Eastern European Jewry. By the eighteenth century the ancient capital of Lithuania had become a major center of Jewish learning in the world, celebrated for its scholars rigorously trained in Talmudic thinking and religious law. In the late nineteenth century Jewish activists contributed further to Vilna's fame by founding secular movements there to bring about cultural and political change.

Today, the Jerusalem of Lithuania no longer exists, but its memory lives on, particularly in the West, where the city's past takes on mythic proportions. In Paris, Jewish Vilna seems to be everywhere: in the cinema and theater; in books and journals; and in the ways the young have recently chosen to return to Judaism, to make a *teshuvah*. Inspired by symbolic, not historical, truth, Vilna (on the Seine) reaches beyond the walls of the Jerusalem of Lithuania. It gathers together the

Once a Jewish man went to Vilna and he came back and said to his friend, "The Jews of Vilna are a remarkable people. I saw a Jew who studies all day long the Talmud. I saw a Jew who all day long was scheming how to get rich. I saw a Jew who's all the time waving the red flag calling for revolution. I saw a Jew who was running after every woman. I saw a Jew who was an ascetic and avoided women." The other man said, "I don't know why you're so astonished. Vilna is a big city, and there are many Jews, all types." "No," said the first man, "it was all the same Jew."

—I. B. SINGER

old Jewish communities that once stood along the Rivers Neris and Neman and across Lithuania's thick forests, embracing an area, known as "Lite" in Yiddish (pronounced *Leetah*), presently found in the Soviet Republics of Lithuania, Byelorussia, parts of Latvia, and Russia (see maps 1, 2, and 3). Those living in the region spoke their own dialect of Yiddish, had special culinary customs, and studied Talmud in a style that distinguished them from Jews who had settled in other parts of Eastern Europe.[1]

The ideas and traditions of the Jews from old Lite have shaped the lives of the most unlikely people in present-day France. More Sephardim from Morocco than Ashkenazim from Byelorussia have joined the Lubavitcher Ḥasidim, a group of Jewish mystics who originated in Lite.[2] Many other French Jews oppose the sect, identifying instead with the Gaon of Vilna, the great Talmudic scholar of eighteenth-century Lithuania who denounced the Ḥasidim as heretics. These new followers of the Gaon study Bible together in French yeshivas modeled on the legendary institutions that dominated the cultural life of Vilna and the surrounding towns. And that is not all. In academic circles we find people of learning comparing French Enlightenment thought to the teachings of rabbis from eighteenth- and nineteenth-century Lithuania, while still others use works by Jewish nationalists from Lite to help them develop autonomous cultures for Jews in the Diaspora today.

For the most part, the people described here are French intellectuals of the generation of 1968. Young faculty members and students in the late 1960s, they participated in the struggle to decentralize the university system. They went on to challenge the ideal of a single French culture and to call for the national rights of ethnic minorities living in France. In the process, they embraced a cause with political roots going back to Lite: As they looked for ways to mobilize minorities in the country today, many studied the strategies proposed by members of the Jewish Bund, a socialist party of secular Jews founded in Vilna in 1897.

Since then, many have broken away from national expressions of their Jewish identity. Following the teachings of the Lithuanian-born philosopher Emmanuel Lévinas, they now find their heritage in the sacred books instead. Today we find Jews of the generation of 1968 reading Lévinas with dedication, discovering through his work the Talmudic tradition of rabbis from Vilna and the neighboring towns.

While ties to Lite seem to be everywhere, studies of Jews in contemporary France speak rarely, if at all, about Lithuanian Jewry. They focus instead on North African Jews and the impact they have had on the old French

MAP I. The Western Part of the Russian Empire on the Eve of World War I.
Drawn by Stuart Fiedel.

• • • • • • Western boundary of Russian Empire in 1914
———— Boundaries of Eastern Europe since 1945

MAP 2. Poland between the Two Wars. Drawn by Stuart Fiedel after map no. 7 in Rachel Ertel, *Le Shtetl* (Paris: Payot, 1982).

MAP 3. Cities and Towns of Western Russian (Political Boundaries of the Late 1980s). Drawn by Stuart Fiedel.

community. When Morocco and Tunisia became independent in 1956 and Algeria in 1962, Jews living in the newly freed protectorates and colonies abandoned their homes by the hundreds of thousands, moving, for the most part, to Israel or *la métropole*. Today, North African Jews represent more than half the Jewish population in France.[3]

The literature also suggests that the Six-Day War in Israel in 1967 led to changes in the French Jewish community, inspiring assimilated Jews to speak out more boldly than they had done before in defense of the Jewish state. It mentions as well the student revolt of May 1968, which provoked ideological crises on the left and the rise of minority nationalism. But it does so summarily, inviting superficial comparisons between activists in France and similar groups in the United States. Few people have traced the unique itineraries of French Jewish radicals as they have made their way back to Judaism, taking several different paths, most of which go through Lite.[4]

In the late 1960s, student activists challenged the assumption, held by many on the left, that conflicts of class interest adequately explained all cases of exploitation in democratic nation-states. They now gave examples of ethnic discrimination, of national minorities whose members were forced, regardless of class, to relinquish their cultural autonomy. Marxist theorists, they claimed, paid too little attention to the restrictions imposed on minority peoples since the late eighteenth century, when the French Revolution endorsed legislation that protected the rights of abstract individuals and sacrificed those maintaining the collective integrity of distinct ethnic groups.

Jean-Paul Sartre had already recognized the difficulties faced by minorities who lived in democratic nation-states, but he continued to favor this political system over any other. In his postwar essay *Réflexions sur la question juive* (*Anti-Semite and Jew*), he described how the democrat defended mankind stripped of all specificity and did not, therefore, protect the Jew as Jew or the black as black.[5] Still, Sartre argued, the democrat was the minority person's best friend: he gave everyone the opportunity to be just like everybody else.

Many young leftists, Jewish or not, disagreed with Sartre's formulation. For them, democracy and cultural pluralism should not be seen as conflicting principles. On the contrary, they believed that in the name of freedom the state should support and encourage ethnic groups to cultivate their own languages and traditions. Coming up with the slogan "le droit à la différence" (the right to be different), they called on the French government to find the necessary funds to help ethnic groups maintain and develop the cultures of their people.

Practicing Jews had a unique way of life that set them apart. They truly had something to preserve. But Jewish students identifying with May 1968 had little they could call their own. In spite of themselves they fit the description Sartre had made in his controversial portrait. According to the philosopher, Jews were Jews, because non-Jews had called them Jews. They embraced no single culture. No national history or set of traditions united them. Thus, once anti-Semites stopped pointing the finger, Jews would quickly fade into the wider society.

Unwilling to accept Sartre's conclusions, many secular Jews found ways to express their ethnicity through forms of nationalism. Some became Zionists and involved themselves in struggles taking place in a foreign land. Others tried to create an autonomous Jewish culture in contemporary France.

According to the typology proposed by Dominique Schnapper in 1980, the Jews described here belong to her category of young "militants," most of whom come from middle-class, assimilated families and identify with the left.[6] Today, these people are no longer so young or so militant. We find them in important positions in the French university system, at the Centre National de la Recherche Scientifique (CNRS), as well as in the media and publishing houses. Marginal at the time Schnapper was writing her book, many of these intellectual Jews now influence the direction of the larger Jewish community in France, a community dominated by three main groups:[7]

> 1. *The Israélites*: Ashkenazim and Sephardim, the majority of whom come from families of assimilated Jews who have lived in France for generations. They belong to the French bourgeoisie, support the major Jewish organizations like the Conseil Représentatif des Institutions Juives de France (CRIF) and the Fonds Social Juif Unifié (FSJU), and give money regularly to Israel. Many, but by no means all, attend "liberal" (reform) synagogues, or the more observant French houses of prayer sponsored by the *consistoire*, the rabbinic assembly established by Napoleon. The Israélites also promote Jewish education in the universalistic tradition—in France and abroad—through programs sponsored by the Alliance Israélite Universelle.
>
> 2. *The Orthodox*: Mostly North African immigrants, but also a small group of Eastern European Jews who survived the Second World War. They tend to be members of the petite bourgeoisie, to

live together in the "Jewish" quarters of Paris—the Marais and Belleville—and to belong to nonconsistorial synagogues where the services reflect the traditions of home.

3. *The Yiddishists*: A group of Jewish immigrants from Eastern Europe who continue to cherish secular Yiddish culture. Like the Orthodox, they too tend to be members of the petite bourgeoisie. Frequently the Yiddishists, together with some Eastern European Orthodox Jews, belong to *landsmanschaftn,* social groups, the members of which all came from the same town or city in Eastern Europe. Many also sponsor educational and cultural programs to promote Yiddish.

We should not exaggerate the role of members of the generation of 1968 and give the impression that they have taken over all programs sponsored by the Israélites, the Orthodox, and the Yiddishists. But we should not minimize their influence either in revitalizing the three groups. Seeking ways to enrich the lives of Jews in France, these new activists have assumed many responsibilities within the community and in the process have sometimes introduced, sometimes reenforced, the ideas and traditions of Eastern European Jews, most notably those developed in Vilna and surrounding towns.

As we look more closely, we find a generational split within the group. Those who were young professors at the time of the famous upheaval became leaders, for the most part, of secular Jewish movements in France. Those who were then in the lycée, or beginning students in the university, followed their professors in the early years, but many went on to seek inspiration from their religious heritage. Some have become Orthodox Jews, others merely students of sacred texts.

Many activists of the generation of 1968 initiated their return to Judaism by studying the history of nation-state formation in Western Europe. They concluded that a country like France prevented diverse cultures from flourishing side by side. Nation-states, they claimed, imposed a single dominant tradition on all peoples living under the same jurisdiction. Critical of the policy, they looked for models to replace the ideal of one nation, one state, and discovered the theoretical writings of minority nationalists and socialist Zionists, of individuals who spoke for movements that took root in Vilna at the turn of the century. As the founding city of the Bund, Vilna was also one of the earliest centers of the newly emerging Po'alei Zion (Workers of Zion). Both groups had large followings in Eastern Europe until the Second World War.

Although many would eventually reject secular movements as the way to express themselves as Jews, the issues raised by socialist Zionists and minority nationalists continue to play critical roles in the debates presently going on in France.

ZIONISM

After the Six-Day War in 1967, the French Jewish community saw a significant rise in the number of young people emigrating to Israel.[8] Even for many of those who remained in France, the eruption of violence in the Middle East awakened a fierce sense of loyalty to the Jewish state. To work for Israel became a way of affirming their ethnic and national identity. But as the crisis deepened in the 1970s, many Jewish intellectuals with ties to the left had difficulty endorsing decisions made in the name of defending Israel's right to annex the West Bank and the Gaza Strip. They refused to join mainstream Zionist organizations and embrace policies they considered to be acts of aggression, but they vigorously opposed the Palestinian Liberation Organization (PLO), too, defying Arab threats to destroy the Jewish state. Caught in the middle, they tried to serve as intermediaries.

A handful of artists and intellectuals had begun to seek ways to do something as early as 1967. Their numbers, however, increased in the 1970s when socialist Zionists started sending representatives to the Middle East on a regular basis to meet with like-minded Israelis and Palestinians. By this time a few individuals had also stepped forward to test their skills as unofficial diplomats.

In his book *Le Fou et les rois,* the painter and writer Marek Halter describes his attempts to negotiate a peace settlement. With cultivated naïveté, he presents his credentials in an autobiographical sketch: his early childhood days in Warsaw in the mid-1930s, just before the outbreak of World War II; his family's escape from Poland to the Soviet Union, where the young Marek meets Stalin; and his parents' postwar decision to move to France. While Halter records extraordinary interviews with Jews and Arabs, he acknowledges with sadness his inability to change the course of history.[9]

Later on, Halter joined others in the generation of 1968 in addressing the problems of diaspora Jewry and questions of cultural memory. By 1983 he had published his internationally acclaimed novel *La Mémoire d'Abraham,* which follows the experiences of one Jewish family over two thousand years of diaspora history.[10] Then, in 1986 he joined those who were making a religious return by organizing a highly publicized month of events concerned with "Judaisms," which, in the end, provoked a great deal of controversy.[11]

As the Israeli-Palestinian conflict continued to escalate in the late 1970s, Jews in France became targets of terrorist aggression. Between 1979 and 1982, bombs killed and wounded innocent people with alarming frequency. In some cases, Palestinian groups were responsible for the attacks; in others, French neofascists. During the same period, Robert Faurisson, a literature professor at the University of Lyon, claimed he had evidence that gas chambers never existed.[12]

For many in the generation of 1968, it was this wave of violence, both physical and ideological, that pushed them to consider the problems of Jews in the Diaspora. And as they focused their attention on the situation back home, they began to look at themselves, wondering why they claimed they were Jewish when they identified so little with their traditions. To correct this embarrassment, some joined groups seeking ways to establish national and secular Jewish cultures in France, whereas others turned to religion.

MINORITY NATIONALISM IN FRANCE

Jews interested in questions of minority nationalism had begun forming circles in the late 1960s to study the experiences of ethnic groups in France and compare them to those of communities living in states where cultural diversity existed. Determined to replace the historical French model of "one nation (culture) within one state," they made alliances with the Bretons, Occitans, and other ethnic groups in the country and eventually found ways to influence government policy. In the 1980s, the French Socialists actually adopted aspects of their program for the new party platform on minority cultures.

In 1967 Richard Marienstras founded Le Cercle Gaston Crémieux. Shakespearean scholar and professor of English literature at the University of Paris, he was one of the first to analyze closely the contradictions imposed on assimilated Jews in France.[13] With a group of one hundred and fifty professors and students, Marienstras studied Jewish history from the perspective of Simon Dubnow, the great Russian apologist for diaspora Jewry, and looked for ways to develop a secular Jewish culture in France. Influenced as well by the Bundists, Marienstras envisioned a national Jewish tradition tied neither to the synagogue nor to the state of Israel. Committed to the development of Jewish cultures in the Diaspora, Le Cercle Gaston Crémieux encouraged Jews to seek ethnic autonomy in a joint political effort with other minorities.

While the Cercle recognized the importance of the state of Israel in the life of contemporary Jewry, it challenged those who would make Zionism the central ideology of Jews living in the Diaspora. Deeply opposed to cultural uniformity and to the expansionist policies of all nation-states, the Cercle often criticized Israel and opposed the willingness of the French Jewish establishment to support virtually every decision made by the Jewish state. The Cercle similarly opposed traditional Judaism, insisting on the importance of the cultural and political lives of Jews outside the religion. To promote a secular Jewish culture in France, the Cercle organized study groups in Jewish history, classes in Yiddish and Jewish cooking, and work-shops to discuss what it meant to be a Jew in the Diaspora today. Most importantly, the Cercle sponsored major events to introduce France to the accomplishments of secular Jewish cultures outside Israel. Although its programs reflected only the contributions of Yiddish-speaking Jews from Eastern Europe, the group endorsed efforts that promoted Ladino, Judeo-Arabic, and even Hebrew cultures in the Diaspora. Identifying neither with the state of Israel nor with institutionalized Judaism, the Cercle wanted to create living Jewish cultures in France that went beyond Israeli nationalism and Western Europe "cultism"—beyond the politics of such influential organizations as the CRIF and the kind of Judaism promoted by the French consistoire.[14]

Given their outspoken positions on Israel and the synagogue, the Cercle never received much support from mainstream organizations in the French Jewish community. Still, members of the group have played an important role in setting the terms of the debate about minority cultures in the country today. Thanks to the Cercle, everybody knows the contemporary French rendition of the Bundist ideal of minority nationalism: "le droit à la différence." Furthermore, even though the group stopped meeting for several years in the mid-1980s, former members of the Cercle continued to generate a great deal of interest in the history and literature of Eastern European Jewry before the Second World War. The number of books, films, cultural events, and university courses on the subject produced by people who participated in the Cercle is impressive, the reception by Jews and Gentiles enthusiastic.

For the most part, older members of the Cercle came from Jewish families of Polish and Lithuanian origin. Richard Marienstras, for example, was born in Warsaw in 1928, into an assimilated middle-class family.[15] When he was three, he and his mother moved to France. His father, an agronomist, stayed behind and died in the Warsaw Ghetto. As a boy, Marienstras never learned Yiddish. He spoke Polish at home with his mother and French with his friends at school.

Many criticize Marienstras for taking a strong stand against Israeli policies in the Middle East. But few realize that the founder of Le Cercle Gaston Crémieux has taken up arms to defend the rights of Jews to live in Europe and in a state of their own. During the German occupation, he was only a teenager hiding out with his mother in the southeast of France, but he was still old enough to join local Resistance efforts in the Department of Drôme (see maps 4 and 5). After the war, he took a job with the American Joint Organization, first as a delivery boy, then as a caseworker in charge of securing South American visas for displaced persons—that is, until doors began closing, at which time he developed new strategies and found places for Jews on boats bound illegally for Palestine. In 1948, the young activist defied the British himself and ran the blockade in order to fight in the Israeli army.

Remaining firmly committed to Jewish causes, Marienstras became editor of *Kadimah,* the journal of the Union d'Etudiants Juifs, in the early 1950s. At the time, this organization of Jewish students attracted members representing a wide range of political persuasions: Communists, Zionists—on the right and the left—and budding minority nationalists like himself. During those years, he also taught English at the Ecole Maïmonide, a Jewish lycée that produced a number of graduates who have gone on to play leading roles in the revival of Judaism taking place in France today.

Like other teachers of his generation, Marienstras had the option of going to North Africa to work in a French-language lycée as a way of fulfilling his military obligations. In his case, he was sent to Tunisia in the late 1950s, right in the middle of the Algerian War. The experience marked him dramatically, making him even more critical than he had already been of the hegemony of French culture. A married man by this time, his wife, Elise, went with him, sharing his experiences and sense of outrage. She too was the child of Polish Jewish immigrants and went on to assume major responsibilities in Le Cercle Gaston Crémieux. Today a professor of American culture and civilization, Elise Marienstras has written extensively on the struggles of Native Americans in the United States.[16]

By the time Marienstras founded Le Cercle Gaston Crémieux and developed a platform for cultural autonomy in France, he had been teaching at the University of Paris for several years and already had an enthusiastic following. A forceful speaker, he had both the brilliance and charisma necessary to influence student radicals eager to abandon the organized left and seek political and cultural fulfillment as secular Jewish activists. Before long,

MAP 4. Modern France. Drawn by Stuart Fiedel.

Names in upper case = Departments.
Names in lower case = cities and towns.
Alsace = the Departments of Haut-Rhin and Bas-Rhin.
Bretagne = the Departments of Finistère, Côtes-du-Nord,
Morbihan, and Ille-et-Vilaine.
Languedoc = the Departments of Haute-Garronne, Aude,
Tarn, Hérault, Gard, Ardèche, Lozère, and
Haute-Loire.

MAP 5. France during the German Occupation. Drawn by Stuart Fiedel.

however, some of his young followers rejected minority nationalism as well and sought answers for themselves in the sacred books instead.

THE RETURN TO JUDAISM AND RELIGIOUS TEXTS

By the mid-1970s, younger members of the generation of 1968 had begun questioning whether national definitions of Jews in the Diaspora had meaning for their lives today. Many of those who had been students during the university revolt shared a similar political history. First they joined the extreme left, dividing themselves essentially between the Trotskyists and the Maoists. As the left became increasingly critical of Israel and, so it seemed, of all Jewish people, many quit their parties and continued to struggle as minority nationalists, becoming members of groups like Le Cercle Gaston Crémieux. But unlike Marienstras and his contemporaries, most of these students could not respond to the ideals of the Yiddishists. While they wanted to know more about the history of Eastern European Jews, they could not see reviving or creating a secular Jewish culture in France. The lost world of Polish and Russian Jews was a haunting nightmare, not a dream for the future. In his book, *Le Juif imaginaire,* Alain Finkielkraut, a prominent spokesman for this younger group, stated the problem this way: "The need for roots is the *mal* of the last quarter of this century. But how can I possibly plant myself in pre-war Galicia or Warsaw? All I know in Polish and Yiddish are a few swear words, a few affectionate expressions, two or three little sayings. This world, assasinated, concerns and haunts me. . . . [Yet] I do not look for myself there, but for who I am not and and can no longer be."[17]

Finkielkraut's target was not Le Cercle Gaston Crémieux—in fact he praised Richard Marienstras in a footnote—but the emptiness today of his own secular Polish Jewish heritage. He could not identify with a way of life that had been monstrously destroyed before he was born. Finkielkraut had not suffered personally during the war, and he had little experience with Jewish secular or religious traditions from Poland or anywhere else. When he used to evoke his Jewishness during the turbulent student years, his declarations were nothing more than a political travesty, he claimed—an image he drew on when it was convenient, his most interesting way of attracting attention. There was no substance to his "Juif"; it was little more than a narcissistic label.

After 1968, when Finkielkraut decided to look seriously at his Jewish heritage, he went to meetings of Le Cercle Gaston Crémieux, but he found the group's Yiddishist program inadequate for his needs. He has since

turned to the study of philosophical texts, becoming a student of Emmanuel
Lévinas and following his mentor in an exploration of the ways Jewish
thought enriches the humanistic ideals of Western European culture. Inspired by the work of a philosopher of Lithuanian Jewish origin, Finkielkraut has rejected the call to elaborate his ethnic differences as a Jew and
returned instead to a radical reinterpretation of universalism and the French
Enlightenment. In the process, he has redefined for himself what it means to
be a secular, assimilated Jew in the Diaspora.

Other members of the generation of 1968 continue to criticize the
universalistic ideals of the Enlightenment in terms similar to those of Le
Cercle Gaston Crémieux. But they too have moved away from minority
nationalism. Embracing particularism with a passion, they eventually broke
with the secular Yiddishists and turned to religion in order to live, in their
eyes, more fully as Jews. Even though they no longer endorse the goals of
the Cercle, they too remain faithful to the Jews of Lite as they study Talmud
with teachers trained in the Lithuanian rabbinic tradition.

In 1976 a few of the younger members of Le Cercle Gaston Crémieux
invited a rabbi, Eliahou Abitbol, to give a lecture on Jewish life in the
Diaspora. Their initiative challenged the group's policy of refusing to sponsor talks by religious leaders. Rabbis, the Cercle maintained, had other
forums in which to speak. Abitbol's talk caused such an uproar that those
responsible for arranging the event decided to leave the group and pursue
their religious interests elsewhere. A couple of them subsequently joined the
Orthodox rabbi's yeshiva community in the Alsatian city of Strasbourg
(Bas-Rhin), a place where young people with little prior background in
Judaism have come to study and live as strictly observant Jews.

Rabbi Abitbol was born in Morocco in the 1930s, into an Orthodox
working-class family. Despite his ties to Sephardic Jewry, he received an
education in the Lithuanian tradition, as did many other Jews of North
African origin. While a young student in the 1950s, he came to France and
attended, briefly, the Ecole d'Orsay, the school organized by the French
Jewish Scout Movement, and a yeshiva that two Lithuanian rabbis had
opened before the Second World War. He then went to Israel to continue his
studies with scholars trained in Lite.[18] Finally, in the late 1960s, the enterprising Abitbol, ordained as a rabbi, came back to France and opened a
yeshiva for French Jews raised in assimilated families who want to make a
teshuvah. Today, La Yéchiva des Etudiants in Strasbourg has more than one
hundred families in its community, and all of them are committed to the
Lithuanian Talmudic tradition.

Among Abitbol's disciples, there is Benny Lévy, the former radical and leader of the French student movement. Known by his alias Pierre Victor, Lévy founded La Gauche Prolétarienne, a Maoist faction in the extreme left, in the late 1960s. He then became the secretary and intellectual companion of Jean-Paul Sartre, during the last seven years of the philosopher's life. With Sartre, Lévy began studying philosophy again, an interest he had dropped during his activist days, and through philosophy he discovered the work of Emmanuel Lévinas, which led him to embrace Judaism.

As Lévy read the sacred texts, he discussed Jewish history and religious thought with Sartre. In 1980, a few weeks before the philosopher died, Lévy published three interviews the two had recorded jointly. Sartre's "last words" caused quite a furor, for, it seemed, the young man had convinced the philosopher to revise his position on a number of issues, including the Jewish question.[19]

Although people differ in their opinions about the meaning of these interviews, most would agree they bear witness to the seriousness with which the philosopher had responded to the changes occurring in Lévy's intellectual and political life. They also suggest that the philosopher had been influenced by his young companion. And Sartre was not alone. As Lévy turned to the sacred texts, he brought many others with him, in particular young activists like himself who had belonged to the extreme left.

Lévy persuaded, for example, a group of former Maoists to support Jewish scholarship through the publication of a series of translations of religious commentaries and treatises, among them *The Soul of Life* by Chaim of Volozhin, the celebrated disciple of the Gaon of Vilna and one of the greatest Talmudic teachers of eighteenth-century Lithuania.[20] The publishers, known as Editions Verdier, run a cooperative in Lagrasse (Aude), at the foot of the French Pyrenees (see map 4). They have lived there since the early 1970s, when they moved back to the land to join the political struggle of wine producers in the area.

The number of Jews in the generation of 1968 making a return to religious Judaism extends far beyond Abitbol's immediate followers and a handful of their friends. Over the past few years, the Orthodox movement has grown dramatically, developing programs across the nation. La Yéchiva des Etudiants has sponsored other communities by sending out teachers to set up schools all over France. Perhaps more important, study groups have mushroomed in Paris and throughout the country.[21] Led by philosophers and rabbis, many of whom oppose the Hasidic movement, these courses attract young Jews with varying commitments to Orthodox Judaism, but many of the students are in the process of making a return. For the most part, those who attend have virtually no Hebrew and little religious background—they come to listen to teachers translate and analyze small sections of the Talmud or a mystical text, perhaps from the Kabbalah, almost always in the rationalistic Lithuanian tradition.

As I have already noted, the Lubavitcher Ḥasidim have also developed a strong following in France. Since this group too comes originally from Lite, some jokingly suggest that French Jews have revived the theological debates that took place in Lithuania in the nineteenth century. Repeating the old pattern, here once again the better educated have embraced the rationalism of the Gaon of Vilna while those with less schooling have adopted the spiritualism of the Baal Shem Tov, the founder of the Ḥasidic movement. On both sides of the divide, we find Ashkenazim and Sephardim.

Major Jewish organizations and the French university system have responded to this booming interest in Jewish studies by introducing a wide variety of new programs. Once again traditions from Lithuania seem to be everywhere. In Paris alone, students have had the opportunity for years to take courses in Jewish languages and culture at the Alliance Israélite Universelle and the Centre Rachi, as well as the Institut National des Langues et Civilisations Orientales (INALCO). Those learning Yiddish at INALCO have been working with the scholar Alexandre Derczansky, who is himself the son of Vilna Jews. In the early 1970s Rachel Ertel added Yiddish to the curriculum at the University of Paris VII. A translator and author of works on American and Eastern European Jews, Ertel is from Lite and identifies closely with the secular Yiddish tradition of the area. She is also a close friend and colleague of Elise and Richard Marienstras and an early member of Le Cercle Gaston Crémieux.[22] But even Ertel's program is old history by now. The true explosion began about ten years later.

In 1982 the Ecole des Hautes Etudes en Sciences Sociales established a special course of study with the help of a grant from La Fondation du Judaisme. Visiting scholars give most of the seminars, but the Ecole has provided the program with two permanent faculty lines, one for the director, the other for an assistant. The director is the sociologist Dominique Schnapper, daughter of the philosopher and sociologist Raymond Aron and author of a major study on Jews in contemporary France.[23] Her assistant is Nancy Green, the American historian trained by Arcadius Kahan, the economic historian born and raised in Vilna. Green has written on the immigration of Russian Jewish workers to France at the turn of the century.[24]

A few years later, the Alliance Israélite Universelle opened a new Collège des Etudes Juives, under the direction of Shmuel Trigano, a philosopher and Jewish activist, known in particular for his analysis of the ways the nation-state has weakened Judaism in Europe.[25] Trigano's program offers courses by people who represent the followers of Eliahou Abitbol and Benny Lévy. In the mid-1980s the Centre Rachi also organized a degree-granting program in religious studies with the University of Paris IV, and here too we find traces of Lithuania—the president of the center, Bernard Kanovitch, is from a Vilna family. Finally, since the 1950s, the French branch of the World Jewish Congress has sponsored annual colloquia for Jewish intellectuals in France, but only recently have the meetings become popular events for those beyond a small circle of specialists. The highlight of these gatherings is the yearly lecture by Emmanuel Lévinas on a Talmudic text, presented in the rationalistic Lithuanian tradition.

I will give other examples of how Lithuanian Jews and forms of Lithuanian Judaism have influenced members of the generation of 1968. But references to the Bund or to the Gaon of Vilna have little to do with the demographic presence of Lithuanian Jews in the nation today. Even without making ethnic or regional distinctions among Jews who came from Poland and Russia, Eastern European immigrants represent a very small minority of the Jewish population currently living in contemporary France. Things were different, however, before the Second World War, and this fact weighs heavily on the conscience of both Jews and Gentiles.[26]

Most of the Jews described in this book confronted the Nazi terror directly or through the experiences of members of their families. For that reason alone the specter of the past demands our serious attention. But there are other reasons for devoting the next chapter to the shame and anger many people feel about Vichy's collaboration with the Germans. Prominent among them is the widespread concern since the late 1970s about the rise of incidents of anti-Semitism in the country today.

As Jewish intellectuals of the generation of 1968 look for ways to express themselves as Jews, some have contributed to the debates going on by writing about Nazi-sympathizers in France during the occupation period. Others have chosen to preserve the memory of those tortured and killed, while still others have exposed the political scandals and acts of violence against Jews that have recently taken the nation by surprise. In the process they have revealed elaborate networks of right-wing neofacists and groups of *gauchistes* who had previously been identified with the student left.

2

Remembering the Past in the Present

In October 1978, Philippe Ganier Raymond, journalist and author of a book on French anti-Semitism,[1] published an interview with Louis Darquier de Pellepoix, commissaire général of Jewish affairs in Vichy France. An infamous figure of the occupation period, the commissaire vanished at the end of the war. The French tried him in absentia in 1947 and condemned him to death, but Darquier de Pellepoix eluded his sentence. Thirty-one years later he turned up in Madrid, having preserved both his life and convictions: "Six million Jews disappeared? Pure invention. A Jewish invention. . . . In Auschwitz they only gassed lice."[2]

For the French, the war years have not faded into the pages of history. Vichy's collaboration with the Germans continues to haunt and humiliate them. Only weeks after publishing the interview with Darquier de Pellepoix, newspapers carried stories about Robert Faurisson, the literature professor at the University of Lyon who claimed that gas chambers never existed. Although nearly everyone objected to his so-called research, a handful of people gave Faurisson their enthusias-

—Monsieur, thirty-six years ago you turned over 75,000 men, women and children to the Germans. You are the French Eichmann.
—What are all these numbers?
—Everybody knows them; they are reported in this document [Serge Klarsfeld, Le Mémorial de la déportation des Juifs de France].
—I was sure of it: a Jewish document. Here we go again with Jewish propaganda. Of course you have nothing to show me but Jewish documents; no others exist.

—Interview with
LOUIS DARQUIER DE
PELLEPOIX

tic support, among them Pierre Guillaume, the leader of a band of extreme leftists.[3]

Guillaume called his group La Vieille Taupe (the old mole),[4] assuming the name of a radical bookstore he and his followers had taken over in 1967. Five years later the comrades closed shop, but the old mole lived on, digging in for a while, and then reemerging in 1978 as a publishing house specializing in "revisionist" accounts of the Nazi period.[5]

La Vieille Taupe issued Faurisson's book (*Mémoire en défense*) in 1980, together with an opening statement by Noam Chomsky, the American linguist (and Jew), recognized for his commitment to causes supported by the left.[6] Chomsky made his case for Faurisson in the abstract terms of liberal theory: Freedom of speech was at issue, not the argument put forth by the literature professor. Others disagreed, and Chomsky's remarks caused an international scandal. Still, the linguist held his ground: he had written an "opinion" as a civil libertarian, not a "preface" as one who endorsed the author's views. In fact, he admitted, he had never read the book.[7]

Guillaume also published a detailed analysis of the reactions people had to Faurisson's claims. It was prepared by Serge Thion, a sociologist previously known for his writings on the Cambodian crisis.[8] In this massive volume, Thion argued that the French had rejected Faurisson on ideological grounds, not on the quality of his research.[9]

Everyone was talking about the "Faurisson affair." In the press, journalists and scholars mounted vigorous campaigns against revisionist accounts of the Nazi period. They alerted their readers to the dangerous alliance that had recently developed among extremists representing the right and the left. But the outcry did not silence Faurisson, who went on to inspire others to pursue the same line of investigation.

In the spring of 1985, the literature professor showed up at the University of Nantes for the doctoral defense of Henri Roques, a retired agrarian engineer and former leader of the fascist organization, La Phalange Française.[10] Following Faurisson, Roques' research questioned the existence of gas chambers, a subject that demanded the scrutiny of historians of twentieth-century Germany. Instead it received the attention of Claude Rivière—Roques' thesis advisor—a specialist in Provençal poetry, whose only credentials for evaluating the study consisted in having spent nearly thirty years of his life serving groups on the extreme right.[11] The rest of the jury, too, lacked the training necessary to judge the man's work.[12] Passing with honors, Roques assumed the title of "Docteur d'université" for nearly a year, until the ministry of higher education investigated the matter and revoked the degree.[13] Thanks to Faurisson, the rejected thesis was subsequently published by the right-wing Editions Ogmios, the house that had recently taken over the distribution of books produced several years earlier by La Vieille Taupe.[14]

Many assumed that Faurisson and his followers had the support of only marginal members of the French academic community. In 1988, however, they learned differently. Faurisson also enjoyed the respect of Jean Beaufret, a distinguished philosopher and celebrated hero of the Resistance. According to an article in *Libération,* before he died Beaufret sent a note to Faurisson, congratulating him on his courage and confessing that he too had doubts about the existence of gas chambers.[15]

Jean Beaufret had introduced Martin Heidegger to post–World War II France, hardly an incidental detail in early 1988. As people read about his correspondence with Robert Faurisson, many were already involved in heated debates about the importance of Nazism to the German philosopher's work. Although Heidegger never denied his party affiliations, for years scholars made distinctions between the man's intellectual contributions and his political choices. While praising the first, some went to great lengths to condemn the second, among them Emmanuel Lévinas and Jacques Derrida.[16] Then Victor Farias published *Heidegger et le nazisme* in 1987 and challenged those who separated Heidegger's work from his politics.[17] Basing his argument on archival materials, Farias claimed that Nazism was intrinsic to Heidegger's thought. Some hailed the new book, but others demurred, refusing to join the campaign to eliminate Heidegger from the roster of great European thinkers.

In two highly regarded essays on the subject, the philosopher Elisabeth de Fontenay confronted Heidegger's Nazism directly while she continued to support the merits of his work.[18] Her first article appeared in April 1987, six months earlier than Farias' book and nine months before *Libération* reported that Beaufret had written to Faurisson. Even though she knew nothing at the time about the correspondence, Fontenay still voiced concern over Beaufret's apparent indifference to Heidegger's ties to the Nazi party. She went on to condemn the German philosopher for his political choices and identified, before Farias, elements of Nazism in Heidegger's writings. In her second article, published after the scandal had broken, Fontenay now cautioned those eager to reject the work of the German phenomenologist. We can use Heidegger against Heidegger, she explained: challenge the inexcusable mistakes he made in his life, and in some of his writings, with arguments drawn from his major contributions to twentieth-century thought.[19]

Revisionist readings of National Socialism have recently burdened the courts, as well. In the spring of 1987, the French tried the German war criminal Klaus Barbie, "the Butcher of Lyon [Rhône]," who had successfully evaded justice for nearly forty years (see map 4). Like Faurisson, Barbie managed to win the support of a handful of people identified with the left. His own lawyer, for example, had previously defended revolutionaries engaged in the struggle for the liberation of Algeria. Now Jacques Vergès made the case for Klaus Barbie by putting France on trial, comparing the activities of this Nazi soldier to those of members of the French army during the Algerian war.[20] Many feared Vergès might embarrass the country further by stirring up memories of collaboration with the Germans.[21]

Another case involves Paul Touvier, a pro-Nazi intelligence officer, who was based in Lyon during the occupation. Known as the "French Barbie," he was finally arrested in 1989, accused of having been "directly responsible" for deporting Jews from France, as well as for having organized the capture and murder of Victor Basch and his wife. Basch was a socialist and a Jew who had been serving at the time as president of the French League for the Rights of Man. According to the prosecution, Touvier remained free for as many years as he had thanks to the help he had received, first from members of the church hierarchy in Lyon, then from a group of ultraconservative Catholics.[22]

Finally, the 1988 presidential campaign had its scandal as well, when Jean-Marie Le Pen noted in passing that Auschwitz was a "minor point," a footnote to history.[23] Running on a ticket for the extreme right (Le Front National), the xenophobic Le Pen spent most of his time criticizing the government's liberal immigration policy for giving away jobs to foreigners. As he toured the country, he made racist remarks against Arabs, mostly, not Jews, but he still reverted occasionally to older forms of bigotry, endorsing the positions of French anti-Semites.[24]

While individuals such as these keep stepping forward to rewrite the past, many more have chosen to preserve the memory of those tortured and killed. More often than not, they focus their attention on Jews of Eastern European origin, on those who endured the greatest losses during the war. In Claude Lanzmann's nine and a half hour documentary on the Final Solution (*Shoah*), the filmmaker interviews a handful of these people who miraculously survived. To the same lulling sound of the freight train that accompanied so many to their death, Lanzmann takes us over endless kilometers of Poland and Russia. We visit sites of mass murder, meet victims, resisters, executioners, trainmen, peasants, and townspeople—all of whom tell in painful detail about what they went through, inflicted, or merely saw.[25]

In 1939, when Lanzmann was growing up, approximately 300,000 Jews were living in France, the vast majority of whom were of Eastern European origin.[26] Five years later, 180,000 remained. More than 75,000 Jews were deported. Only 3,000 of them ever returned.[27]

Of all the Jews hunted down in occupied France, Eastern Europeans suffered the most. Thousands of them had come to the country between the two wars to find work, education, and freedom from persecution. When the Germans defeated the French in 1940, the Gestapo targeted these immigrant Jews for early deportation. Decidedly unassimilated, they were easy prey for the Vichy police who, following directives from Darquier de Pellepoix, descended on their neighborhoods and rounded them up.

Serge Klarsfeld records the fate of these Jews who disappeared in cattle cars and never returned. Gathering his data from German archives, he published the names of 75,721 individuals, along with their birth dates, places of origin, citizenships, and the numbers assigned to the convoys that led them to their death. Well over half the people listed in the *Memorial to the Jews Deported from France* came from Eastern Europe.[28] How many more were from families who had settled in France only a generation before?

Scholars and journalists have written at length about Jewish leaders in occupied France and the decisions they made when faced with the horror of deportation. Some condemn them for having taken part in the Union Générale des Israélites de France (L'UGIF), the French Judenrat, or council of prominent Jews established by Vichy to help keep order in the Jewish community.[29] Others defend them for having done the best they could to protect as many Jews as possible.[30] But almost everyone agrees that they made distinctions between immigrant and French Jews that jeopardized the Eastern European population.[31] In the Resistance too, there were cases of native-born fighters discriminating against foreigners, Jews and Gentiles— even sacrificing them, if they had to, in order to save their own lives.

In 1985, the filmmaker Mosco produced a documentary for national television about immigrant workers (*Des Terroristes à la retraite*), the majority of them Jewish, who had joined the Communist resistance during the Second World War. In the autumn of 1943, a group of these fighters were ambushed in and around Paris, and the Germans shot most of them, including their leader, the Armenian, Missak Manouchian. Before he died, Manouchian wrote a letter to his sister in which he seemed to accuse his French comrades of having framed the immigrant fighters. At the time, the Communist party chose not to investigate the matter thoroughly. Years later, they vehemently objected to Mosco's film, challenging the evidence, but doing little to clear the names of party members charged with taking part in the betrayal.

Mosco's film described how the French Communist party created combat units composed only of immigrant fighters. Such a policy made it possible, the documentary suggested, for party leaders to sacrifice some of their soldiers, without taking the lives of native Frenchmen. After segregating them, the Communist resistance then assigned a group of foreigners to the Paris region, under the command of Manouchian.[32]

People concerned with the problem of anti-Semitism in France have not only documented the tragedies of the past, but have focused on those taking place in the present, as well. Within months of the interview with Darquier de Pellepoix, responsible sources reported a rise in the number of acts of aggression against Jews in France, many of them life threatening.[33] And the violence continued at regular intervals until 1982.

In the face of these attacks, Henri Hajdenberg founded Le Renouveau Juif (the Jewish Renewal) in 1979.[34] A young lawyer of Polish Jewish origin, Hajdenberg called on French Jews to challenge Giscard d'Estaing for having recognized the PLO. In doing so, Hajdenberg argued, the president had encouraged Palestinian militants to come to the country, where they committed acts of terrorism against Jews. For the most part, the Jewish Renewal attracted its members from young Jews in the North African community whose families had abandoned their homes twenty years earlier when France's colonies and protectorates had gained their independence. By 1980 the movement was so popular it could draw tens of thousands of people together for pro-Israeli demonstrations[35] and for marches of protest against incidents of violence in France.[36] People even began talking about a "Jewish vote." But during François Mitterrand's first term as president (he took office in 1981), things quieted down and the Jewish Renewal subsided.[37] By the mid-1980s, the group had virtually disappeared as a political force.[38]

In June 1979, the French Jewish establishment responded to the violence by creating a research and communications center, staffed by members of the generation of 1968, to study anti-Semitic factions in the country. André Wormser, a member of the executive committee of the CRIF, stepped forward to sponsor the project. Calling the center CERAC (Le Centre d'Etudes et de Recherches sur l'Antisémitisme Contemporain), Wormser gained the support of several national and international Jewish organizations, including the CRIF, the French branch of the World Jewish Congress, and the London-based Institute of Jewish Affairs. As the promotional pamphlet explained, the center hoped to serve France by alerting Jews and Gentiles alike to developments of "anti-democratic, totalitarian, fascistic and racist ideas or forces" in the nation.[39] CERAC continued its activities for seven years until it eventually closed down for lack of funds.

André Wormser is a member of a distinguished family of bankers whose ancestors have lived in France since long before the French Revolution. His father, Georges Wormser, had been chief of staff of President Clemenceau's cabinet, an observer at the discussions that led to the Balfour Declaration in 1917, and a participant in the peace negotiations after the First World War. He had also served as president of the Paris Consistoire, then president of the Central Consistoire of France and Algeria. While in hiding in Lyon during the Second World War, Georges Wormser helped organize the CRIF,[40] the creation of which marked the first time in the history of French Jewry that a single body represented both secular and religious groups and both French and immigrant Jews.[41] Today, André Wormser continues his father's active involvement in the French Jewish community by assuming the leadership of a number of important organizations.

In 1979, in an interview published in *La Tribune juive,* André Wormser explained the need for creating CERAC with the following remark: "I am rather philosophical by nature and am not easily upset by a vile or stupid slogan scribbled on the wall of a building or in the subway, nor by some act of desecration in a cemetery. A French Jew like myself, who is over fifty years old, has learned to live with the taunts of such abject and infantile people. Out of self-respect, we refuse to yield to the provocations of these hateful little bands who never seem to give up. But today, the situation has grown more serious. It demands our attention and an immediate response.[42]"

Among the many acts of violence that occurred in France between 1979 and 1982, three incidents stand out, all of them in Paris: the bombing of a Jewish students' restaurant on the rue de Médicis (March 1979); the attack before a synagogue on the rue Copernic (October 1980); and the gunning down of people at Jo Goldenberg's restaurant, in the old Jewish quarter (August 1982).

On March 27, 1979, between forty and fifty students had gathered at noon in the Foyer des Etudiants Juifs to have lunch in the only kosher university restaurant in the Latin Quarter. Founded in 1920 by the Paris Consistoire, the Foyer had a long history of serving the Jewish community;

it was the obvious target for an anti-Semitic act of aggression. At 12:30 P.M., a bomb went off, wounding about thirty people, three of them seriously.[43]

Since the attack took place the day after Israel and Egypt had signed the Camp David Treaty, many assumed that Palestinian terrorists had planted the bomb. The French news agency, Agence France-Presse, had in fact received a call from an "autonomous collective . . . against the Zionist presence in France and against the Peace Treaty that neglects all the problems of the Palestinian People." But then somebody else phoned in as well to deny that the group had had anything to do with it.[44] In the end, nobody came forward to assume responsibility, and the PLO vehemently denounced the action. Ibrahim Souss, the organization's representative in France, declared: "We will carry on our struggle in the occupied territories, not in France." He further announced his intention to send "sympathy" and "regrets" to the chief rabbi of France.[45]

In the days following the incident, journalists blamed the aggression on a general rise of race hatred in the country and not on any specific political group.[46] Agreeing with this analysis, André Wormser added that such violence against Jews reflected the emergence of a "new right" in France, and the passive acceptance by the public at large to open expressions of anti-Semitism: "Since the publication of the interview with Darquier de Pellepoix, we have seen the build-up of a chain reaction that has led to a kind of explosion. Some, like that fraud Faurisson, assume they now have the right to spread their theses. Others, who have kept quiet for thirty years, feel that the moment has come to proclaim once again their anti-Semitism. We might almost say that those expressing anti-Semitic opinions had recently gained the right to speak out freely, and this is dangerous, for soon we might find ourselves headed toward the formation of a new fascist party."[47]

In autumn of 1980, as further acts of anti-Jewish violence shook France and other parts of Europe, many joined André Wormser in voicing their concern about the possible rise of a new fascist party.[48]

On October 3, 1980, shortly after 6:30 P.M., two men on motorcycles left explosives on top of a car parked in front of the synagogue on the rue Copernic, located in the fashionable sixteenth *arrondissement*. The bomb was timed to go off just as the congregants finished their Sabbath eve prayers and left the temple to go home. Three hundred people had gathered for services that evening.

Fortunately the rabbi went on a little longer than usual. When the bomb exploded, the worshipers were still inside. Four passersby died in the blast. Thirty-one people were wounded, eleven of them seriously. Among those rushed to the hospital, many were Jews who had come to the synagogue to pray.[49]

Later that evening, Prime Minister Raymond Barre appeared on television and clumsily grieved with the nation: "This hateful assault, aimed at Jews attending synagogue, struck innocent French people crossing the rue Copernic." Although Barre added that "the Jewish community is a French community, respected by all the French," his unfortunate slip provoked violent reactions. Critics used it as further proof of the insensitivity of Giscard's government to the plight of French Jews.[50]

A few days before the rue Copernic bombing, the president had already come under attack for declarations made by Christian Bonnet, his minister of the interior. Newspapers quoted Bonnet complaining that people exaggerated the seriousness of recent acts of violence directed against Jews in the country.[51] After the tragedy, the minister showed little interest in investigating accusations made by reliable sources that neo-Nazis had infiltrated his police force.[52] Angered by the man's unconscionable response to the dangers facing the Jewish citizens of France, the Socialist party demanded that Giscard dismiss Bonnet. The Communists insisted that Bonnet appear before the National Assembly. Jewish groups, too, voiced their outrage as they participated in demonstrations across the nation.[53]

On October 7, more than one hundred thousand people took to the streets of Paris to protest the rue Copernic bombing. Representing a cross-section of political and religious beliefs, Parisians came out in force to express their solidarity with Jews living in France.[54] They also insisted that Bonnet purge his police force of neo-Nazis and prosecute the murderers. But again, nobody really knew who had planted the bomb.

This time, Agence France-Presse received a call from someone claiming to represent the FNE (Faisceaux Nationalistes Européens), a neo-Nazi organization that had replaced the infamous FANE (Fédération d'Action Nationale Européene). But their leader, Marc Fredriksen, said the group had had nothing to do with it.[55] Some continued to blame neo-Nazis, while others accused Palestinians, the KGB, and Libya's Qaddafi.[56]

In the days following the tragedy, newspapers published countless articles about the treatment of Jews in occupied France, reminding the French of the dangers of racism. As journalists, philosophers, and historians drew clear connections between the ideology of National Socialism and the "new right," they provided compelling arguments for blaming neo-Nazis for the recent wave of violence.[57] Over the weeks, however, the evidence pointed increasingly to groups based in Cyprus and Lebanon,[58] leading others to repeat warnings about alliances being made between extremists on the left and the right.

Having studied the pattern for several years, CERAC's researchers, Nelly Gutman and Jacques Tarnero, stated conclusively: "We must note that certain groups on the extreme left (those for whom the struggle against Israel and Zionism plays a central role), have joined forces with people who long for the rehabilitation of Hitler. Together they back Faurisson and produce the political equation, Israel = the New Nazi State. Denying that the Genocide ever took place, they dismiss the evidence as a huge hoax fabricated in order to justify the creation of the state of Israel (and, incidentally, to deceive the Germans). In this way, they have come up with yet another way to blame the Israelis."[59]

Factions such as these could only gain strength when new conflicts erupted in the Middle East. In June 1982, Israel invaded Lebanon. And on August 9, five or six assailants carrying submachine guns and a grenade entered Jo Goldenberg's restaurant in the heart of the Marais. Within seconds they had killed six people, wounded twenty-two, nine of them seriously, and escaped on foot through the narrow streets of the Jewish quarter. A few days later, two bombs went off in other parts of the city.[60]

At the end of the week, Bernard-Henri Lévy added his voice to those who assumed the existence of a coordinated network of killers. While the "new philosopher" of the generation of 1968 has not always enjoyed the unanimous support of his peers, this time he spoke for many when he said: "The two recent bombings have left me, like everybody else, entirely flabbergasted. I am only sure of one thing: A chain of disasters like this one could not be the work of a single murderer, of somebody who fits the classic image of a romantic, anarchistic desperado out to settle his obscure grievances with bourgeois society."[61]

Indeed, the August massacre gave every indication of being a well-organized operation between bands of "little local" terrorists and the international "big professionals."[62] From Paris, a group of leftist terrorists called Action Directe claimed a major role. Soon after the attacks, their leader, Jean-Marc Rouillan, announced to the papers that his men were responsible for three bombings against "Jewish targets." Mitterrand's government responded by declaring Action Directe illegal and ordering the police to begin making arrests.[63]

Many Jews of the generation of 1968 broke with the extreme left and the Communist party over the question of Israel. But some of them also took stands against individual actions of the Jewish state, and their numbers increased with the invasion of Lebanon in 1982 and the massacres at two refugee camps, Sabra and Shatila.[64] Committed to Israel and identified with the left, they joined groups which were looking for ways to recognize the rights of Israelis and Palestinians.[65]

Pierre Goldman is one of the most dramatic examples of an extreme leftist who broke with the Trotskyists because he differed with them about Israel, among other issues. For many, this young radical has come to symbolize the struggle of Jews on the left to remain true to the ideals of socialism while they also defend the rights of their people. Describing himself as "a Polish Jew born in France," he devoted the last years of his life to trying to bring his politics and personal history together.

Two gunmen shot Pierre Goldman down on September 20, 1979, at the place des Peupliers, in the thirteenth arrondissement. He was thirty-five years old. A neo-Nazi group called Honneur de la Police assumed responsibility for the killing, explaining to the press that they had taken the law into their own hands because the French authorities had been too conciliatory.[66] In the days following Goldman's death, *Le Monde* described the radical as a "Jew, political activist, gangster, writer."[67]

Pierre Goldman was born in Lyon in 1944 to Jewish parents, originally from Poland, who had joined the Communist resistance in France.[68] When the war ended, his parents separated, in part, Goldman suspected, because his mother had remained faithful to Soviet communism and his father had not, but he never heard the full story. He only knew that his mother stayed on in Paris for nearly three more years and worked for the Polish embassy or consulate. In 1948 she received instructions to return to Poland, and she fully expected to take Pierre with her. But Goldman's father intervened at the last minute and kidnapped the child with the help of some friends. Even though the man had previously shown little interest in his son, he could not bear the thought, he later explained, that his boy would grow up in a country where millions of Jews had recently been exterminated and where anti-Semites and Stalinists now ran the government. And so Pierre Goldman remained in France, living first with an aunt, then, beginning in 1950, with his father and his father's new wife.

Raised in the family's radical political tradition, Goldman went on to participate in the Communist youth group affiliated with his lycée, a boarding school he attended in Evreux (Eure). In 1963, he joined the Union des Etudiants Communistes (UEC) at the Sorbonne. Politics rapidly became his major concern, and within a year he had dropped out of school and was training full time to fight with the *guerrilla* movement in Latin America.

In 1966 Goldman took a job on a Belgian freighter to pay his way to the Americas. When the boat docked in New Orleans, he jumped ship, went to Texas, and stole across the Mexican border. He did not get very far, however, before immigration caught up with him, sent him back to New Orleans, and threw him into jail. A few days later the Belgian captain agreed to assume responsibility for Goldman, and the young radical returned to Europe on the same ship that had brought him to the United States.

In 1967, soon after the Six-Day War, Goldman took off once again, but this time he had the necessary funds to fly directly to Cuba. There, he met with revolutionaries who had operations in Venezuela, and they invited the French, Jewish, Polish radical to join them. But first they told him to go back to Paris and wait for instructions, and this took nearly a year. As a result, he was still around for the student uprising in May 1968. His struggle, however, was elsewhere. He showed little interest in what was happening in France.

Goldman did not write much about the fourteen months he spent in Venezuela, but he did say that he lived a clandestine existence there with a group of rebels whose mission had failed. In September 1969 he went back to Paris and settled down on the edges of society, earning his reputation as a gangster. The following December the police placed him under arrest and charged him with armed robbery and murder. Sentenced to life imprisonment, Goldman used his first years in jail to complete two degrees with honors: a *licence* in philosophy and a masters in Spanish. He also wrote his now famous memoir, *Souvenirs obscurs d'un Juif polonais né en France*, in which he told his life story, describing himself as an outsider, the typical Jew in exile: "To be or not to be French, that was never the question. I didn't think to ask it. I believe I always knew that I was simply a Polish Jew born in France."[69] "I was only a Jew in exile with no promised land. Exiled indefinitely, forever, for good. I did not belong to the proletariat, but I, like a member of the working class, was a man without a country, with no homeland other than this absolute exile, this Jewish exile in the Diaspora."[70]

In his memoir, Goldman also pleaded his case. He had not killed the pharmacist or his assistant, on the rue Richard-Lenoir. If given another chance he could prove it. Pressured by the public's response to the book, the authorities relented and gave him a second trial. This time, with the help of civil rights lawyer Georges Kiéjman, the political radical cleared his name of the charges of murder. Still, Goldman had committed armed robbery and returned to jail in May 1976 to finish out six more years of what had now been reduced to a twelve-year term. Five months later the courts released him on parole.[71]

During the remaining three years of his life, Goldman wrote articles for *Libération* and other journals and served on the editorial board of *Les Temps modernes*. He also published a novel,[72] and was working on a philosophical manuscript. Politically, he continued to identify with the extreme left, but he no longer belonged to a party.

While Goldman maintained close ties with the Trotskyist Ligue Communiste Révolutionnaire, he could not entirely endorse the position of this group. As he explained in an interview published in their paper, he disagreed with them on a variety of issues, including the question of Israel.[73] A diaspora Jew to the end, Goldman felt exiled in Israel as well,[74] but this in no way weakened his belief that the Jewish state had a right to exist.

Had Goldman lived to witness the recent troubles in Lebanon and the West Bank, he might well have joined other Jews of the generation of 1968 in voicing his objections to Israeli policies in the Middle East. Like them, he too would probably have done so without any thought of challenging the state's legitimacy in the area. He might also have worked with a group of Jews and Gentiles who founded SOS Racisme in 1984, a movement dedicated to combating racism in France, the main victims of which are not Jews, but Moslem immigrants from North Africa. What we know for sure is that when he died he was still struggling with the meaning of his Jewish identity, sounding tortured and confused, but reflecting the feelings of many of his peers.

In an interview he gave a few weeks before he was shot, Goldman spoke at some length about being Jewish:

> To be Jewish means, perhaps, nothing more than to come from a family influenced by customs, by Jewish culture. My life is not filled at the conscious level with Jewish culture. There is no Jewish music, or Jewish books, or Jewish religion. Within me, there are many things that have nothing to do with being Jewish. Still, they are part of my Jewishness. To be Jewish is not what I have, but my condition. Not even that. It's a space that I fill existentially with this and that. My books are not Jewish, but in each and every one of them, there is the past of a Jew. To be Jewish is to convey the past. And why is this so important? Because of anti-Semitism. Because of the hatred. The only answer to the question of what it means to be a Jew, is Auschwitz. The Holocaust has renewed Jewish identity for centuries.[75]

When these observations appeared in *Le Monde* just after his death, Laurence Podselver recognized herself and many of her friends in his portrait of the Jew. A descendent of Lithuanian immigrants on her father's side, Podselver today is an anthropologist who writes on Ḥasidim in France. In September 1979, she was a graduate student and a Jewish-identified activist: "Pierre Goldman represents our whole period, even though we do not share or approve of his former gangster activities, which he himself later analyzed and condemned. His ideas touch us deeply. I am sending you this article which we read [in France] on the eve of Yom Kippur. Like all gifted people, he knew how to express a great deal of what many in my generation think about their Jewish identity. As you will see, it is full of contradictions and obscure passages. These contradictions are ours."[76]

The journalist Luc Rosenzweig wrote a *Kaddish* for his friend, who had worked with him at *Libération*. A veteran of the students' movement and a secular Jew, Rosenzweig composed a mourner's prayer, instead of an obituary, honoring Goldman's decision to express himself publicly as a Jew. Promising to carry on his friend's struggle, Rosenzweig added, "We found your hatred of anti-Semites at times excessive and anachronistic, [but] we now embrace it entirely and completely and will act on it."[77] Rosenzweig kept his word and wrote a book (with Bernard Cohen) on the Nazi past of Kurt Waldheim, the former secretary general of the United Nations and the newly elected president of Austria.[78]

Like Pierre Goldman, many Jewish intellectuals of the generation of 1968 were born into a world dominated by the evils of National Socialism. Even for those who came after the war, the specter of Auschwitz formed them, pushing many into radical politics and leading them out again as extremists made alliances with their enemies. While some of these activists would eventually withdraw into Orthodox religious communities, many of them experimented with socialist models of minority nationalism first, "becoming Jewish the way the Occitans became Occitans."[79] In the process they discovered the richness of Eastern European Yiddish culture. Determined to retrieve some of what the Nazis had destroyed, these Jewish intellectuals joined Le Cercle Gaston Crémieux, and parallel groups, to study and republish works by Jewish socialists and former Communists, by those who had created a secular Yiddish culture in the Diaspora.

3

The Right to Be Different

A few weeks before the Six-Day War, a group of twelve left-wing intellectuals circulated a manifesto that subsequently appeared in several journals. Drafted by Richard Marienstras, it began with these words: "The recent events in the Middle East have revealed the malaise that Jews on the left have been living with in France. Uninterested in the religion, having no desire to emigrate to Israel, fully considering themselves citizens of their own country, most of these people have still felt the need to take a stand as Jews. Given the diversity of options open to them, it came as a surprise to see so many respond in the same way."[1] The manifesto proclaimed that like-minded Jews should come together and define their position in relation to (1) the left which has misunderstood them; (2) the French Jewish establishment, which has limited the choices for Jews to the synagogue and/or Zionism; and (3) Israel, which has reduced expressions of Jewish nationalism to the Western European model of the nation-state. Challenging Zionist assumptions about the centrality of Israel for Jewish people living in other parts of the world, the tract recalled the long history of diaspora Jewry, a

The liberating forces of freedom destroyed the cultures of the French provinces through assimilation, reducing the traditions of the people living there to a kind of folklore, turning their languages into a shameful vice. In the same spirit, these forces of freedom offered the defenseless Jews a deal they could not refuse: Emancipation at the expense of their Jewish national dimensions. To become citizens, Jews would have to give up their collective way of life.

—RICHARD MARIENSTRAS

period stretching over more than two thousand years, during which time communities in Europe, North Africa, and Asia Minor shaped most of the religious and secular traditions we identify as Jewish today. Approximately one hundred and fifty individuals responded to the call and formed Le Cercle Gaston Crémieux, associating their project with that of a nineteenth-century socialist and Jew, a political activist who lost his life a few months after the fall of the Paris Commune.

With this name, the group placed itself in clear opposition to members of the French Jewish establishment who frequently celebrated another Crémieux, cousin Adolphe, the founder of the Alliance Israélite Universelle and the architect of a decree that recognized Algerian Jews as French citizens. While one Crémieux defended the interests of Jews by accommodating the system, the other risked his life to bring about radical political change. Lawyer, journalist, and poet, Gaston Crémieux participated in the revolutionary movement that was gaining strength in France during the last years of the Second Empire. Imprisoned for his political activities, he was subsequently freed by representatives of the Republican Revolution in September 1870 and went on to play a major role in the south, where he helped create the radical Ligue du Midi, and became president of the commission representing the Bouches-du-Rhône Department.

In March 1871, when socialists in Paris successfully took over the French capital, Gaston Crémieux proclaimed solidarity with the insurrection on behalf of the people of Marseille. The Paris Commune, however, lasted only two months. As the "forces of order" gained control once again, they arrested the Jewish radical, executing him in November of the same year. Could anyone have saved him? According to the Cercle's biographical sketch, the prisoner had hoped his well-connected cousin would try, but apparently he did not.[2]

The Cercle drew on French history for more than its name. Using the analysis of their founder Richard Marienstras, they traced the problems secular Jews had in defining themselves in contemporary France to the days of the French Revolution and to the political circumstances that led to the creation of the Central Consistoire by Napoleon. As Marienstras explained in his path-breaking article, "La Vocation minoritaire," during this period Jews were forced to sacrifice their "national" identity in order to gain their political emancipation.[3]

If they wanted to enjoy the rights of citizens, Jews had to assimilate and become "Frenchmen of the faith of Moses," culturally homogeneous members of society who merely went to a Jewish house of prayer. Granted religious freedom, they lost the possibility of developing their national autonomy. In other words, they could attend synagogue, as French Catholics and Protestants went to church, but they had to become members of the French nation: speak the same language and identify with the same cultural heritage. Nearly two hundred years later, the Cercle challenged the legitimacy of the contract and called on France to drop its eighteenth-century stipulation that there be only "one nation" within the state.

Although May 1968 interrupted its activities for a while, the Cercle came together again in 1973. By this time, members claimed, they represented even more Jews than they had before: "The Cercle has more reason to exist today than it ever had before and its potential audience is much larger; for official Judaism, polarized by the synagogue and Zionism, has lost its appeal to young Jews (perhaps it never had one), to people who are clearly looking for a way to rediscover themselves, to affirm themselves as Jews outside the usual options."[4]

Young Jews would have new options, the Cercle suggested, once minority nationalism developed in France the way it had in Eastern Europe between the two wars. French Jews should read about the cultural and political movements that had flourished in Vilna, Warsaw, and elsewhere in Eastern Europe before 1939. Inspired by the work of the Russian historian Simon Dubnow, the celebrated theorist of diaspora Jewry, Marienstras did not propose a nostalgic return to the past, but a serious search for models that might serve the interests of ethnic groups living in the Diaspora today:

> We might ask, more concretely: what can we do today in France? What programs can we offer to enhance the cultural life of Jews beyond the ones that already exist at this time? What role should community institutions play? Briefly, we propose the study of Jewish history, all of it—that of the Sephardim and the Ashkenazim, of speakers of Yiddish, Ladino, Hebrew, Aramaic, of religious Jews, secular Jews, mystics or revolutionaries, Bundists or students of the Bible. We should also renew our efforts to provide instruction in the various Jewish languages—not just Hebrew—and to create a systematic course of study to prepare people to make translations for those unable to learn these other tongues.[5]

Marienstras opened a debate that many soon joined, including Albert Memmi who had already written two books on the Jewish question.[6] Drawing on Sartre's analysis, the Tunisian-born philosopher expressed surprise that anyone would want to remain Jewish in France and develop a separate culture. To do so meant accepting an oppressive identity defined by others. The modern world, Memmi claimed in 1978, had rejected religion and offered people only one way to affirm themselves as Jews: to become citizens of a Jewish nation-state. Even though Israel did not exist when Sartre wrote *Anti-Semite and Jew,* it does now, providing a happy conclusion to the Jewish question, one that concerned Memmi only as a matter of academic interest. Having chosen freely to embrace French culture and nationality, Memmi had little desire to live authentically as a Jew. He suffered no sense of personal loss, he added, for having made the decision he did.[7]

Shmuel Trigano, on the other hand, agreed with Marienstras that Jews should reject the model of the nation-state and the form of Judaism practiced in the West. He did not, however, support minority nationalism or any other secular definition of Jewish culture. In his view, Jews needed to live in a state infused with the values of Judaism. Critical of present-day Israel, he called for the development of a spiritual center, one that eliminated the restrictions of Western European definitions of culture and looked for models in the historical experiences of Sephardic Jewry.[8]

Trigano is an Algerian Jew who identifies with the "Oriental" tradition, but he, like Marienstras, bases much of his vision on the ideas of a Russian Jewish thinker—in his case, those of Aḥad Ha-Am (Asher Ginzburg), the philosopher who envisioned Palestine becoming the spiritual center for Jews living throughout the world. Trigano, in fact, has made a clearer commitment to the Jewish values Aḥad Ha-Am wrote about than did the Russian thinker himself, for Aḥad Ha-Am remained an agnostic and an unobservant Jew throughout his life, whereas Trigano has chosen to follow the *Halakhah* (religious law). Acknowledging his intellectual debt, Trigano has challenged Marienstras in ways that recall the arguments used by Aḥad Ha-Am in the early years of the twentieth century, when he contested Dubnow's commitment to diaspora Jewry.[9]

To join the debate, we must step back and consider some of the issues framing the controversy, first by reviewing briefly the history of the nation-state and minority nationalism in relationship to the Jew. The discussion that follows begins with an analysis that takes the position of Le Cercle Gaston Crémieux, but it soon moves on to look at an aspect of the problem that spokesmen for the group have rarely addressed: the description here focuses on the impact Western European ideas about culture have had in shaping the political platforms of minority nationalists who lived in the Austro-Hungarian and Russian Empires.

When progressive Jews in Eastern Europe began leaving Orthodox Judaism in the last decades of the nineteenth century and identifying them-selves as members of a national Jewish minority, they did so by translating Western European ideals into Hebrew and Yiddish, embracing, in the pro-cess, aspects of the very philosophy that ended cultural diversity in France. Celebrating the humanism of the French Enlightenment, they modeled themselves on philosophers and artists who were either living in nation-states or were themselves influenced by the West. For the most part, literary movements in France, Germany, and Russia determined the universal stan-dards used by Jewish artists for measuring the quality of their cultural productions. As Jews developed their secular traditions, they abandoned much of their own cultural specificity, conforming instead to the values emanating from Western European nation-states.

THE NATION-STATE, MINORITY NATIONALISM, AND THE JEWS

Historians often trace the idea of the nation back at least as far as medieval times.[10] Modern nationalism, however, dates to a much later period. It took shape in Western Europe during the seventeenth and eighteenth centuries, as political philosophers debated the wisdom of forming bourgeois democratic states. Recognizing the symbolic power of ethnic attachments, progressive theorists argued that people would feel a greater sense of patriotism if they identified with the culture and heritage of the state.

Jean-Jacques Rousseau was perhaps the first to develop a program for preparing people to become loyal citizens, capable of participating actively in a democratic nation-state. Following Plato's description of the ideal city-state, Rousseau began with the education of children, but he had a more complicated problem on his hands, involving individuals who spoke differ-ent languages, belonged to different cultures, and lived scattered over a large territory. To turn people like these into dependable citizens who shared common interests and goals, Rousseau recommended they be taught to identify with a single history and set of traditions: "National education belongs only to the free; they alone live a national life, they alone are truly bound by law. . . . At twenty a Pole should be nothing else; he should be a Pole. When he learns to read, he should read of his country; at ten he should know all its products, at twelve he should know all its provinces, roads and towns, at fifteen all its history, at sixteen all its laws; there should not be in all Poland a noble deed or a famous man that he does not know and love, or that he could not describe on the spot."[11]

Soon, other voices joined in. Democracy required cultural uniformity: "one nation within one state." Before legislating that all men were created equal, everyone had to become the same. With this principle in mind, progressives came up with a policy to emancipate the Jews. In 1791 Count Stanislas de Clermont-Tonnerre made his famous declaration in defense of the Jews: "We must refuse the Jews everything as a nation and give them everything as individuals; they must constitute neither a political group nor an order within the state; they must become citizens as individuals."[12]

During the late eighteenth and early nineteenth centuries, enlightened Jews understood the limitations of this emancipation, but they eventually accepted the terms. They agreed to compromise, to give up their collective cultural autonomy in order to gain individual political freedom. Although Jewish communities across the country varied considerably—culturally, socioeconomically, and politically—some favoring emancipation and others vigorously opposing it, the French Revolution did not offer Jews much of a choice.[13] Emancipation was thrust upon them. They became "Frenchmen of the faith of Moses" and agreed, for the most part, to do away with many of their own traditions so that they might conform to the national mold.

As the Enlightenment moved east in the early nineteenth century, it held out promises of freedom by means of assimilation. Here, too, many Jews embraced the future by learning Russian, German, sometimes Polish as well, educating their children in the traditions of the wider society as they patiently waited for emancipation to reach czarist Russia and the Austro-Hungarian Empire. In the mid-1800s, dramatic waves of nationalism swept across Europe, providing yet another way for enlightened Jews in the East to join the modern world. While some remained European assimilationists, others became Hebrew nationalists.

Unlike the assimilationists who tried to become Russians or Austrians of the faith of Moses, Hebrew nationalists stimulated the development of a secular Jewish culture, posing a serious threat to Orthodox communities there. Many Hebrew nationalists, it is true, remained committed to Judaism—a point often forgotten in the literature—but they also insisted on the importance of defining Jewish traditions outside the synagogue, giving rise to the idea that one could be a nonpracticing Jew. By the end of the nineteenth century, Hebrew nationalism had become Zionism, and Yiddish movements had emerged as well, devoted to creating a secular Jewish culture in the Diaspora.

It is easy to see how Jews changed as they accommodated French, German, or Russian national traditions, but the process is less clear when we turn to Jewish movements. If we look closely, we see that they too embraced Western European ideals about what constituted a national culture. Even social democrats like the Bundists, who opposed territorial nationalism, shared similar beliefs about the need to develop their own cultural traditions.

In 1897 in Vilna, a group of Jewish socialist intellectuals and workers founded the General Jewish Workers Union in Lithuania, Poland, and Russia. They called their party the Bund (Union) for short. Influenced by Russian populism and socialism, they joined others to form the Russian Social Democratic party in 1898, but they maintained their political and cultural identity as Jews. By 1903 they had left the Social Democratic party and gone their own way. After the revolution of October 1917, Lenin outlawed the Bund, condemning it for its "separatist" and "nationalist" tendencies. Rejected in the Soviet Union, after the First World War the Bund became a major political force among Jews in the newly constituted state of Poland—Vilna had gone to the new Polish state—and, to a lesser extent, in Lithuania.

During the early years of the Bund, the party underwent a number of ideological shifts between European assimilationists and Yiddish cultural nationalists. By 1917, however, members of the Bund were fairly united in their demand for national and cultural autonomy. Their platform combined the ideals of socialist internationalism with those of cultural specificity.

The Bund developed strong, well-articulated positions against Zionism and religious Orthodoxy. Opposing the instruction of Hebrew, the party celebrated Jewish holidays only in nonreligious settings. Passover, for example, became a secular festival of the liberation of Jews from slavery. Most importantly the Bund promoted the teaching of Jewish history and the creation of a secular workers' culture based on the language of the masses, namely Yiddish.[14]

The Bund flourished in Eastern Europe during the 1920s and 1930s together with several other Jewish national parties, some Zionist, others "diasporist," some preferring Hebrew, others Yiddish. In Polish Vilna, secular Jews organized primary schools, gymnasia, and teaching seminaries so that children could study math, literature, and history in the languages of their people. Then, in 1925 at a meeting held in Berlin, Yiddish-identified intellectuals decided to create a research institute in Vilna with smaller supporting establishments in Warsaw, Berlin, and New York City. Known as YIVO: The Jewish Scientific Institute, the Vilna center played a major role in defining the national traditions of Yiddish-speaking Jews throughout Eastern Europe. When the Nazis occupied Vilna in 1941, they destroyed YIVO, but the director of the institute, Max Weinreich, escaped and came to the United States, where he took over YIVO's New York branch, turning it into the most important center of Yiddish scholarship in the world. Known today as YIVO: The Institute for Jewish Research, its library in New York has recovered tens of thousands of volumes from the original archives, some of which had been hidden successfully in the Vilna Ghetto during the war and others retrieved from warehouses in Germany.[15]

Back in Vilna during the interwar years, YIVO sponsored students of anthropology and folklore to study the culture of shtetl Jews before this way of life entirely disappeared.[16] Many writers and dramatists embraced the same cause, creating modern pieces of art out of the folk culture of Jews. Ansky's *Dybbuk* is an excellent example of the kind of work enjoyed as reading at the time. A pioneer in the field of Jewish folklore and a socialist, he created the script for the play after leading a Jewish ethnographic expedition to the Ukraine, through the villages of Volhynia and Podolia (1911–14). Ansky first wrote *The Dybbuk* in Russian, then translated it into Yiddish, incorporating changes suggested to him by the director of the Moscow Art Theater, Konstantin Stanislavsky. In December 1920, thirty days after Ansky had died, the play premiered in Warsaw in the new Yiddish version, performed by the Vilna Troupe.

Offering a socialist interpretation of the plight of shtetl Jews, *The Dybbuk* describes the fate of Khanan, a poor yeshiva boy who has fallen in love with the daughter of a rich man. Desperate to keep his Leah from marrying another, Khanan resorts to the magical powers of the Kabbalah and spirit possession. He dies in the process, taking the soul of his beloved one with him. What is denied to him in life for social reasons, he takes through death.[17]

Although artists like Ansky rejected the shtetl for themselves, preferring instead the wider, more cosmopolitan world of Russian intellectuals, the spirit of populism led many of them back to Yiddish culture to preserve for posterity the customs of their people. As they recorded the traditions of Jews who still lived in these backward towns, the Yiddishists introduced the hope of a liberated future, one that would free the poor from both Jewish and non-Jewish constraints. Such a dream necessarily required the emancipation of Jews from Orthodox Judaism and their assimilation into European culture.

Others used Yiddish as a vehicle for participating in the literary movements that dominated the works of prominent Russian, French, and German writers. Reviewing the history of Yiddish letters, the literary critic Benjamin Harshav summarizes their contributions in the following way:

> In the last third of the nineteenth century, three "classical" writers of Yiddish literature—Mendele Moykher Sforim, Sholem Aleichem and I. L. Peretz—gave prestige to a rapidly expanding literary institution. In a short period, dozens of important writers created a literature with European standards, moving swiftly from Rationalist Enlightenment through carnivalesque parody to Realism, to Naturalism and psychological Impressionism, and then breaking out of these conventional European modes into the general literary trend of Expressionism and Modernism.
>
> This became possible because of the secularization of the Jewish masses and the trend to join the general world of modern culture and politics in the language they knew. The growing political parties, especially the Diaspora-oriented Folkists and Socialists, supported Yiddish culture and education, seeing it at first as a tool for propaganda and a way to break out of the traditional religious framework and, later, as a goal in itself. . . . Hundreds of periodicals and newspapers appeared in Yiddish. . . . Libraries sprang up in hundreds of towns. A modern secular school system developed all over Eastern Europe and was echoed in part in both Americas. Massive translation efforts brought to Yiddish readers the works of Tolstoy, Kropotkin, Ibsen, Zola, Jules Verne, Rabindranat Tagore, Lion Feuchtwanger, Shakespeare, Sergey Yesenin, Ezra Pound and many others.[18]

While Jewish national movements took root in the nineteenth century, they grew dramatically in the years following the First World War. This was a time when ethnic minorities in Central and Eastern Europe gained official recognition from the League of Nations. With the dissolution of the Ottoman Empire, Austria-Hungary, Prussia, and czarist Russia, the Versailles Treaty established fourteen new states. But even these were not enough to satisfy the national longings of every group. A compromise had to be reached, and the Allies found one by introducing a radical reinterpretation of the nation-state to the recently constituted republics, one that ironically supported many of the goals of the Bundists and Austro-Hungarian Marxists.

Had the Allies imposed the same innovation on their own peoples, they might have received a better response from the leaders of the new states.

Instead, they maintained the principle of one nation within one state back home, while they legislated ethnic diversity in the East—thanks to the Versailles Treaty, minorities gained the right to preserve their collective identities if they lived in any of the fourteen countries created at the end of the war. This arrangement enraged the Poles, among others, for they had expected to develop a single national culture on the Western European model.

When the Allies drew up the Versailles Treaty at the Paris Peace Conference in 1918, they appended to it fourteen separate treaties in which they spelled out the rights of minority peoples who now found themselves living in the new states. Using Poland as a type case, the Allies patterned the thirteen other charters on the one they wrote for this country. The Polish Minorities Treaty determined who was a citizen (articles 7 and 8) and carefully instructed the government in the ways it must treat those falling under its jurisdiction: defend the life and liberty of everybody "without distinction of birth, nationality, language, race or religion" (article 2). In other words, while the Allies granted Poland sovereignty over its territories, they did not give it exclusive sovereignty. Officially recognized minorities had the protection of the League of Nations in ways comparable ethnic groups did not have in the West. Poland, for example, had inherited sizable communities of Ukrainians, Byelorussians, and Jews, and the treaty expected the government to set up primary schools in the languages of these peoples (article 9). Hospitals, as well as other public facilities, were supposed to be staffed with personnel fluent in the appropriate tongues. The treaty also included a series of regulations prohibiting Poland from passing legislation that could interfere with the Jewish Sabbath and dietary practices. Elections, for example, could not be held on Saturdays.[19]

Important English, French, and American Jewish lobbies at the Paris Peace Conference worked particularly hard to give Jews living in the newly formed states the same opportunities that members of the faith had in the West. Others were more ambitious: they hoped to obtain separate representation for these Jewish minorities at the League of Nations. While the international organization never gave them a seat, Eastern European Jews won the right to preserve their collective identity, a right they had not enjoyed in the West since the end of the eighteenth century.[20]

Famous for opening its doors to people from around the world, even the United States discouraged its citizens from holding on to their different cultures. The national school system taught newcomers to pour their pasts into the great melting pot, and immigrants eagerly tried to blend into the

American way. But when Woodrow Wilson returned from Paris to campaign for the Minorities Treaties, he gave the impression that he represented a country committed to ethnic diversity:

> We of all peoples in the world, my fellow-citizens, ought to be able to understand the questions of this treaty and without anybody explaining them to us; for we are made up out of all the peoples of the world. I dare say that in this audience there are representatives of practically all the peoples dealt with in this treaty.
>
> You don't have to have me explain national ambitions to you, national aspirations. You have been brought up to them; you learned of them since you were children, and it is those national aspirations which we sought to realize, to give an outlet to in this great treaty.[21]

Offering a more straightforward analysis of the treaties protecting the rights of minorities, the British diplomatic historian Harold W. V. Temperly explained why the Allies only endorsed cultural pluralism in the newly formed states, while they continued to discriminate against ethnic groups back home. Publishing his voluminous study of the Paris Peace Conference in 1921, Temperly made the following observations:

> The objection was raised at the time in Poland and in other quarters that it was difficult to justify procedures by which the Polish State, a friendly and allied Power, was subjected to an invidious control of its internal affairs, from which Germany herself was exempt. . . .
>
> The ultimate truth is this. If the principle of these Treaties had been applied to Germany, it would have been very difficult eventually to refuse a demand that it should be applied universally to all established States, but to do this would have been, as we have seen, a quite unprecedented innovation. No one with any knowledge of the condition of opinion on this matter can believe that such a proposal would have had any chance of acceptance or that it would have been wise to press it. This principle, if once adopted, could have been interpreted in such a way as to bring Negroes in the Southern States of America under the protection of the League; it could have been applied to the Basques of Spain, to the Welsh and the Irish.[22]

Poland, we know, did not respect the rights of its ethnic minorities for very long, if at all. Objecting to the way the League of Nations had meddled in their domestic affairs, the Poles officially refused to comply with the treaty in 1934. By then fascistic groups had enough control over the government to pass legislation that discriminated against Jews.[23]

Still, Jewish nationalists took advantage of the West's encouragement and enthusiastically developed their national culture. Considering journalistic activities in Yiddish alone, by 1926 there were twenty daily newspapers in that language in Poland, sixty weeklies and three monthlies. Eleven years later there were twenty-seven dailies, one hundred weeklies, and eighty-five monthlies.[24]

In sum, the idea of building a national Jewish culture took shape in the nineteenth century. But it was only after the First World War that Jews began developing their secular traditions on a massive scale. The Allies, it is true, supported cultural diversity in the East for self-interested reasons, but Jewish nationalists welcomed the decisions reached at the Paris Peace Conference. Zionists and Yiddishists alike, those who sought a Jewish homeland and those who joined the international struggle of the working classes as Jewish-identified socialists—all of them opened schools and other cultural centers to promote the secular and religious traditions of the Jews. What occurred in the 1920s and 1930s had roots that went back nearly one hundred years, but the intensity of activity in the theater, the press, in education and the political arena, clearly reflected the outcome of the war and the decisions made in Paris to legitimize the dreams of ethnic minorities in the East.

As Jews became a national people, they transformed their culture, for "not only politics, but culture too undergoes drastic change in the propagation of nationalist doctrine."[25] What is more, the decisions Jews made were not arbitrary. They followed instead a set of criteria established in eighteenth-century France and Germany for defining a bonà fide national culture.

Over the years, nationalist ideologies have traveled back and forth across Europe, serving a wide range of political and social movements and adapting to different geopolitical contexts. Now, since the late 1960s, we have seen an Eastern European Jewish version developing in France, largely thanks to the efforts of Le Cercle Gaston Crémieux. As members of the group criticized France for supporting the principle of one nation within one state, they have based their arguments on the Bundists' platform for cultural autonomy in a multinational state.

But what kind of a culture did Yiddishists seek to develop for their autonomous Jews? One that used the language of the Jewish masses to produce a literature that would conform to standards set by artists committed to the humanistic values emanating from Western Europe. Paradoxically, therefore, as French Jewish intellectuals have promoted the ideals of Yiddish nationalists and tried to establish their own secular Jewish traditions in France, they have returned to the universalistic vision of culture expressed by Enlightenment philosophers in the newly emerging nation-states.

MINORITY NATIONALISM IN FRANCE

"To attack the language and culture of a people is to inflict the deepest of wounds. We proclaim the right to be different." François Mitterrand made this declaration during his campaign for the presidency in March 1981.[26] While the Socialist government did not live up to Mitterrand's promise, its minister of culture, Jack Lang, created a National Commission of French Cultures and invited people to submit project proposals to help develop a national program for assisting the country's diverse ethnic groups develop their autonomous cultures. In February 1982 Lang received a lengthy position paper entitled, "Démocratie culturelle et droit à la différence." Its author, Henri Giordan, is a researcher at the CNRS and a frequent participant in the activities sponsored by Le Cercle Gaston Crémieux.

Written in consultation with Richard Marienstras, among others, Giordan's report asked implicitly that the government assume the role the Cercle had been playing in trying to unite the efforts of ethnic minorities living in France. For several years already Marienstras had been organizing meetings with individuals active in the Breton, Occitan, and Armenian movements. Now the time had come for the minister of culture to take over this responsibility.

Combining the ideas of Bundists and Austro-Hungarian Marxists with the material realities of present-day France, Giordan's program concerned not only the cultural development of peoples who had stayed together in isolated areas of the country. With the exception, perhaps, of Corsica, Giordan maintained that regional nationalism would not solve the problems facing minorities living in France for at least three reasons: (1) Regions were no longer homogeneous; (2) Minority peoples did not necessarily live in the regions of origin; (3) There were nonterritorial minorities living in France who should also enjoy the right to develop their cultures.

According to Giordan, a series of external and internal pressures had challenged the historical ideal of building a democracy through the diffusion of one dominant, "legitimate" culture. Worldwide economic factors had forced the national market to yield to an international one, permitting a continuous flow of foreign goods that replaced many aspects of traditional French culture. What is more, in recent years, France has had to face the challenge of minorities who refuse to accept the eighteenth-century principle of one nation within one state and have demanded the right to develop their own traditions instead.

How should the French government respond? By recognizing formally the cultural autonomy of its minorities: "Every community of citizens, wherever it may be, must have the right to organize an autonomous cultural life."[27] Giordan presented a plan for the promotion of minority histories, languages, and cultures, including the organization of research projects of an ethnographic and linguistic nature and the formation of programs to sponsor minority literatures, theaters, music, and the visual arts. As he offered suggestions about how to teach minority languages, Giordan also recommended that the French government subsidize the cultural autonomy of its recognized minorities in ways similar to the platform drawn up by social democrats earlier this century.

Endorsing the proposal, Jack Lang created a National Council of Regional Languages and Cultures in 1986 with the hope of coordinating the efforts of all the minority peoples living in France. He had in mind members of such regional language groups as the Basque, Breton, Catalan, and Corsican; the speakers of Franco-Germanic dialects (Alsatian, Flemish, Francique) and of Oc; and the users of Oïl dialects (Gallo and Picard). Under the influence of Henri Giordan and Le Cercle Gaston Crémieux, he also included members of the following nonterritorial language groups: Arabic, Armenian, Berber, Creole, Hebrew, Judeo-Spanish (Ladino), Portuguese, Romany, Soninke, Spanish, Turkish, Vietnamese, and Yiddish.[28]

Unfortunately, the council got off to a slow start before the right gained control of the National Assembly in March 1986, installed its own prime minister and cabinet, and interrupted many of the progressive programs initiated by the Socialist government. Still, the national council continued to exist on paper, and Jack Lang returned to his post as minister of culture in 1988, when the Socialists came back to power.[29]

The Jewish minority has two representatives on the council: Rachel Ertel for the Ashkenazim and Lucette Valensi for the Sephardim. Rachel Ertel was born in Poland and is a native speaker of Yiddish. A literary critic and translator, she has specialized in Eastern European and American Jewish culture. She is also a founding member of Le Cercle Gaston Crémieux and has played a central role in organizing Yiddish courses in Paris at the University of Paris VII. Tunisian-born Lucette Valensi is a social historian who has written extensively on Jews in North Africa and the Middle East.[30]

When it comes to the politics of minority nationalism in France, Yiddishists have clearly been more influential than the "Orientalists." Nevertheless, Lucette Valensi's presence on the council reflects the interest Sephardic Jews have also shown in defining their culture in national terms. Within the community many have joined the Sephardic Jewish cultural organization Vidas Largas and studied Judeo-Spanish and Judeo-Arabic; others have worked with Yiddishists to clarify the problems facing secular Jews in the Diaspora. During the first years of the movement, a number of Sephardic activists even joined Le Cercle Gaston Crémieux, but they soon broke away to form other groups that openly sought ways to combine the efforts of Ashkenazim and Sephardim.

As for Le Cercle Gaston Crémieux, it stopped all activities in 1985, but former members began meeting again in 1989. Even in the intervening years, representatives of the generation of 1968 continued to promote Yiddish culture outside the university, as well as within, thanks to a group of teachers and students who formed L'Association pour l'Etude et la Diffusion de la Culture Yiddish in 1981. A leading force in this organization is Itzhok Niborski, an Argentinian of Polish-Jewish origin, who offers classes in Yiddish at the University of Paris VII with Rachel Ertel and at the Bibliothèque Medem, the Yiddish library in Paris named after the founder of the Bund. When the association first organized itself, about thirty people attended weekly meetings, which were conducted entirely in Yiddish. They also initiated at the time collective translation projects, and this inspired many of them to go on to do serious work in Yiddish within the French university system.

Before most of its activities were absorbed by academic programs, the association sponsored four highly successful Yiddish festivals in Paris. Depending on the year, they attracted between one and two thousand people from all over the city who flocked to the fairs to purchase books, journals, and records in Yiddish, as well as publications in French that promoted minority nationalism and the right to be different in Mitterand's Socialist France. Visitors also came to enjoy Eastern European-style snacks and entertainment in Yiddish.[31]

In the late 1970s another group of minority nationalists decided to publish a journal which they called *Combat pour la Diaspora*. While they mostly came from Sephardic backgrounds, those serving on the editorial board have shared many of the same political positions as members of Le Cercle Gaston Crémieux. They do not, however, limit themselves to the Bundist and Yiddishist tradition. Instead, they also feature work concerned with the history and culture of Sephardic Jews, soliciting for that purpose contributions by people like Haïm Vidal Sephiha, France's most distinguished specialist of Judeo-Spanish. Interested as they are in promoting the heritage of both Ashkenazic and Sephardic Jews, over the years the editors have encouraged debates in the journal on the tensions existing between the two communities today, both in Israel and in France.

In the mid-1980s *Combat*'s founding editor, Bernard Chouat, asked Henri Minczeles to help edit the journal. A regular contributor of articles about Eastern European Jewry, Minczeles was born in Paris in the late 1920s and grew up in a Yiddish-speaking home with Bundist sympathies. Remaining faithful to his cultural and political heritage, he has participated actively in a number of Yiddishist groups within the French Jewish community, both those founded by members of the old immigrant community (Arbete Ring) and by younger Jews who identify with the generation of 1968. In the early 1980s, Minczeles retired as an accountant in order to devote himself full-time to his political and intellectual activities. Since then he has gained recognition for the many articles he has published in Jewish periodicals representing a wide spectrum of Jewish opinion (*La Tribune juive, Les Nouveaux cahiers,* and *Combat pour la Diaspora*) and for his radio program on diaspora Jewry. In 1985 Minczeles decided to do a doctoral dissertation on the history of Vilna.[32]

Another important contributor to *Combat pour la Diaspora* is the Lacanian psychoanalyst Jacques Hassoun. Coming originally from Egypt, he was raised in a religious home, hardly the background usually associated with Jewish minority nationalists. Hassoun, however, managed to break away from Orthodox Judaism when he was a young man and join the Communist party. In 1954 he came to France where he earned a degree in psychoanalysis.[33] Since then, he has published extensively in his field as well as on the Jews of the Nile.

Hassoun's more polemical pieces dismiss the importance frequently given to customs that distinguish Sephardim from Ashkenazim. Enthusiastically embracing the politics of minority nationalism, he calls on all Jews to identify themselves as a single ethnic group and to seek ways to establish meaningful dialogues among Jews living in different parts of the world. With this goal in mind, he gives historical examples of mutual respect and understanding between European and Oriental Jews.

In one issue of *Combat,* Jacques Hassoun tells the story of Schleymen Adler, a Talmudic scholar from Galicia who settled in Alexandria at the beginning of the century. Calling him "my dear *ḥakham* Schleymen Adler," Hassoun describes how the sage happily joined Egyptian masters of sacred learning. He blended in harmoniously and received recognition for his considerable gifts, despite a strong Ashkenazic accent in Hebrew and Yiddish inflections in Arabic. Hassoun concludes with other examples of mutual respect between European and Oriental Jews, using them to challenge those who stress the ethnic differences between the two groups, often at the expense of Oriental Jews:

> Why do people insist on calling Jews from the Middle East underdeveloped? By what criteria? In the old days, when an Oriental Jew visited a shtetl in Eastern Europe, he was received as if he were a descendant from the House of David. When the Gaon of Vilna wanted to condemn the excesses of the Ḥasidim, he asked Kabbalists from the "four cities" (Jerusalem, Safed, Tiberias, and Hebron) to help him. He also requested assistance from communities of Jewish mystics in Aleppo, Damascus, and Cairo. And, when the great ḤIDA [Chaim Yoseph David Azulai] of Jerusalem came to France and appeared before the Court of King Louis XV, the Sephardic leader called the Lithuanian Gaon "the shining light of the century."[34]

But to make the case, Hassoun gave examples of religious Jews only, a strange choice for a man committed to minority nationalism, yet an honest one. He would have found it harder to develop the argument had he drawn on anything else. Scholars in the field who focus on Jewish secular traditions have even debated whether Sephardim represent a single ethnic group among themselves. Haïm Vidal Sephiha, for example, is doubtful. He prefers to stress the differences that exist among speakers of Judeo-Spanish, Judeo-Greek, and Judeo-Arabic, identifying each language community as a distinct national group.[35] Although Shmuel Trigano sees unity, he categorically rejects the notion of a national people in the first place: "The Sephardic Jew is not an ethnic category. Nor is it a racial, linguistic, or chauvinistic one. It is a way of being. The arguments people engage in about the term are ideological (people never question, incidentally, the term Ashkenazim) and are entirely *off base*. They misrepresent the Jewish experience. Take David, the "greatest man" of Israel. His mother is Ruth, the Moabite."[36]

Clearly there is little agreement about how to describe the culture (or cultures) of Jews from the Middle East and North Africa, but as activists and scholars debate the matter, they have given the French the opportunity to learn a great deal about the languages and traditions of Sephardim. People like Valensi, Sephiha, Hassoun, and Trigano have published many articles and books on Jews from the area and sponsored cultural events to promote their music and literature. Members of *Combat pour la Diaspora,* for example, helped organize a series of debates and presentations at the Centre Georges Pompidou. Called "Journées de cultures juives méditerranéennes et orientales" (September 1980), it took place nearly two years after several people from Le Cercle Gaston Crémieux joined efforts to coordinate the "Journées de la culture Yiddish" (November 1978). To the outrage of many, the Sephardic event was scheduled for the second day of Rosh Hashanah.[37]

In addition to *Combat pour la Diaspora,* another journal, *Traces,* came into existence to explore a range of political and cultural possibilities open to Jews who lived in France beyond those proposed by the Jewish establishment or Le Cercle Gaston Crémieux. Most of the founders of *Traces* were born just after the Second World War. If they had any background in Jewish culture at all, they had usually received it in youth organizations affiliated with the socialist Zionists (for example, Ha-Shomer Ha-Za'ir). When it came to Judaism, the religion, they knew almost nothing about it. As teenagers many abandoned their Jewish groups, joined the French student left and went on to participate actively in May 1968.

Ten years after the student revolt, they returned to their Jewish heritage and in 1981 founded *Traces.* The magazine remained in existence for four years, surviving on a shoestring budget. Forced to close down in 1985, several members of the editorial board decided to join the new scholarly journal, *Pardès,* which Shmuel Trigano and his professor Annie Kriegel were in the process of forming that very year.

As the name suggests, the founders of *Traces* hoped to gather fragments of the past in order to give meaning to Jews living in France today. But they also wanted to publish articles on contemporary issues by important Jewish thinkers, such as Vladimir Jankélévitch, Emmanuel Lévinas, and Léon Poliakov, all of whom came out of the Russian Jewish tradition. Defining their goals in cultural terms, the editors claimed to have no unified political agenda: "We have come together to work on what is essentially a cultural project: to bear witness to what we have called 'a bountiful renewal of Jewish culture in France.' We have each taken our own place on the chess board of politics according to our own understanding of the problems, establishing in the process individual positions vis à vis Israel."[38]

Still, for the most part, the founders of *Traces* continued to identify with the left. In their eyes, they were outsiders to virtually everybody in the Jewish community, from the extreme Orthodox, to the establishment, to rebel organizations like Le Cercle Gaston Crémieux. Refusing to identify with any existing group, they drew on many sources, political and religious, Ashkenazic and Sephardic, as they tried to develop a notion of what it meant to be a Jew in France today.

Traces grew out of two earlier projects initiated by its founder, the journalist Luc Rosenzweig. In 1979, a few weeks before Pierre Goldman was murdered, Rosenzweig published a collection of essays written by young Jews who identified with the generation of 1968. Called *Catalogue pour des Juifs de maintenant,* the volume consisted of a series of self-conscious sketches by people who had little or no familiarity with their Jewish heritage, but who wanted to define a political and cultural place for themselves as Jews in contemporary France.[39] The following year Rosenzweig published several interviews with members of this same generation of Jews, and he gave the book the title *La Jeune France juive,* an allusion to *La France juive,* a slanderous volume written in the nineteenth century by the self-proclaimed anti-Semite Edouard Drumont.[40]

When he first decided to write about Jews, Rosenzweig sought the support of one of the most outspoken older critics of the French Jewish establishment, Wladimir Rabi (Rabinovitch): a man whose ideas and background fascinated many former radicals during the early days of minority nationalism in France, a period when Jewish students on the left tended to identify with Eastern European Jews of working-class origin.[41] Rabi was born in Vilna at the turn of the century and died in Paris in 1981. Beginning his education in Lithuania, he went to a Russian-language school and soon spoke only that tongue, rejecting Yiddish, which he had heard at home. When his father went bankrupt, the Rabinovitches moved to Paris, arriving there in 1910 and settling down on the Left Bank, in the part of the city preferred by political refugees of the czarist empire. Soon Rabi and his two sisters learned French and dropped Russian.

During the years before the First World War, the family lived in terrible poverty. Like many other Jewish immigrants of the period, Rabi's father had taken a job in a sweatshop—he sewed fur coats. The work paid so badly, however, that he finally gave it up and opened a restaurant for students in the family's apartment, engaging his wife as the cook and displacing the children, who spent a great deal of time looking after themselves, playing outside in the streets, and escaping the crowds and bustle in the flat. Not an easy way to grow up, perhaps, but Rabi's sister, Sonia Rabinovitch Grinberg, remembers these days as being very exciting, for Russian revolutionaries frequently stopped by for a meal and stayed on for hours, involving everyone in heated debates. Family legend has it that Trotsky ate at the apartment.

The restaurant stayed open on the Sabbath, but Friday evenings remained sacred, the special day of the week when relatives and friends came by to eat together. On the major Jewish holidays, however, Rabi's parents closed down and went to synagogue. In the early days, his father attended a small Eastern European-style *shtibl* on the rue de l'Hôtel-de-Ville, but he soon switched over to the newly constructed Polish-Lithuanian establishment on the rue Paveé, an imposing structure located in the heart of the Marais. Eager to assimilate, Rabi's mother preferred the consistorial temple on the rue des Tournelles.

The children had little formal religious training, but they remained identified with Judaism. In their teenage years, they joined the Union Universelle de la Jeunesse Juive, a group made up of Zionists and anti-Zionists, religious and nonreligious Jews. The union had a student newspaper called *Shalom,* which Rabi edited for a while. It also ran a lecture series in which major figures of the French Jewish community came to speak—for example, Edmond Fleg, the poet and philosopher, who translated Judaism into the French universalistic tradition.

Despite poverty, Rabi managed to get a good education and to study law. Receiving his degree in the interwar years, he practiced the profession in Paris until the late 1930s, at which time he married and moved to Briançon (Hautes-Alpes) to accompany his wife, an art teacher and a Gentile, who had a job there in a lycée. Rabi soon became a judge in the local court and gained the respect and affection of the community (see map 4). When the Germans occupied France, the residents of Briançon demonstrated their friendship by helping Rabi secure false papers for himself and other members of his family, including his sister Sonia and her husband.

Author of two controversial books, Rabi has also written many provocative articles criticizing mainstream Jewish organizations.[42] What is more, he took an active part in the Colloque des Intellectuels Juifs de Langue Française where he continued to lambaste the Jewish establishment for claiming to speak for everyone in the community.

In the lead article of *Catalogue pour des Juifs de maintenant,* Rabi endorsed the desire of the new generation to do away with institutionalized forms of Jewish life. But in the process, he also challenged the positions of

Marienstras and Trigano. In his eyes, one ignored the importance of Israel, whereas the other refused to accept the significance of the Diaspora.[43] In 1981, a few weeks before the publication of the first issue of *Traces,* Rabi died in a car accident.[44]

Another hero for those who eventually founded *Traces* was Moshe Zalcman, a Polish Jewish tailor and former Communist.[45] Born in Zamosc at the turn of the century, he came from the same town as the revolutionary Rosa Luxemburg. As a young man, Zalcman joined the outlawed Polish Communist party and took many risks carrying out his political activities. In 1929 it grew too dangerous for him to remain in Poland, so he went to Paris where he became a member of the Main d'Oeuvre Immigrée (MOI), the French Communist organization for immigrant workers.

Zalcman fled once again in the early 1930s, this time to Kiev in the Ukraine to serve Soviet communism as a tailor. But he was not safe there either. During the Stalinist purges, he was arrested for crimes he had never committed. Surviving ten years of hard labor in Siberia, he spent another nine in a community on the outskirts of the prison camp. Finally a tribunal cleared his name in 1956 and publicly admitted that he had been falsely accused. Zalcman left the Soviet Union a few months later and returned to Poland, where he encountered more disappointments.

In the early 1960s, Zalcman abandoned Poland and communism for good and moved back to Paris. He arrived there in fragile health and with an ailing wife, but he managed to find work as a tailor once again, as well as the freedom he needed to record his memoirs. Published in Yiddish, the book was a great success in the French Yiddish-speaking community, and it came to the attention of members of the generation of 1968 through Zalcman's nephew Frederic Dajez.[46]

Thanks to the efforts of Dajez, Luc Rosenzweig, and a few other friends, the Polish tailor's story appeared in French translation in 1977, together with a short preface to explain the importance of the work for young Jews like themselves. The editors admitted that they felt completely cut off from Zalcman's world. There was no going back. But through his memoirs they had found a way to face the tragic circumstances responsible for severing the ties that should have connected them to the ideals and traditions to which Zalcman had devoted himself in his youth.

This group of young Jews wanted the book to appear in French so that people outside the Yiddish-speaking community could read Zalcman's story. But that was not the only reason. They also wanted his experiences to become part of a wider project aimed at inventing a kind of *Yiddishkayt* for

Jews in France today. Acknowledging the contradiction, they nonetheless sought ways to establish a Jewish cultural tradition for themselves through French translations of remnants of a heritage that had little to do with the lives of Jews born after the Second World War.[47]

Zalcman's memoirs served an additional purpose: they justified the decision made by many student activists to abandon the extreme left and to join Jewish-identified groups. By the time the book was published, Jews of the generation of 1968 had already formed several different factions among themselves, and they did not agree on a number of issues. But when it came to the question of the Stalinist purges, they joined forces once again.

Over the years, members (and former members) of Le Cercle Gaston Crémieux, *Traces,* and *Combat pour la Diaspora* have continued to expose the extent of the betrayal of Jews under Stalinism, borrowing generously from each other's research. Perhaps one of their most successful efforts was Nat Lilenstein's television documentary, *Les Révolutionnaires du Yiddishland.* Rachel Ertel served as the main historical consultant for the project, and she worked closely with a team of five specialists who represented the various groups.

Lilenstein's film appeared on prime-time national television in 1984, and it became, in a sense, the official French Socialist version of the history of minority nationalism in Eastern Europe.[48] Presenting the story largely from the political perspective of Rachel Ertel's book *Le Shtetl,* the documentary also supported the efforts of those in the government working to promote cultural autonomy for ethnic groups living in France in the 1980s.[49] A great critical success, the film describes the rise and fall of Jewish minority nationalism in Eastern Europe. Taking a strong stand against Soviet communism, it blames Stalin, as well as Hitler, for destroying Jewish socialist movements. The film interviews former revolutionaries who explain what life was like for Jews in Poland and Russia at the turn of the century and in the interwar years. For the most part, these people no longer believe in the ideals that gave meaning to their lives when they were young, but the documentary itself remains faithful to the dreams of Jewish socialists and continues to endorse platforms promoting minority nationalism.

As Jews of the generation of 1968 try to salvage Eastern European culture from the ravages of history, they look for guidance from those who participated in Jewish minority movements during the 1920s and 1930s and who have continued to make contributions to Yiddish culture today. Even though these survivors have lost faith in their earlier political ideals, many have maintained strong ties to the rich literary tradition that existed in

Poland and Lithuania between the two wars. Rachel Ertel grew up with these people, and she now interprets their artistic endeavors for the French-reading public.

Among Ertel's many achievements, there is her translation of *Vintn* (*Le Vent qui passe*), a novel written by her mother, who goes by the pen name Menuha Ram.[50] Basing the plot on her own experiences, Menuha Ram tells the story of a Jewish woman and her infant daughter during World War II, of how they were deported from eastern Poland by the Soviet army in 1939 and sent to Kazakhstan, a small village in Siberia. The little girl was Rachel Ertel.

Menuha Ram came originally from Žetl (Zdzieciol), a small town in Byelorussia that went to Poland after World War I (see map 2). Her father, a scribe (*soyfer*), earned a modest living making copies of holy books. When she was old enough to leave home, she went to Vilna to study. There, she joined the Bund and married Rachel's father, who was also a member of the party. A carpenter by trade, he went on to become a union organizer for the Bund.

Rachel Ertel was born in Slonim in 1939, in what was then eastern Poland. When the Soviet troops invaded the city a few months after her birth, they arrested and jailed her father for his political activities. Even though they did not imprison him for long, by the time he got out, his wife and daughter had been exiled. Unable to find them, he remained in Slonim, joined the Resistance, and died there fighting the Germans.

After the war, Menuha Ram returned home with her daughter and discovered she had lost everyone. She then went to Lodz, previously known for its large, working-class Jewish population. In the devastated city, she found a job as a teacher for orphaned children and made arrangements for her daughter to attend the I. L. Peretz School, the same institution in which Marek Halter was studying. Several months later Menuha Ram met Moshe Waldman, a poet and an activist on the Zionist left, and she remarried.

In 1948 the family moved to Paris and settled down in the newly constituted Yiddish community. Receiving a warm welcome, Moshe Waldman found work as a journalist and writer and continued his political activities. By this time Menuha Ram had given up her Bundist loyalties and become a Zionist too. Like many other survivors she now firmly believed that Jews needed a nation that they could call their own.

As socialist Zionists from Eastern Europe, the Waldmans maintained their commitment to Yiddish culture and passed down the language to their children, speaking it at home, making it the source of the family's Jewish tradition. Grateful to them for having raised her in Yiddish, Rachel Ertel later dedicated her book *Le Shtetl* to "my parents [the Waldmans] who gave me the key to this universe."[51]

Shortly after she arrived in France, the young Rachel lost her ability to speak Russian and Polish, replacing these languages with French and English, which she learned in school. After passing her baccalaureate exam in 1957, she decided to spend a year abroad studying at Columbia University.

On the streets of New York, Rachel Ertel marveled at the ethnic diversity. Her experiences in New York convinced her that it was still possible to create a society where peoples practicing different traditions could live side by side. Ertel went on to specialize in the work of writers representing minority cultures in the United States and eventually prepared a doctoral dissertation on American Jewish literature.[52]

When the student revolt occurred in 1968, Rachel Ertel was teaching at the Sorbonne and was well placed to participate in the new programs developing in the university system. Teaming up with those interested in working on minority cultures, she accepted a position in 1969 at the Institut d'Anglais of the University of Paris VII. So did Richard and Elise Marienstras.

From the beginning, Paris VII attracted scholars concerned with feminist and ethnic studies. Those working on aspects of American culture offered courses on the history and literature of women, blacks, Native Americans, and Jews. By 1970, Ertel had established the Centre d'Etudes Judéo-Américaines at the Institut d'Anglais, and this rapidly evolved into a successful program of Yiddish culture, with four levels of language courses, as well as seminars on a wide range of topics. Today, in addition to Rachel Ertel, there are several other instructors of Yiddish at the institute, among them, the Argentinian Itzhok Niborski.

According to Ertel, in the years immediately following 1968, her students in Yiddish were activists identified with the left who were looking for ways to return to their political roots, to make a connection between their private and public lives. Despite their agenda, Rachel Ertel held on to her own and conducted these courses in the early 1970s, with the goal of preserving cultural diversity in a multinational state. Given the new, more flexible university system and the rise of minority nationalism in France, she already saw the possibility of the Socialist party winning the elections and providing opportunities for ethnic groups in the country to develop their own cultures.

Now, as she recalls those early days, Ertel insists that neither she nor Marienstras ever imagined recreating a working-class Yiddish culture in France. They were not living in Eastern Europe in the interwar period where the Bund could count on the Yiddish-speaking masses. In the late 1960s, the Jewish proletariat was small and, for the most part, of North African origin. Le Cercle Gaston Crémieux could only hope to attract intellectuals to their movement. And this they did.

Actually, even if it were possible, Rachel Ertel would not have tried to revive Eastern European culture. She wants only to preserve its memory and apply some of the political insights associated with the tradition to contemporary France. Yiddish belongs to an annihilated people, she explains, who should never be forgotten, but whose past should not be trivialized either by folkloric imitations.

Ertel has defined her task as an interpreter and teacher. She trains students to make the world of secular Yiddishists accessible to the French-reading public. Rejecting all attempts to reconstruct what no longer exists, she uses translation as a way of transposing one culture onto another, transforming and adapting as she goes along, creating a new secular Jewish tradition in France. While she feels she still has much to accomplish, Ertel hopes her work has contributed to the collective effort of minority groups in France to break down the monolithic French system that recognizes only one nation within the state.

In the early 1960s Rachel Ertel began publishing translations of Yiddish literature. Twenty years later she became the editor of a series of books which presents the writings of Eastern European Jews to the French, first at L'Age d'homme and now at Le Seuil. One of her recent projects has involved the work of the poet Abraham Sutzkever, a collection of whose poems and prose pieces she brought out in 1988 (*Où gîtent les étoiles*).[53]

Considered to be one of the greatest Yiddish poets in the twentieth century, Sutzkever belonged to "Young Vilna," a circle of writers who lived in Vilna between the two wars. A hero in the ghetto resistance, Sutzkever was instrumental in hiding many books and manuscripts from YIVO's library. After the war, the poet moved to Tel Aviv, where he founded the literary journal *Di Goldene Keyt* (The Golden Chain) in the late 1940s. His celebrated publication continues to thrive today.

Rachel Ertel has trained young Jews of the generation of 1968 to become capable translators, dedicated to the task of conveying in French the richness of the language and culture of Eastern European Jews. With her encouragement, this new group of Yiddishists has also studied with a man of Lithuanian Jewish origin, who goes by the pen name Litvine. A translator of French poetry into Yiddish, Mordecai Litvine has inspired a number of people who identify with the goals of minority nationalism. But instead of endorsing the efforts of those who promote cultural autonomy for ethnic groups in France, he has dedicated his life to interpreting the works of Western European writers for members of the Yiddish-reading public.

Litvine, the subject of the next chapter, challenges generalizations frequently made about Eastern European Jews of his generation. And the translator is not alone. Emmanuel Lévinas, Jacob Gordin, and Olga Katunal, whose life stories appear in later chapters, do not fit the stereotype either. Raised in families imbued with Jewish and European traditions, they all found ways to maintain their people's heritage while they embraced the cultural ideals of the French Enlightenment. Children of *maskilim* (enlightened people), they received an education that combined the traditional values of Jewish and European cultures.

Scholars frequently describe the Haskalah of czarist Russia as being quite different from the Jewish Enlightenment of Germany and France. Jews in the West, the argument goes, became culturally indistinguishable from everybody else. Many still held on to their people's religion, but they did so by forcing Judaism to conform to the demands of the wider society. In the East, however, as enlightened Jews prepared for their emancipation, they supposedly abandoned Judaism to the very Orthodox and either joined the dominant culture as atheists or Christians, or became secular Jewish nationalists.

In his book *Rédemption et utopie,* Michael Löwy draws on Rachel Ertel's analysis of the process as he contrasts intellectual Jews living in the czarist empire at the turn of the century with their contemporaries residing in Germany:

> In order to understand better the atheistic and secular orientation of the revolutionary intelligentsia of Eastern Europe, it is necessary to examine closely the religious aspect of the *Haskalah* and the consequences of this movement. In Germany, the Haskalah effectively succeeded in "enlightening," modernizing, rationalizing and Germanizing the Jewish religion. . . .
>
> This was not the case in Russia: reform synagogues had few followers except for a small group of upper class Jews. What is more, the iconoclastic attack that maskilim launched against Orthodoxy only made the traditionalists more rigid and obstinate. . . . It became necessary to liberate oneself from the religion first, become atheist or "enlightened," in order to gain access to the outside world.[54]

Enlightened Jews in the East did not, it is true, develop a reform movement comparable to the one that emerged in the West. Nevertheless Litvine's story introduces a note of caution, as do those of other people from Lite, for he grew up in a world where many middle-class Jews remained faithful to Judaism while they embraced Western European humanism and the culture of the wider society. With the eye of an ethnographer, Litvine carefully describes the compromises made by his father with regard to Jewish law. Recalling the way his family observed the Sabbath and other religious holidays, Litvine explains how his father rejected Orthodoxy but maintained the integrity of Judaism, according to his own enlightened beliefs.

Jewish families like Litvine's considered themselves "traditionalists." Although Löwy used the term in the passage above to identify strictly observant Jews, in Lite traditionalists were those between the very religious and the nonpracticing Jews. They did not follow all the restrictions, but they observed kashrut, celebrated the Sabbath and the holidays, and instructed their children in Hebrew and the Bible. Although Litvine eventually abandoned the religion and joined the secular Yiddish literary tradition, to this day he still speaks with pride about the education he received as a boy, one which combined religious learning with the study of secular subjects in Yiddish, Hebrew, and Russian.

Lévinas came from an even more assimilated family than did Litvine. Whereas Litvine grew up speaking Yiddish and Russian, Lévinas spoke only Russian at home. But he too was raised as a traditionalist. While still a young boy, Lévinas received lessons in Hebrew and the Bible, and he has remained a practicing Jew. Faithful to the traditions of the Haskalah in Lite, Lévinas engages the ideas of European and Jewish thinkers in his philosophical work.

Jacob Gordin and Olga Katunal came from families who had broken with strictly Orthodox forms of Judaism to an even greater extent than those of Litvine and Lévinas. But even in the homes of nonreligious Jews, the children were knowledgeable about their Jewish heritage. No matter how diluted their education might have seemed to Orthodox Jews from Eastern Europe, in all four cases these sons and daughter of maskilim grew up in families that maintained important ties to the religion and to Jewish national customs while embracing modernity and Russian culture. Comfortable in several languages and traditions, Litvine, Lévinas, Gordin, and Katunal all had the background necessary to participate in the major political, literary, and philosophical moments of their times, sometimes as cosmopolitan intellectuals, sometimes as Jews, and frequently as both.

4

The European Enlightenment in Yiddish Translation: The Life Story of Mordecai Litvine

Many Lithuanian Jews enjoy tracing their ancestry back to Talmudic scholars, preferably to eminent ones like the Gaon of Vilna, Chaim of Volozhin, the Gaon's favorite disciple, or members of the great Soloveichik dynasty. Mordecai Litvine takes great pride in coming from a family of famous rabbis, recognized since the eighteenth century for its contributions to religious learning.[1] Few people can produce a lineage as distinguished as his, with ties to prominent Soloveichiks, and to Chaim of Volozhin as well.[2]

The first important Soloveichik was Joseph ha-Levi, head of the Jewish community in Slobodka, a suburb of Kovno (see map 3). In the late 1750s, when Lithuania still belonged to Poland (it became a province of Russia in 1795), this rabbi went to Warsaw and convinced the king to rescind a new law that expelled the Jews from Kovno. The written account of Joseph ha-Levi's negotiations with the monarch, stamped with all the official seals, remained in the family until 1915.

The Jews of Kovno celebrated their local victory annually on Purim with the reading of a second Megillah, the story of their expulsion from the city and of Joseph ha-Levi's visit to the king.[3]

For the occasion, yeshiva boys from Slobodka came down to the home of the Kovno branch of the Soloveichik family to participate in the festivities. During the holiday the students honored the memory of Joseph ha-Levi, as well as that of the rabbi's grandsons, Moses and Abraham Soloveichick, who brought further fame to the family in 1772, by building the great synagogue of Williampol-Slobodka.

In the late eighteenth century, Moses Soloveichik's son Joseph, rabbi of Kovno, married Relka, daughter of Chaim of Volozhin. They had two sons, one of whom, Isaac-Ze'ev, broke with tradition and agreed to become the first Crown Rabbi of Kovno, an office created by Nicholas I in 1844 for Jewish communities throughout the empire. Determined to assimilate the Jews of Russia, the czar signed a decree (*ukaz*) ordering the establishment of two crown rabbinical seminaries, both in Lithuania, to prepare religious leaders to be civil servants of the state.[4] Many Jews ignored the ukaz and continued sending gifted sons to Orthodox yeshivas, but some complied, timidly at first, as they pondered the dangers of modernizing Judaism. And so, from the mid-1800s until the Russian Revolution, many Jewish communities had two kinds of rabbis: those who rigorously maintained the ways of the past and those who served the religion as representatives of the czar.[5]

Isaac-Ze'ev had five children, three boys and two girls. One daughter was Relka, Litvine's maternal grandmother. Among his sons, there was Joseph Baer, chief Orthodox rabbi of Brisk, and Chaim-Simḥah, who was also destined for the rabbinate, but refused ordination.

Litvine's great uncle Chaim-Simḥah found ways to remain religious—at least in his eyes—while he welcomed the Jewish Enlightenment. As a young man, he spoke Russian and German, played a good game of chess, and engaged peripherally in dangerous political activities, lending support to revolutionaries. According to family legend, Chaim-Simḥah even saved the life of Lev Hartmann (Gartman), a member of the Narodnaya Volya (People's Will), the populist group responsible for assasinating Czar Alexander II in 1881. Hartmann himself had played a central role in an earlier attempt on Alexander's life that ended in failure in 1879.[6] Although the details are hazy, Hartmann fled Moscow for Kovno in search of a sympathizer who might take him out of Russia. Somehow he met Chaim-Simḥah who agreed to help. As the story goes, Chaim-Simḥah, the son of a long line of rabbis, disguised himself as a peasant, hid Hartmann in a wagon under a load of cabbage, and drove the revolutionary to the German border. Litvine's great uncle also became a friend of Pavel Akselrod, a Narodnik who went on to form the Group for the Liberation of Labor in 1882, the first genuine "Marxist unit" in Russia.[7]

When his parents died, Chaim-Simḥah inherited the Soloveichik home in Kovno and took in his sisters, Relka and Sarah. The two women had independent incomes, for Isaac-Ze'ev had left his daughters property in the Kovno fish market, which they rented out to merchants. Still, the sisters preferred to live together in the family's house. Sarah was a widow by then, and Relka, though married, was alone most of the time, because her husband spent much of the year tending his business in the Latvian port city of Libau (Liepaja). He exported and imported herring and grains.

Like her brother, Relka was an enlightened Jew, open to new ideas and languages. While still a young girl, she studied modern Hebrew with the famous writer Abraham Mapu. After she married, Relka wore a wig, following the Orthodox tradition, and maintained a kosher home, but she remained committed to the goals of maskilim Jews, eager to read European and contemporary Hebrew literature and to participate in the culture of the wider society. According to Litvine, his grandmother knew German poetry so well she could recite Heine and Schiller by heart.

Relka had two daughters. To prepare them properly for the modern world, she engaged private tutors to teach them Hebrew and Russian. One of these instructors was a young man from Radin (Radun), a small town located between Vilna and Grodno.

The tutor came from a modest family, but he had had an excellent religious and secular education. In his youth, he studied Torah and Jewish ethics with the celebrated scholar Ḥafez-Chaim (Israel Meir ha-Kohen). Like many in his generation, he subsequently embraced the Enlightenment and turned his attention to modern languages and literature.

Relka's daughter Sarah-Rivkah fell in love with the young man from Radin and wanted to marry him. Although children rarely had their way in such matters, Relka supported her daughter's wish, a bold decision in the face of their status-conscious family. The Soloveichiks did not normally approve of husbands who had neither wealth nor commitment to a life of Talmudic learning.

Married in 1891, Sarah-Rivkah gave birth to a healthy male child a year later. Soon afterward, she had a second son, then a daughter, both of whom died in infancy. Her fourth child, Mordecai, did not arrive until the early years of the twentieth century, after the family had left Kovno and moved to the nearby town of Shavli (Šiauliai).

During the early years of their marriage, Mordecai's father took a job in

Shavli with the Kagan Chocolate Factory, leaving his wife and their first son in Kovno, much as his father-in-law had done a generation before. When he became head accountant of the factory in 1899, he sent for his family. By the time Litvine was born a few years later, his parents had abandoned the Soloveichik home. They did not even return for summer vacations, but went to neighboring Latvia instead to visit his grandparents, who had settled permanently in Libau soon after their daughter Sarah-Rivkah had moved to Shavli with her family. Litvine got to know Kovno only as a teenager, when he went there to study in the early 1920s.

Before he was ten, Litvine's mother passed away, leaving him with few memories of her. Still, he recalled that the emancipated Sarah-Rivkah had never worn a wig. His older brother claimed that she had never been to a mikveh (ritual bath) either.

Mordecai's father did not marry again. To help run the household and care for the children, he employed a Lithuanian maid, a woman who spoke Yiddish well, even though she was not Jewish, and knew how to maintain a kosher kitchen. During those years, the family lived in a large, beautiful home with a small garden, right on the grounds of the factory.

As head accountant of Kagan's, Litvine's father received the house rent-free. He also earned a good salary, for pre-World War I Shavli, something on the order of 100 rubles a month. This allowed him to raise his sons in comfort. His father, however, Litvine explained, was not a rich man, for he owned no property and could make no capital investments.

Trying hard to compete with the famous George Bohrmann Chocolate, the owners of Kagan kept the business going seven days a week. But they nonetheless managed to respect the religious traditions of their employees. A Jewish firm, Kagan hired Lithuanian Catholics for most of the unskilled labor and Jews for the semiskilled and skilled. Following the ethnic division of the work force, management closed the white collar office on Saturdays and the factory on Sundays.

Mordecai's father opposed Orthodox Judaism. Proud to be a Jew, but eager to enter the modern world, he joined other maskilim of his generation and redefined his relationship to the religion. While he remained kosher, he gave up many of the daily practices of strictly observant Jews. He also modified the way he celebrated the Sabbath and holidays. On Friday evenings, for example, he donned a skullcap, lit the candles, and recited the blessings to welcome the Sabbath.[8] But after chanting the traditional prayers over the wine and bread, he took off his *yarmulke* and reverted to his secular self, paying no further attention to ritual. Instead of saying grace after the meal, Mordecai's father read stories by Sholem Aleichem or Peretz to the children.

Frequently Mordecai's father attended synagogue on Friday evenings to greet his friends and wish them a good Sabbath. During the cold months, he often went to services the next day as well, but when summer came, he preferred to spend his Saturday mornings in the garden reading the newspaper.

Whereas observant Jews did not cook on the sabbath, Litvine's father wanted his children to eat freshly prepared food. For the sake of tradition, he occasionally had the Lithuanian maid make a *cholent* in advance and send the potato stew over to the baker's oven to keep warm. But more often than not, he employed his housekeeper as a *"Shabes Goye"*9 and asked her to prepare something special for the noon meal on the morning of the Day of Rest. After lunch, when the weather permitted, father and sons took long walks along the railroad tracks and through fields of rye, to the home of some peasants who sold them milk and bread for a snack. Only years later did Litvine learn that Jews were not supposed to carry money on the Sabbath.

Litvine associates every holiday with its special dishes. On Rosh Hashanah, for example, they ate apples and honey, like Jews throughout Europe, to bring in a sweet year, and raisins too, but the real treat was watermelon which turned ripe in the Ukraine in the month of Elul (August/September), just before the big celebration. The Jews of western Russia honored the fruit by serving it for the first time on the eve of the New Year. Before taking a bite, they recited the traditional *Sheheheyanu* prayer to thank God for keeping them alive long enough to enjoy the harvest of the new season. Gefilte fish was served as well, presented in the skin of the pike or whitefish, complete with its head and tail. Mordecai's father cut off the head of the fish and recited the famous saying: "May it be God's will that I be a head and not a tail." Pronouncing the words carefully in Hebrew, he would smile to himself, as he thought of the jokes people made about tails in Yiddish.10

As Litvine remembers it, the most delicious holiday of all was Shavuot. A festival known for its dairy dishes, Lithuanian Jews served cheese blintzes on the first day, fried lightly in butter, the way Jews did all over the Russian empire. On the second day, however, they ate a regional variation (pronounced *shal-teh-no-seh*) : deep-fried square dumplings, also filled with cheese.

One year when Mordecai was still a young boy, the eve of Shavuot fell on the same day as Pentecost. Having nothing to do in the early afternoon, he went next door to play with the child of their Catholic neighbors, whom he found helping his family get ready to celebrate the revelation of the Holy Spirit. In preparation for the festivities, Lithuanians gathered green branches and attached them to the outside of their houses. As evening drew near, Litvine's father called his son home to join them in the commemoration of the giving of the Ten Commandments. Even though the boy adored Shavuot, he was disappointed that he could not celebrate his holiday in the open air too.

Despite this childhood memory, Litvine rarely felt torn between being a Jew and a member of the wider society. In his own life, he never encountered the dreariness he read about in works of fiction, written by maskilim rebelling against the conservative forces of traditional Judaism. While still a young boy, Litvine found a copy of the famous Hebrew novella by Mordecai Ze'ev Feierberg, "Whither?", which describes the stark life of the son of a Ḥasidic rabbi in terms so dramatic that he never forgot them. Litvine was particularly struck by the episode in which the father, Reb Moshe, admonishes little Naḥam for playing with his friends:

> A Jew mustn't fill his mouth with laughter in this world. We're here to worship God and to study His Law; we mustn't even think of spending our time in such foolery.
>
> Ah, son, don't you say every day in your prayers, "And let not the Evil Urge [yeẓer ha-rah] have power over us? What a great prayer it is! But the Evil Urge does have power over us because of our sins. Every moment of pleasure and enjoyment is put there by the devil to drag us down into the vanities of this world, so as to rob us our place in the next. We mustn't take pleasure, son, we mustn't ever take pleasure in this world!"[11]

Litvine attended classes in a modified *ḥeder* until he was seven, but his father was dissatisfied with the program there. Taking him out of the school, the former teacher hired a maskil tutor to come to the house to give lessons to his son and three other children—a cousin and two boys of friends of the family—in Hebrew, Bible, modern Hebrew literature, Russian, and arithmetic. Although this arrangement was a big improvement, Litvine's father eventually joined other enlightened Jews in Shavli and helped organize a school similar in outlook to the Tarbut institutions that became popular in Eastern Europe during the interwar years. This precursor of the Tarbut was recognized by the czar in 1913, and it provided classes in modern Hebrew and Russian and had a Zionist orientation. Strictly Orthodox Jews rejected the experiment, and they would go on to oppose the Tarbut schools a few years later.

In the morning, students had four hours of Jewish instruction: Bible (Tanaḥ), Talmud, Hebrew language and modern literature and history. Except for the Talmud, which they studied in Yiddish translation, Jewish subjects were taught in Hebrew. After a two-hour lunch break, students returned for three hours of math and Russian language, literature, and history, all taught in Russian.

Influenced by his father, Litvine was an avid reader. Like many other maskilim of the period, the former teacher had wanted his sons to be literate in Yiddish, Hebrew, and Russian, and he encouraged the boys to use the family's vast library, with its selection of books in several languages. In Yiddish, Litvine could choose from among the classics of this relatively young literary tradition: the works of Mendele Moykher Sforim, I. L. Peretz, and Sholem Aleichem, as well as from those of more contemporary novelists, poets, and playwrights. There was also a large collection of books by European authors translated into Yiddish, rather poorly, Litvine observed critically. As far as he was concerned, only Jules Verne read reasonably well. In contrast, Litvine found that translations into Hebrew were usually excellent. He therefore did most of his reading as a young boy in this language, enjoying fairytales, Dickens, Swift, Mark Twain, and Shakespeare, not to mention the works of such modern Hebrew writers as Bialik, Mapu, Smilanski, and Feierberg.

By the time he was seven, Litvine was reading Russian as well, and had discovered the great classics, most of which his father had in the library. There were many books in German too, but since Litvine did not learn that language until later on, his first introduction to Goethe, Schiller, and Heine was in Russian translation. Finally, came the section of religious books: the Torah, the Talmud, and a goodly number of commentaries, but no Kabbalah.

Although Litvine's father never joined a political party, he sympathized with the Zionist left and the Russian socialists. His leanings determined the newspapers he subscribed to: *Der Haynt,* the Zionist Yiddish daily from Warsaw, and *Hed Ha-Zeman,* a Hebrew journal from Vilna. He also bought *Denj,* a progressive Russian daily from St. Petersburg. It is not surprising, given this exposure, that Litvine's brother and then Litvine himself went a step further than their father and eventually became Communists, at least for a while.

The political evolution from one generation to the next expressed itself in many ways, even in the music father and elder son brought home. Litvine remembers his father playing the violin and teaching the boys folk melodies in Yiddish and Zionist songs in Hebrew. His brother then added the Bund's anthem in Yiddish—he joined the party in 1905—Bolshevik airs in Russian, and the "Marseillaise" in the version preferred by the German Social Democrats.

In 1913 Litvine's brother left czarist Russia to avoid the draft and joined the huge colony of Lithuanian Jews who had emigrated to South Africa. By doing so, he escaped two world wars and the hardships that threatened Litvine's life. He was also spared the political conflicts that led his younger brother to reconsider his earlier ideological convictions.

The Germans declared war on Russia in the summer of 1914. As Prussian soldiers invaded the czarist empire, the Grand Duke Nikolay Nikolaevich, head of the Russian army, expelled masses of Jewish residents who lived near the German border. A notorious anti-Semite, the grand duke claimed that Yiddish speakers were natural allies of the enemy. Within twenty-four hours, more than a million Jews had been forced to leave their homes. Moving southeast, Litvine's father first took his son to Lida (Vilna Province), where he had relatives. Then they continued into the Ukraine, with the hope of taking refuge in the city of Slavyansk (see map 3).

The road to Slavyansk was choked with frightened people forced to leave home. In the crush, it was easy to get separated, and Mordecai lost his father. There was no turning back to look for him; he had to keep going and assume they would meet once they reached their destination. When he arrived, however, Litvine discovered that his father had died on the way. He never learned how.

Mordecai moved in with an aunt and uncle and remained in Slavyansk until after the Bolshevik Revolution. These were difficult years for the boy, but he had the good fortune of being able to study in a local Russian gymnasium. He did so without even having to take the highly selective entrance exam usually imposed on Jewish children of his generation for the purpose of excluding most of them from attending government-run schools. Litvine avoided the ordeal, he explained, because his family had settled in a part of town where very few Jews lived. The school, therefore, did not worry about quotas and never bothered to administer the test.

When the war ended in 1918, Lithuania declared itself an independent nation, and all residents of the former Russian province automatically became citizens of the new democratic republic—even those living in exile.

Litvine's aunt and uncle qualified. In 1921 they finally left the Soviet Union and returned to Kovno (now called Kaunas), taking their nephew with them and enrolling Litvine in Kovno's Russian-language gymnasium.

At school in Kovno, Mordecai had many Jewish friends, and he and his classmates participated in groups that promoted the development of a modern Jewish culture. He joined, for example, the student newspaper where he had the opportunity to publish translations of Gorky in Hebrew and pieces of criticism in Russian. While he enjoyed the work immensely, Litvine later observed that he found his literary voice only when he started to write in Yiddish in the late 1930s.

Like many intellectuals from the Baltic states, upon graduating from gymnasium, Litvine went to Berlin with the intention of attending university there, once he had gained a working knowledge of German. Having studied the language in high school, it took him only one year to finish preparing himself adequately. In autumn of 1923, he was ready to take classes in history, philosophy, and political economy, as well as in literature, his major course of study. Within five years he had successfully passed the highly competitive *Staatsprüfung* exam that qualified him for a doctorate. Litvine, however, dropped out of the program before finishing his degree— he needed to start earning a living.

In the early postwar years, Germany's desperate economic situation had made the country cheap for foreigners. Even poor students could manage on tight budgets. At one point during 1923, Litvine remembers inflation rising so high that one American dollar was worth twelve million marks. Since Lithuania's currency was reasonably stable, with four or five *lits* to the dollar, a few coins from back home produced a fabulous sum. But every day the value changed, and Litvine had to be careful not to cash too much money at a single time. As a result, he and his friends pooled resources, using his lit one week and somebody else's the next.

Then all of a sudden inflation stopped. By the end of 1923, the mark had settled at 4.20 to the dollar and remained there until 1939. While the new situation forced many students to leave the country, Litvine hung on, scraping along. His biggest concern was to have enough money to cover rent and university tuition. When it came to food, he made do with very little.

Litvine found the German equivalent to a bed and breakfast. In addition to lodging, this provided him with two rolls and a cup of coffee every morning. For lunch he tried to have four rolls and tea, with a lump of sugar if he could afford it, without it if he could not. On a lucky day, he went home with a friend for supper. If he had no invitation, he did without, unless he felt rich enough to treat himself to dinner at the Aschinger Brasserie. For twenty-five *pfennigs* you could get a simple split-pea soup; for fifty the cooks added a chunk of lard. With the soup you could have as much bread as you wanted.

Litvine left university in 1929 and found work as an economist for an import-export firm. In no time his days of poverty were over. But when Hitler came to power in 1933, Litvine was drafted into the Lithuanian army and had to return home for a few months of military service.

As the threat of Nazism continued to grow, Litvine went back to Berlin, where he joined the Resistance. He arrived in March 1934. Nine months later the Gestapo arrested him, threw him into jail, and kept him there for more than a year without giving him a trial. Then in January 1936, the courts found him guilty of having abused German hospitality as a Jew and a foreigner and sentenced him to twelve years of solitary confinement.

Had he served his full term, Litvine would probably have died. But he spent only two and a half years in jail before he and three other Lithuanian prisoners were exchanged for four Nazis who had been condemned to life imprisonment in Lithuania. Several people intervened on Litvine's behalf, among them the chief rabbi of Kovno, who knew Litvine's Soloveichik relatives well.

Returning to Kovno in July 1938, Litvine began working almost immediately as a journalist for the *Volkstsaytung,* the Yiddish newspaper of the Folkist party. Neither Zionist, or anti-Zionist, the Folkists endorsed the position of their founder Simon Dubnow, who believed in developing an autonomous Jewish culture in the Diaspora at the same time he supported the creation of a Jewish homeland. The *Volkstsaytung* gave Litvine the first opportunity he ever had to write in Yiddish professionally. Drafting his articles with care, he strove to eliminate the German constructions that had slipped into his mother tongue over the years.

Although he was happy to be free, Litvine knew he was still in danger. Like other politically active people of the period, he recognized the seriousness of the Nazi threat and despaired every time England and France made concessions to Germany in the vain hope of avoiding another war. The Allies had initiated this fruitless strategy while Litvine was still in prison.

In March 1938, England and France offered Hitler no resistance as Nazi troops annexed Austria to the Third Reich. When the Allies met in Munich with Mussolini and Hitler the following September, they agreed to let Germany absorb a part of Czechoslovakia (the Sudetenland), as well. Then, in early 1939, the Führer's soldiers took over the rest of the country and also annexed Klaipeda (Memel), the Lithuanian port city on the Baltic Sea and the surrounding region (see map 3).

When the Nazis invaded Klaipeda, Litvine knew that Lithuania would soon fall the way Czechoslovakia had. Since the courts in Berlin had warned him that he would finish out his term if they ever caught him on German territory again, he decided to leave the country while he still had the chance. Securing a three-month student visa to France, he said good-bye to his aunt and uncle and went to Paris in August 1939, one month before war was declared. He never saw his guardians again.

Litvine spent the first year of the war in relative safety. When the Germans invaded France in May 1940, the French government responded by interning thousands of immigrants who had settled in the country over the last two years, but even then he managed to stay free and legal, registering as a Jew with the Préfecture de Police, and maintaining his status as a foreign student.[12] Litvine, however, took no chances either.

By the time the Germans reached Paris a month later, he had moved to Montpellier (Hérault), leaving on one of the last trains to depart from the Austerlitz Station. This southern city was in the Free Zone (see map 3), in the part of France that came under the jurisdiction of Pétain's collaborating government (see maps 4, 5). Even if Vichy had Jewish laws too, Litvine felt safer there than in German-occupied France. Faithfully checking in with the authorities at regular intervals, he spent two years in Montpellier, living openly as a student and attending classes in French literature at the university there.

The summer of 1942 was the turning point. With the help of the French police, the Gestapo deported more than 32,000 Jews from France during July and August of that year, arresting them in both the occupied and free zones.[13] When they came looking for Litvine in Montpellier, he was innocently vacationing in a small village nearby, unaware of the danger. Friends found him quickly and told him not to return.

Litvine took refuge in the home of a village priest. Although he was safe and had permission to stay, he wanted to fight in the Resistance. He was strong, in good health, and experienced in the horrors of Nazism. A few months later he joined the *maquis* in the Tarn, near Albi, in the historic region where the Albigenses defied the Church of Rome in the twelfth century.

Litvine was the only Jew in his unit, but this did not bother him. He was used to it. With the exception of the one year he had spent in Kovno before coming to France, from 1924 to 1945, he had had little contact with the Jewish world. His political and intellectual concerns at the time went beyond the specific problems of his people, and his friends, he observed, were frequently not Jewish. Nevertheless, he did not hide his identity.

Litvine spent his free time in the maquis cultivating his literary interests. While still a student in Montpellier, he had purchased a pocket edition of Baudelaire's *Les Fleurs du mal*. Now, in the middle of the Tarn, surrounded by French peasant hamlets, he began to translate "Invitation au voyage" into Yiddish. Litvine had already worked with poetry in Russian and German, but this was the first time he had tried to do anything with the French.

After the war, Litvine returned to Paris and found a job with the Communist Yiddish newspaper *Di Naye Prese*. Within a few months he became editor of the literary page, a highly sensitive position that caused him considerable trouble. Committed as he was to European humanism and the ideals of a universal culture, Litvine rejected the paper's policy of judging art by a set of political criteria established by Stalin and followed by the French Communist party. Instead, he insisted on publishing the work of such Yiddish writers as Abraham Sutzkever and Chaim Grade, who passed through Paris after the war, having abandoned Communist Russia and Poland. Unwilling to toe the party line, Litvine refused to censure these exceptional artists just because they had criticized the Soviet experiment. Such independence on his part angered Litvine's superiors and eventually cost him his job.

In November 1947 the person in charge of the Palestinian page took a leave of absence and *Di Naye Prese* transferred Litvine temporarily to his post. At the time, the Soviet Union supported the creation of the state of Israel and the national struggle of the Jews. Litvine's opinions, therefore, coincided with those of the paper, and the editorial board allowed him to include more or less what he liked in his articles about the Middle East. Taking advantage of the situation, he quoted liberally from the poems of Chaim Nakhman Bialik and the Zionist extremist Jacob Cahan, both of whom celebrated Jewish nationalism in their verses. Then in 1948, when Truman recognized the state of Israel, the situation grew more complicated, and Litvine had to be careful. Soon, the regular editor returned to his post, and Litvine stepped down. Unhappy with the nationalistic tone that had crept into his articles, *Di Naye Prese* now refused to let Litvine write about international news. They assigned him instead to carry out technical services: make translations of articles from French papers about local matters and to write on apolitical subjects of concern only to the Yiddish-speaking audience in France.

Even in this work, relations remained tense, and Litvine was fired in 1951. A year later, however, they rehired him, for they could not do without him, Litvine noted triumphantly. He knew how to do everything: from writing an article to setting the print.

When Stalin died in 1953, the political situation eased up, and in 1954 Litvine became the literary editor of a quarterly review called the *Parizer Tsaytshrift*. But before long he ran into similar difficulties with other members of the editorial board about the role Yiddish culture should play in the party. As Litvine interpreted their differences, he wanted to publish the work of gifted artists who expressed themselves in Yiddish, while the *Parizer Tsaytshrift* favored writers who provided Yiddish readers with ideologically correct literature. In 1956 Litvine left the magazine, and two years later he broke definitively with the Communist Yiddish community.

During these same postwar years, Litvine worked as a ghost writer, helping survivors record their memoirs about life in Eastern Europe before 1939 and about the ways they resisted the Nazis—in ghettos, in camps, and in the forests with the partisans. But he could not make a living from this alone. Finally, in 1960, after having passed a national exam, he got a job as an official guide for Russian- and German-speaking tourists visiting France. Extremely knowledgeable about the nation's history, art, and architecture, Litvine enjoyed accompanying tourists around the country and introducing them to the cultural monuments of France.

In the mid-1970s Litvine retired and since then has turned all his attention to his life's major work: the translation of French poetry into Yiddish, a project inspired by his deep belief that a literary tradition grows through its interaction with the achievements of artists who write in other languages. Today, he enjoys international acclaim among readers of Yiddish, for both his translations and his essays in literary criticism. A regular contributor to Sutzkever's Israeli-based journal, *Di Goldene Keyt,* he has gained special recognition for his rendition of selections from *Les Fleurs du mal*. In 1968 Litvine published his first comprehensive book of translations of French poetry into Yiddish—for which he received the I. Manger Prize in 1973— and it contained many poems from that work. A second volume came out in 1986, and this too had translations of Baudelaire.[14] While he still has a way to go, Litvine has promised himself and his enthusiastic public to finish the entire cycle before he dies. In 1989, Mitterand's minister of culture, Jack Lang, joined Litvine's many admirers and recognized the importance of the translator's work by making Litvine a chevalier (knight) of the Order of Arts and Letters.

Why continue working in Yiddish when so few people still read it? For aesthetic reasons, Litvine replies. Isaac Bashevis Singer gives the same answer, adding ironically that, when the Messiah comes and millions of Jews rise up from the dead, they will surely ask for something to read and expect to find new books in Yiddish.[15] With few exceptions, Litvine continues, writers work best in their native tongue. Even in his case, where he left the Yiddish-speaking world for many years, he found his literary voice only when he returned to the language he had learned at home.

Dedicated to the idea that writers should translate, as well as create, original pieces of literature, Litvine today spends long hours training Jewish students in Paris to render Yiddish poetry and fiction into French. With his guidance, a new generation is expanding the repertoire available in French and familiarizing the public with the extraordinary complexity of Eastern European culture. Among Litvine's disciples there is also the Argentinian Itzhok Niborski, who has humbly stepped forward to continue working in Yiddish, to extend the language's literary legacy for yet another generation.

Born in 1947 in Buenos Aires to Jewish immigrants from Poland, Niborski learned Yiddish before Spanish and considers his parents' language his national tongue. Since 1979 he has resided in France, where he devotes himself full-time to keeping secular Yiddish culture alive. Defying history he struggles on, unwilling to see his rich heritage disappear into French translations. As he explained in a letter:

> Those who claim to practice a non-religious form of Judaism cannot, it seems to me, do so without a language of their own. It is already quite difficult to create a Jewish-identified movement that does not follow the Commandments, but to come up with one that does not have a language either is simply going too far. I do not mean to argue that it is indispensible or even desirable to want to remain Jewish; assimilation may be an ideal solution for those who choose it. But if you want to be Jewish, then you should give yourself the means needed to claim this identity. To show an interest in Yiddish and its literature by translating works from that language [into French], or by reading the translations of others, is a nice thing to do, but it is not necessarily Jewish. It is rather like reading or translating French literature into Spanish, which could hardly be taken for an expression of being French.[16]

Following Litvine's example, Niborski hopes to provide Yiddish readers, no matter how few of them remain, with translations of great works from other traditions, preserving the commitment secular Yiddish writers have had since the late nineteenth century to developing a body of literature open to the ideas and aesthetic sensibilities of the world around them. In the process, Niborski challenges those who have represented Yiddish culture as quaint folklore, and on this point he joins the efforts of Rachel Ertel and her students. With Litvine's help, those translating Yiddish into French have corrected misconceptions about the culture of Eastern European Jews by introducing the French public to the wide range of talent and cosmopolitan concerns of writers in this Jewish tongue.

Through their translations, Yiddishists of the generation of 1968 have carried forward the universalistic ideals of the eighteenth century Enlightenment that inspired Yiddish writers at the turn of the century and between the two wars. Niborski has accomplished this by continuing Litvine's project of providing Yiddish renditions of the literature of other people. Rachel Ertel and her students have done the same by making the work of Eastern European Jews accessible to those who represent the very cultural tradition that influenced Yiddish writers in the first place.

Recently, other members of the generation of 1968 have taken a less circuitous route back to the values that inspired Yiddish writers. Giving up on cultural nationalism, they have returned to the principles of the Enlightenment in the original. But they, like the Yiddishists, want to do so *as Jews*. In their search, they have found inspiration from the teachings of Emmanuel Lévinas, one of France's most distinguished philosophers.

Lévinas, unlike Litvine, has no background in Yiddish culture and little interest in it. He puts the future of Judaism and the Jewish people in the hands of those who study and teach the sacred texts. Still, Lévinas shares a common goal with the Yiddish translator: he too wants to bring together Jewish culture and the universal traditions of European humanism.

5

The Lithuanian Jewish Enlightenment in French Translation: Emmanuel Lévinas and His Disciple Alain Finkielkraut

Emmanuel Lévinas was born in 1906 in Kovno. At the time, the city had a population of approximately 80,000 people, thirty percent of whom were Jewish. The area around Kovno was known for its yeshivas, but many Jews in the region still embraced the Enlightenment and adopted the Russian language. This did not mean that assimilated Jews abandoned their people's heritage. Mixing little with members of other ethnic groups, they remained among themselves, creating their own relationship to Russian and Jewish traditions. When, for example, they rejected Orthodox Judaism, they frequently continued to keep kosher and celebrate what they called the "national Jewish traditions."[1] This even remained true for maskilim who moved out of the old Jewish quarter and settled down in the new part of town, the way Lévinas' family did when the philosopher's father opened a bookshop there, specializing in Russian publications.

Lévinas grew up speaking and reading Russian. As a toddler, he deciphered the letters of the Cyrillic alphabet off the label of a container of cocoa used to make his morning cup of hot chocolate. When he was about six years old, his

A few years ago, an Israeli born in Eastern Europe paid me a visit. Upon entering my house, he noticed that I had the complete works of Pushkin on the book shelves: "You can see right away," he said, "that this is a Jewish home."

—EMMANUEL LEVINAS

parents engaged a private tutor to start preparing the young boy for the qualifying exam he would eventually have to pass to enter a Russian gymnasium. He also received lessons in Hebrew, taught in the modern way, as a living language. Lévinas read the Torah, for example, as if it were a piece of contemporary literature, in storybook form, unaccompanied by the traditional commentaries he would later consider essential to understanding the sacred text.[2]

Forced to leave Kovno during the First World War, the family moved to Kharkov in the Ukraine, where Lévinas continued studying at home (see map 3). In 1916 he successfully passed the highly competitive entrance exam that had been established, essentially, to control the number of Jews accepted into Russian schools. Lévinas was one of four Jewish children admitted to his gymnasium that year, an achievement greeted with much celebration at home.[3]

When the czar abdicated in 1917, Lévinas was still too young to understand the complexities of what was going on, but he knew his parents were frightened. For bourgeois Jews like themselves, the revolution was dangerous. Trying to maintain a semblance of order, Lévinas' parents held on to their old values and encouraged their son to continue working hard in school. What mattered most in the world was that he should study.[4] Lévinas obeyed his parents and never engaged in the political struggle, but he felt drawn to Leninism and the promises communism held out for the future.

In 1920 the family left the Soviet Ukraine, and returned to "a normal life" in the newly constituted bourgeois Republic of Lithuania. For a fourteen-year old boy who had just lived through a major social revolution, to be back in Kovno (now called Kaunas) was a bit of a letdown. Now he was forced to watch the Russian people make history without him. This sense of longing, of wishing to be part of the action instead of looking on from the sidelines, stayed with him until he left Kovno a few years later to continue his studies in France.[5]

But life in Lithuania had memorable moments, too. Lévinas went to secondary school in Kovno's Hebrew gymnasium, where he had what he later called, "my first contact with Europe": "The director of our gymnasium was a German Jew who had discovered Eastern European Judaism during his captivity in Russia. He was a doctor of philosophy, and it was he who taught me German. When he used to say, 'das ist goethisch' (this is like Goethe), a chill went up and down everybody's spine. During this period, I found it a personal embarrassment never to have visited the cathedral in Cologne!"[6]

In 1923, when he was seventeen years old, Lévinas left home to attend the University of Strasbourg (Bas-Rhin) (see map 4). Although contemporaries of his from the Baltic republics usually went to Germany, not France, by the time Lévinas was ready to go, the economic situation in the Weimar Republic has become extremely unstable. Anti-Semitic outbursts occurred occasionally, and Jewish students of foreign birth faced certain restrictions.[7] France was far more hospitable, and the prestige of its language and culture very attractive.[8]

Lévinas says that he chose Strasbourg over other cities in France because it was the university town closest to Lithuania. Perhaps he went there as well because people spoke German in the Alsatian capital, a language he already knew and could use while he improved his French. Within a year, he was able to read Pierre Corneille and George Sand in the original. Developing a true passion for his newly acquired language, to this day Lévinas expresses his sense of patriotism in terms of linguistic nationalism. "For me this language is the soil of France. . . . I still speak very good Russian and do fairly well in German and Hebrew. I also read English. But I often thought at the beginning of the war of 1939 that we were fighting to defend the French language."[9]

At the University of Strasbourg, Lévinas spent a year studying Latin. He then majored in philosophy, a discipline he had never worked in before in a systematic way, for philosophy as such did not exist in his gymnasium. As a result he did not have the background French students had when they came to university. He quickly discovered, however, that he still had the preparation he needed thanks to courses he had taken in Russian literature back home.[10] What he lacked in formal training, he more than compensated for by having read Pushkin, Turgenev, Lermontov, Dostoevsky, and Chekhov, all of whose work brimmed over with "an abundance of metaphysical uneasiness."[11] Lévinas also found he could draw on his familiarity with the Bible, a source he exploited more fully after World War II.

During his early days in France, Lévinas took a course with Maurice Pradines on the relationship between the ethical and the political. To demonstrate how ethics could win out over politics, his professor gave the example of the Dreyfus Affair. This made a deep impression on him: "Everywhere in Eastern Europe, Jews knew about Dreyfus. Old men with long beards, who had never read a letter of the Latin alphabet in their life, spoke of Zola as if he were a saint. And then, all of a sudden, there was this professor before me, in flesh and blood, who talked about the Dreyfus Affair. What an amazing world!"[12]

These were exciting years to be a student. Lévinas discovered the work of Henri Bergson, the French thinker of Jewish origin whose pathbreaking ideas had led to the emergence of a "new philosophy": "I believe that all the new ideas developed by philosophers during the modern and postmodern periods, in particular the venerable newness of Heidegger, would not have been possible without Bergson."[13]

After he completed his undergraduate degree in 1928, Lévinas went to Freiburg for a year to study with the German philosopher Edmund Husserl, the founder of phenomenology, who was teaching there at the time. His experience in Freiburg formed him intellectually in critical ways and provided him with one of the greatest philosophical moments of his life: his encounter with the work of Martin Heidegger. Although he has since criticized himself for his youthful ingratitude, Lévinas appreciated Husserl at the time mostly for having given him the preparation he needed to be able to study with Heidegger, who was also in Freiburg that year. As Lévinas read *Being and Time,* and attended Heidegger's lectures, he was fascinated by the way the philosopher managed to develop Husserl's phenomenological approach in exciting new ways. Comparing the two, Lévinas observed: "Husserl seemed less convincing because he seemed less unexpected. This may sound paradoxical or childish, but everything in Heidegger's work came as a surprise: the wonders of his analysis of affectivity, the new ways he approached daily life, the distinction he drew between being [*sein*] and beings [*seindes*], that famous ontological difference. The rigor of Heidegger's thinking, through the brilliance of his formulations, was truly impressive."[14]

Despite his preference for Heidegger, Lévinas wrote his doctoral dissertation on Husserl for the University of Strasbourg. Published in 1930 (*Théorie de l'intuition dans la phénoménologie de Husserl*),[15] Lévinas' thesis gave Sartre his first formal introduction to the work of the phenomenologist. Sartre had heard about Husserl in 1933 from his former classmate Raymond Aron, who had gone to study with the German philosopher in Berlin. Terribly excited by what Aron had told him, Sartre immediately went out to buy Lévinas' book, the only serious work on the man's ideas available in French. As Simone de Beauvoir recalls: "Sartre purchased Lévinas' book on Husserl on the Boulevard Saint-Michel and was in such a rush to read about the philosopher that he leafed through the work while he was walking along, before he had even cut the pages."[16]

Sartre too wanted to study with Husserl. He arranged to take a leave of absence from the lycée in Le Havre (Seine-Maritime), where he was then teaching and to find a place for himself at the Institut Francais in Berlin for a year. Husserl quickly became Sartre's "master," his inspiration. Dedicating himself to the man's work with passionate devotion, Sartre studied virtually nobody else for six years.[17] At one point, he tried reading Heidegger as well, but gave up after fifty pages, concluding: "I made the mistake of believing that you could *study* two philosophers as important as they, one right after the other, the way you can learn about foreign trade in two European countries."[18]

When Sartre finally turned to Heidegger, he, like Lévinas before him, identified with the philosopher's new reading of phenomenology and followed Heidegger's efforts "to pass beyond the essentialism of Husserl."[19] Gaining inspiration from Heidegger, Sartre and Lévinas both went on to develop their own existentialist visions of the world and to write at great length about human freedom and the individual's relationship to the other. Despite their similar itineraries and overlapping interests, they came up with different conclusions on a number of basic questions, including the nature of human relationships: "For Sartre, to be human has to do with one's immediate relationship to others. Others are my hell, but they also make me be. They are at my side, my equals, my companions in existence. Lévinas is wary of 'this group called we, of the feeling that the other is at a person's side and not facing him.' He writes: 'Instead of this group of friends, we propose the group of I-Thou which comes first.'"[20]

The description Lévinas gives of the relationship between I and Thou separates him as well from the Jewish thinker Martin Buber, the leader of a movement of religious existentialists based in Berlin during the interwar years. In 1923, Buber published his classic essay *I and Thou,* in which he compared the relationship I-Thou (what two people have with each other) and I-It (what the individual has with an object). For Buber the I-Thou interaction was reciprocal; for Lévinas it was assymetrical.[21]

Lévinas differs with Buber over some of the teachings of Hasidism, too. In particular, he does not agree that one should give priority to developing a personal relationship with God. According to Lévinas, one should begin with the Torah, with what has already been written, not with spontaneous prayer. Still, Lévinas joins Buber in giving serious thought to the bonds that tie Jews to their Supreme Being, a concern that sets him apart yet again from Sartre, who claims that God does not exist.[22]

The God Lévinas describes in his writing, however, has little in common with the one Sartre rejected. This is not the Jehovah of the Catholics who treats humans as "eternal children," awarding those who behave (or confess) and punishing those who do not. God's presence or absence cannot be tested either, as atheists seem to assume, by the degree of goodness or evil found in the world.[23] This other God, the God of the Jewish people, has no direct authority on earth. He appears through the teachings that Moses handed down to the Israelites on Mount Sinai and that men have passed on, without Divine intervention, from generation to generation: "The relationship between God and man is not a sentimental communion of love with an incarnate God, with a deity possessing body and flesh, but a relationship between minds who meet through instruction, through the Torah. It is precisely the word of a God without a body that assures that God lives among us."[24]

Many have called Lévinas a Jewish thinker, a title he accepts, but with some qualifications: He identifies himself with the Jewish people and observes many of the traditions of a practicing Jew. In his philosophical work, he frequently refers to the sacred texts. However, and this is very important, Lévinas does not seek to prove philosophical truths on the basis of biblical verses. To do so would require him to demonstrate the validity of a passage in the Torah in phenomenological, not theological, terms. What Lévinas does is quite different. As he seeks a philosophical truth according to the rules of the phenomenological method, he might illustrate a point—but he does not prove it—with a verse from the Bible or a piece of Talmudic wisdom. Much of his writing, however, is not philosophical in the first place. It is religious commentary, and as such it can and does accept the authority of a biblical passage.[25]

In 1935 Lévinas began reading Franz Rosenzweig's *Star of Redemption,* a work that inspired him to consider seriously the relationship between European philosophy and Judaism.[26] For Lévinas, Rosenzweig led the way to a truly modern approach to Jewish thought, one that had gone through the process of assimilation and then returned to Judaism without rejecting European history. Rosenzweig gave Lévinas a way to think about the reconciliation between Christianity and Judaism, not by means of a "synthesis," but a "symbiosis," the result of a privileged relationship of neighbors who share a common world. Thanks to their close association with Christians, Jews, for example, gained access to art:

> Great art is non-Jewish art, accessible to Jews thanks to the fact that they live among Christians. There is no confusion here or syncretism, but a symbiosis, which for Rosenzweig is deep and tied to the very structure of truth. It is as if there were an additional

enrichment, a surplus. Truth in Judaism might be described as that which is given to a people already "close to" the Lord and who do not [given this proximity] see the world. In Christianity to attain truth one must travel first along the road of the world on the way to the Eternal One. But this experience on the road and in the world is also given to Judaism, thanks to its nearness to Christianity. Is what I am saying here theologically heretical, or does it give meaning to a destiny that is unquestionably and essentially linked? I believe it is the latter . . . for even the State of Israel must live with the Christian world, read Christian authors: Shakespeare and Racine and Victor Hugo; come to terms with all this Europe, which is undeniably great and unquestionably Christian. That is what Rosenzweig also means to me.[27]

But Rosenzweig died in 1929, before Hitler came to power. As a result, his work only reached the "age of puberty," Lévinas explains. It did not mature through the Shoah, the final test for Jews in the modern period.[28]

Naturalized in France in 1930, Lévinas was mobilized in 1939 and fought with the French army until the Germans caught up with him in Rennes (Ille-et-Vilaine) in the spring of 1940 as his regiment was retreating. Lévinas spent the next few months in an internment camp in France before being sent to Germany as a Jewish prisoner of war, a discriminatory status segregating him from his Gentile friends, but one that also protected him from the fate of Jews arrested as civilians. Despite their determination to exterminate the Jews, the Nazis upheld the agreement they had made with Vichy and treated Jewish members of the French army with the respect due a soldier captured in battle.

Lévinas spent the war doing slave labor in the German forests like any other military prisoner. Occasionally bits of news drifted in from the outside world, but for the most part he was unaware of what was happening to Jews elsewhere in Europe. Only afterward did he learn that his entire family in Lithuania had perished, along with millions of other victims of the Final Solution.

In captivity, Lévinas spent the war doing backbreaking physical labor and reading. Books arrived, nobody really knew from where, providing him and his fellow prisoners with cultural sustenance during their leisure time. "I read Hegel, of course. But also many philosophical texts of other origins. Works I had not had the chance to read before: more Proust than ever, the authors of the eighteenth century, Diderot, Rousseau, as well as writers who did not fit into any specific program of study. And then, all of a sudden, I wondered why I bothered? But in this life of daily physical work in the forest—watched over by guards who were not violent—these months were not a waste of time when considered from a cultural point of view."[29]

After Liberation, Lévinas returned to Paris, where he resumed the administrative position he had held before the war at the Alliance Israélite Universelle, helping to coordinate the organization's educational programs. Since the second half of the nineteenth century, the Alliance had been running schools for Jews in North Africa, the Middle East, and Asia Minor with curricular programs based on France's revolutionary principles that every individual should have the opportunity to participate in the same, universal culture. In 1946 Lévinas became director of the Ecole Normale Israélite Orientale, where young people received training before going out to teach in Alliance schools in France and abroad. He held that position until 1979.[30]

During the early postwar years, Lévinas continued to develop his own relationship to philosophy and Judaism, studying the works of Husserl, Heidegger, and Rosenzweig and taking classes with Shushani, a Talmudic scholar he met in Paris in the 1940s.[31] The first three helped Lévinas define a place for himself within the European philosophical tradition and modern Judaism. The fourth introduced him to a way of thinking long associated with his native Lithuania, but one he had known little about before he began studying Talmud in Paris with this "wandering Jew."[32]

Shushani was not his real name, but that was what everyone called him. According to Lévinas and others, the man knew Torah, Talmud, and Zohar by heart. He could also recite the *Rig-Veda*, the sacred text of the Hindus. And that was not all. Among his many other achievements was a brilliant command of modern mathematics and physics. He also spoke thirty languages fluently.[33]

Some say Shushani was from Lithuania.[34] Lévinas notes that he spoke the Yiddish of Lite, distinguishing this linguistic accomplishment from the way he communicated in the other languages he knew—with remarkable skill, but with a strong foreign accent.[35] Others insist that he came from Israel, or Turkey, or North Africa.[36] The man himself refused to talk about his origins.

Soon after Shushani died, Elie Wiesel received a visit from somebody who claimed to be the Talmudic scholar's nephew. Arriving with photographs and documents from his uncle's past, he cleared up the mystery. But before he left, the nephew made Wiesel promise never to reveal what he had learned.[37]

Dressed in baggy clothing, Shushani used to appear and disappear at whim, accept room and lodging from people for a few weeks, or months—he lived with Lévinas for a while—then pack up with no warning and leave town. When he returned, he arrived unannounced and picked up where he had left off, gathering students around him who wanted to study the Talmud—or perhaps something else.

By the 1960s Shushani had supposedly left Europe for good and moved to Montevideo. Lévinas had heard he was giving lessons there in nuclear physics.[38] Wiesel, too, thought Shushani had settled down in South America until he saw somebody who looked just like him near the Sorbonne, in the late 1960s. As he approached, he found Shushani's double so deeply involved in conversation with a student that Wiesel did not dare interrupt to verify whether or not this was his former teacher.[39] What we know for sure is that Shushani died in Uruguay soon after his possible appearance in France.

There are many stories about Shushani as a teacher. Impatient and demanding, he wasted not a minute with gracious pleasantries. Knowing every page of the Talmud by heart, he stood before his disciples with no book in hand, correcting the smallest error a student might make as he read through a passage. Shushani's prowess extended beyond his formidable memory: Possessing prodigious analytical skills, he interpreted the texts with profound wisdom.

As they studied with their irascible teacher, Shushani's students knew they were in the presence of a true master. For Lévinas, the man was "a frequentation."[40] "What remains of this contact that filled me with wonder, made me anxious, and caused me sleepless nights? A new way to approach rabbinic wisdom and to understand what it meant to be human. Judaism is not the Bible, it is the Bible as seen through the Talmud, through the wisdom and questions of rabbinic religious life."[41]

When Lévinas met Shushani, he was trying to come to terms with "the teaching of Auschwitz." How could Judaism speak to people whose families had disappeared in gas chambers and who had themselves, in many cases, suffered unspeakable deprivation and torture in the camps? Lévinas had no desire to challenge the despair of others. Committed to the asymmetrical relationship between I and Thou, he knew he did not have the answer for everyone. But did he have one even for himself? Could he remain faithful to a religion like Judaism which held out so few promises? As he pondered the question, Shushani led him back to the sacred books: "Certainly the Holocaust played a much more important role than the encounter with this man in determining what happened to my Judaism, but Shushani gave me reason again to have confidence in the books. The phrase I frequently use now: 'the books are deeper than consciousness and the inner-self' comes from this period of my life when I studied with him.'[42]

Today, Lévinas uses "the books" to enhance the ideals of European universalism and the Enlightenment. His project goes beyond the intention of eighteenth- and nineteenth-century Jews in Germany and France who tried to demonstrate the compatibility of the Torah with the "noble models of the West." Lévinas calls for more. He wants to "translate into Greek"— into the language of European philosophy—a set of ethical principles found among the ancient Hebrews, but not among the peoples of Greece. Speaking metaphorically, he does not mean to make a new translation of the Old Testament into Greek, but to engage the tradition that inspired modern philosophy with the ethical concerns of the ancient Hebrews. He would like to examine philosophically, for example, the biblical assertion that Jews should demand more of themselves than they do of others.[43]

Given his ambitious program, Lévinas does not fit the general description of Yosef Hayim Yerushalmi has made of contemporary scholars of Judaism. In his remarkable essay on history and memory (*Zakhor*), Yerushalmi contrasts the concerns of present-day specialists with those of individuals who lived in the Middle Ages. People today, he suggests, look at historical, not philosophical issues, whereas those in the earlier period did just the opposite:

> There has been little genuine interpenetration between Jewish and general philosophy, but a deep and ubiquitous interaction with modern historicism. By this I mean simply that while there was a common realm of discourse and mutual influence among Jewish, Muslim, and Christian philosophy in the Middle Ages, this has not been true of Jewish and general philosophy in modern times. . . .
>
> In the Middle Ages, Jewish philosophers felt a need to effect a reconciliation between a Greek truth and a revealed Judaism of whose truth they were equally convinced. Those Jews in the early nineteenth century who first felt an imperative to examine Judaism historically did so because they were no longer sure of what Judaism was, or whether, whatever it was, it could still be viable for them.[44]

As the exception to the rule, Lévinas would undoubtedly agree that scholars today devote most of their time to historical issues. While he does not wish to dismiss the importance of such endeavors, Lévinas believes that historical studies have contributed to creating a false problem for contemporary Jews. Our fascination with the past has led many to conclude that they must choose between assimilation or a folkloric form of Judaism made up of the inessential, of those sentimental memories of family traditions and dialects. In his opinion, Jews should create a new science of Judaism, based on the Hebrew language and the sacred texts of the Jewish people:

> This science is impossible without a return to Hebrew. The "inner cathedrals," constructed four thousand years ago in the texts, must reappear on the horizon. Be assured, they will not destroy the beautiful accomplishments found in the modern countryside. These ancient texts teach a universalism, purified of the particularism of any one land, of the memories of the plants of any one soil. The texts teach that human beings belong to a single nation unified by ideas. The state of Israel and our commitment to this state will certainly nourish the Judaism of Jews who live in the Diaspora. But Israel alone cannot look after the Jewish flame in homes overwhelmed by the burning light of the West which outshines the fires borrowed from elsewhere. The reawakening of a curiosity for the great books of Judaism . . . is the underlying condition for the survival of Jews in the Diaspora.[45]

Basing his Judaism on religious texts more than on an abstract belief in the Supreme Being, Lévinas has devoted himself for more than four decades to studying the Five Books of Moses, the Talmud, and the commentaries. In the process, he has led the way for others to make their teshuvah by "loving the Torah more than God."[46] Over the years, he has shared his insights with students at the Ecole Normale Israélite Orientale, the University of Poitiers, and the Sorbonne. Since the late 1950s, he has spoken on the subject before general audiences at the Colloque des Intellectuels Juifs in Paris, where his annual *lectures talmudiques* have become major events in the French Jewish intellectual community.

For years now Lévinas has enjoyed the admiration of contemporary philosophers in France. Jacques Derrida, for example, published an important essay on his work in 1964.[47] But only recently has Lévinas' influence extended beyond a small circle of specialists to include many members of the generation of 1968.

According to some, Lévinas has contributed to the interest we see today among young Jews in studying the works of Lithuanian religious scholars. The philosopher rejects the idea, but proudly takes credit for being the first to write about Chaim of Volozhin in French. He also recognizes that he has introduced many to a method of reading sacred texts that has roots in the rationalistic Lithuanian tradition, a tradition he embraced long after he had studied European philosophy.[48]

Among those who have been inspired by the work of Lévinas, some have made a liturgical return to Judaism and observe the laws of the Halakhah (the laws of the Talmud). Others have remained secular Jews who study the "history of the subject [Judaism]," as Lévinas put it, "and ask the question, is there a truth?"[49] In both cases, these young Jews have come to Lévinas with strong backgrounds in European philosophy, training that prepared them, as it had their teacher, to appreciate the intellectual rigors of the Talmudic tradition of Lithuania.

While they warmly acknowledge their debt to Lévinas, the philosopher's students rarely adopt their mentor's complete program. In recent years, for example, as some have returned to Orthodox Judaism, they have chosen to separate themselves from the surrounding society, withdrawing into yeshiva communities modeled on the ones that existed in Lithuania before the Second World War. They have no interest in translating the teachings of Judaism "into Greek." Others endorse Lévinas' commitment to the values of universalism, but reject the religion. They share a historical, not practical, interest in the world of Talmudic study, endorsing in abstract terms Lévinas' mission, without devoting themselves to acquiring the skills necessary to engage in highly technical debates about Jewish thought and European philosophy. Still, they have embraced a kind of ethical Judaism that reflects the humanistic education they received in secular French schools and a new awareness about some of the fundamental questions posed by "the books."

Alain Finkielkraut is one such secular disciple of Lévinas. A prolific writer, in many of his essays he defends the principles of the Enlightenment and gives credence to his teacher's conviction that European culture can lead individuals back to the questions raised by Judaism. In 1986, when the Fondation du Judaïsme presented the young writer with an award for his contribution to Jewish letters, Lévinas made a speech in his honor, concluding with praises for the French intellectual tradition that had produced him: "The imaginary Jew, standing on the threshold of the Talmud has, perhaps, not yet knocked at the door, even though he has come very close. Nevertheless, we Jews in the West are happy to note that once again, in the land of Montaigne, Descartes, and Pascal, in the land of Molière, Hugo, and Proust, in the land of Blanchot, the roads lead where they should."[50]

A SECULAR DISCIPLE OF LEVINAS

Alain Finkielkraut was born to Polish Jewish immigrants in June 1949, one year after the founding of the state of Israel and four years after the Second World War.[51] His father, originally from Warsaw, came to Paris in the 1930s. Deported to Auschwitz during the German occupation, he was one of the few who miraculously survived.

Finkielkraut's mother was originally from Lvov. Her family moved to Germany before the rise of National Socialism, and she remained in that country in the 1930s, protected by false identity papers. Later she escaped to Belgium, where she survived in the same way. After the war, she came to Paris, met her future husband and married in 1948. The newlyweds had lost almost everyone in their families, "in Auschwitz, the Polish forests or the Lvov Ghetto."[52]

Finkielkraut's father made a living in the leather business while his mother stayed at home to devote herself full-time to caring for their only child, whom she smothered with love and attention. Commenting on his home life in *Le Juif imaginaire*, the young writer noted with irony and affection that mothers such as his raised their sons in the tradition caricatured by Philip Roth in *Portnoy's Complaint*: "You never really recover from such adoration. Egocentric and infantile, the children of a 'Yiddishe Mama,' are easy to recognize. No matter how hard they try, members of the brotherhood of Portnoy cannot sneak by unnoticed. As adults they have the vulnerability and look of a child who has been loved too much. What makes them Jewish is not the wisdom of wandering, or the sadness of persecution, as they would like to believe, but the impotence of being a big, over-protected baby."[53]

Perhaps they share psychological problems, but Alexander Portnoy and Alain Finkielkraut grew up in very different worlds. Jewish traditions lingered on in Portnoy's home in Newark, New Jersey, in the 1930s and 1940s, but they did not in Paris in Finkielkraut's family nearly twenty years later. Deeply scarred by the war, Finkielkraut's parents responded like many other survivors and chose not to pass down Jewish traditions to their son, either religious or secular. For them, Yiddish culture had disappeared in Poland, together with their families and friends. Their Alain would be culturally French, free of every trace of his Polish Jewish origin.

Finkielkraut went to some of the best schools in Paris. When the students rebelled in May 1968, he was completing a two-year program at the Lycée Henri IV (*hypokhâgne* and *khâgne*) to prepare for the exam he had to pass in order to enter the Ecole Normale Supérieure de Saint Cloud, where he planned to major in French literature. Identifying with the movement, Finkielkraut sacrificed his studies for a year and participated actively in the political upheaval.

In 1969, Finkielkraut entered Saint Cloud, and for the next few years he took courses there, as well as at a number of other campuses in Paris, including the University of Paris VII, where he studied Yiddish with Rachel Ertel and Shakespeare with Richard Marienstras. Influenced in particular by Marienstras, Finkielkraut joined Le Cercle Gaston Crémieux, but he had difficulty identifying with the group's platform on minority nationalism. He remained loosely connected to the Cercle all the same for a number of years, while he looked around for other ways to affirm himself as a Jew.

Finally, Finkielkraut withdrew. He could no longer endorse the Cercle's attempts to defy history and apply the strategies of minority nationalists from interwar Poland to the problems of Jews living in contemporary France. Immigrant Jewish culture could not serve as a model for him. While Marienstras spoke glowingly of "this atmosphere . . . that Jewish immigrants know how to create for themselves in the country of their second exile," the young writer saw things differently. His experiences growing up with Polish Jews in France had convinced him that "this environment bears testimony to an already weakened Judaism."[54]

Finkielkraut went to the Cercle for the last time in 1980 and presented the group with *Le Juif imginaire,* his third book, but his first attempt to analyze the Jewish question for himself and other members of the generation of 1968. In contrast to Marienstras, he did not blame the hegemony of French culture for the emptiness of his own Jewish identity today. Instead, he criticized himself for claiming to be different from non-Jews when he had never demonstrated much interest in or knowledge of his people's culture. Writing in an autobiographical voice reminiscent of Sartre's in *The Words,* Finkielkraut observed: "'I am Jewish,' said I, and this phrase condensed all that I knew about Judaism, my profound truth, my dignity refound. The only language I spoke was the one that made demands. Settling down to a life of *defiance,* I spent many happy days on the edges of the social order, enchanted with the part I was playing. It was this posing of mine that kept me away from Jewish culture more than social pressure or any obligation to assimilate."[55]

Finkielkraut evoked Sartre for more than stylistic reasons. As he looked for his own answers to the Jewish question, he studied the *Anti-Semite and Jew,* a text he admired and considered basic to an understanding of the problem,[56] but one that encouraged Jews of his generation to transform meaningless gestures into expressions of heroic "authenticity": "Sartre said to me with unquestioning rigor that I was an *authentic* Jew, that *I assumed* my condition and that it took courage if not heroism to claim loud and clear that I belonged to a people held in such contempt. The terms chosen by Sartre literally made me drunk: In them I read my life, written in a sublime style. Through them, my proclamations of loyalty seemed like true acts of bravery."[57]

When Finkielkraut looked at himself honestly, he knew he had little in common with the authentic Jews Sartre described in his essay, with those people in his parents' generation who had lived through terribly dangerous times and had bravely chosen to assume their Jewishness. Spared by history, he was raised in comfortable, overprotected surroundings that permitted him to assert his identity with no fear of reprisals, to wear it like a costume, or wave it about like a political banner, the way many students did in May 1968, when they took to the streets, crying: "We are all German Jews."

And what provoked this expression of solidarity with Jewish immigrants? The expulsion from France of Dany Cohn-Bendit, the German student of sociology whose visa was revoked after he led the historic uprising at Nanterre (University of Paris X) in May 1968. More than ten years later, as he thought about the slogan, Finkielkraut observed cynically: "All German Jews? Come on now, we were all imaginary Jews."[58]

Finkielkraut claimed that history did more than spare his peers the sufferings of those who had lived through major tragedies.[59] History had literally passed them by. Reduced to spectators, but eager to find a role for themselves, they tried to play a number of parts from the sidelines, before assuming the empty shell of their own. Over the years they had dressed up as colonized natives with Frantz Fanon, as American blacks with Malcolm X, as guerrilla fighters with Che, Giap, and Ho Chi Minh.[60] Now they were playing Jews and in doing so reversing the famous formula associated with their people's emancipation in the eighteenth century: they had become universal men at home and Jews in the street.[61] Asserting their right to be different in public, they returned to their usual assimilated selves once they went home.

Finally, many in the generation of 1968 grew tired of "ornamental Judaism." They wanted to be Jews in private as well as in the street, a wish some of them fulfilled by rediscovering "the austere charms of the tradition," adopting, ironically, many of the rituals their parents had chosen not to impose on them. But as they obeyed the restrictions of the Jewish legal code, observing the Sabbath and the laws of kashrut, they did not necessarily accept the existence of God. Their teshuvah was not a profession of faith, but a declaration of belonging to a people. God, for them, was optional.[62]

Religion, Finkielkraut explained, had become the only choice for Jews living in the Diaspora: "ritual or nothing; repetition or disappearance; the tradition—with or without God—or nothingness." With the exception of Israeli state nationalism, all other expressions of Jewish life had been destroyed. There was no bringing them back: "The rites which we carry on with the timidness of beginners and the clumsiness of amateurs are not the center or the precious jewel of Judaism: they are its residue. The deteriorating remains of a people who have been killed off or turned into quaint 'folk' by other cultures. These rituals now serve as our only fragile chance to escape the fate of becoming imaginary Jews."[63]

Despite the *we* evoked here by the author, Finkielkraut did not join those who had turned to Jewish rituals. He defined for himself a kind of ethical Judaism instead, inspired by the work of Emmanuel Lévinas, whose influence we see most prominently in his book *La Sagesse de l'amour*. But even before he wrote on the wisdom of love, he drew on the philosopher's ideas in significant ways in the two volumes that followed *Le Juif imaginaire*. Challenging a number of groups on the left for positions they took in the Faurisson affair (*L'Avenir d'une négation*) and the Lebanese crisis (*La Réprobation d'Israel*), Finkielkraut relied on Lévinas to help him develop his argument as a Jewish moralist.

In *L'Avenir d'une négation*, Finkielkraut claimed that extreme leftists of the generation of 1968 came to question the existence of gas chambers for ideological and philosophical reasons that had little in common with those espoused by neo-Nazis. They were not anti-Semites eager to rehabilitate Hitler, but radical socialists who wanted to save Marx: "Those who deny the existence of gas chambers do not hold it against the Jews for being Jews (that is for being different, monotheistic, obscurantist, or greedy), but for mixing up the historical process, for *conspiring against the dialectic* by claiming to be victims of a wrong that is greater than the one endured daily by the working class."[64]

For these "metaphysicians of history," Finkielkraut continued, Auschwitz was unthinkable. Consequently, it never happened. Agreeing with others who have written on the subject (Gutman, Tarnero, Fresco, Vidal-Naquet), Finkielkraut added that Faurisson appealed to certain individuals on the pro-Palestinian left, for he undermined, they believed, the moral reasons for supporting Israel.[65] If Faurisson could demonstrate that gas chambers had never existed, the saviors of Marx would no longer have to face the national demands of those claiming to be survivors of the Final Solution. Eliminate the "myth" of Nazi atrocities, and the world will start giving its full attention to the real victims in the Middle East, namely the Palestinians.

Such demented reasoning, Finkielkraut argued, is only part of the problem. We have to deal, as well, with the historical distortions presented today by people claiming to *preserve* the memory of Auschwitz, by popularizers of the subject who have created "the Holocaust effect" and turned one of the greatest tragedies of the twentieth century into television soap opera. As these self-appointed chroniclers of Jewish suffering reduce the unthinkable to sentimental schmaltz, they often portray Jews as Christ figures, the idealized symbol of martyrdom: "Irony of ironies: the Jews became likable by becoming Christ. This marvelous misunderstanding made them popular (even, at times, to themselves): they were good because they were victims. But this sentimental new image contradicted the message of Judaism, one which refuses to confuse suffering with justice, to value victims for being victims."[66] Finkielkraut's reading here of Jewish doctrine comes directly from Emmanuel Lévinas, whom he quotes in the next paragraph. According to Jewish law, the philosopher explains, the just man is worthy not because he suffers, but because his sense of justice rises above his suffering. There is nothing magical in his pain.[67]

What interests the young writer most in Lévinas' work, however, is the philosopher's analysis of the other, which Finkielkraut examines briefly in *La Réprobation d'Israel*, then in considerable detail in *La Sagesse de l'amour*. Calling Lévinas "our greatest philosopher," Finkielkraut offers his interpretation of his mentor's ideas in the following way:

> The other person, writes Lévinas, wakes me up from my trance-like spontaneity, breaks the quiet and innocent imperialism of my determination to be, and puts me in the impossible position of invading the world like a piece of wild vegetation, like pure energy, like a moving force. My freedom does not have the last word, I am not alone. Without announcing himself, the Other, my fellow man, enters my life, his naked face, impregnable, both exposes and takes away my powers, indicts me. This intrusion, this bother, gives birth to my sense of scruples. The other man is the untimely presence who comes before I invite him to challenge the dogmatic naïveté of my own way of living.[68]

The other invades my world, puts limits on my freedom, forces me to take him or her into account as I live my own life. Confronted with the naked face of the other, with a vulnerable, unarmed being, I must assume responsibility for this intruder, who is outside myself, who is not me, who will never become just like me, but will remain the other in an asymmetrical relationship to me. As Finkielkraut considers the ethical implications of this formulation, he contrasts Lévinas' view with the position held by the Nazis, who not only rejected any sense of obligation toward those outside themselves, but who actually tried to wipe the others out.

Nazis attributed dangerous powers to Jews that nobody could see. Like microscopic germs, Jews supposedly brought about social illness and decay, threatening Aryans by invisible means, not by their external physical or cultural characteristics.[69] Nazis hated Jews, Finkielkraut explains, because they were "other," not because they were "different," a distinction he borrows from Lévinas and sees as essential if we are to understand European forms of racism and imperialism. Unfortunately, Finkielkraut continues, in *La Défaite de la pensée,* many people fail to make this distinction, among them activists involved in Third World struggles and left-wing intellectuals who express their solidarity with minority movements in the language of French structuralism.[70]

Finkielkraut singles out Frantz Fanon, the Algerian theorist of colonialism, and Claude Lévi-Strauss, the founder of French structuralism for special attention. In their works, he claims, the two thinkers have vigorously accused Europeans of being unwilling to accept the differences found among other peoples. Concerned, in particular, about the influence Lévi-Strauss has had on Western philosophy, Finkielkraut presents the structuralist's position at some length before he criticizes it. Let us do the same.

A STRUCTURALIST READING OF HISTORY

Europeans raised on Enlightenment philosophy have discriminated against those who stand out: the unknown, the marginal, people who come from someplace else, whose unique ways threaten Europeans by their strangeness. Justifying their use of violence with ideological explanations, they claimed that they alone represented civilization and had to defend their way of life from the barbarism of strangers. As they protected themselves from cultural diversity, they also imposed their narrow worldview—their ethnic specificity—on others, calling it everybody's world view, the universal culture: "Western civilization has sent out soldiers and missionaries all over the world. It has set up bars and plantations. It has interfered, either directly or indirectly, with the ways people of color live. It has turned their cultures upside down, from top to bottom, either by imposing Western traditions on them or by creating the conditions that would cause existing forms to crumble without replacing them with anything else."[71]

Lévi-Strauss rejects the teachings of Enlightenment-period universalists, identifying instead with the earlier philosophical tradition of Montaigne, which challenges ethnocentrism and promotes cultural pluralism. And Lévi-Strauss is not alone. Since the end, so-called, of European colonialism in the Third World and the subsequent rise of the new nation-states, Montaigne's position has gained popularity with progressives in the West, influencing a number of public figures to question long-held assumptions about Europe's cultural superiority. Individual leaders have slowly begun to consider the possibility that other ways of life are as legitimate as their own. What is more, the indigenous inhabitants of former colonies have learned to take pride in the heritages of their people and to identify with the traditions of their ancestors. They no longer feel they have to choose between cultural inferiority and assimilation.

Those who endorse the recent turn of events take pleasure in observing that we in the West now play a more modest role in the world. Our cultural ideals no longer dominate, but stand side by side with other equally valid traditions. We have had to accept that our belief system reflects only the historical circumstances of those living in the West, nothing more, nothing less. What we think is right is not necessarily so for people with entirely different experiences and backgrounds.

Given Finkielkraut's political and intellectual history, and his ongoing commitment to the left, it is hard to imagine that he would challenge the structuralists' position. He does so, however, suggesting that many of the school's most influential voices have fallen victim to their rhetorical call for equality. As we Europeans try to assume a more humble role in the world, proclaiming ourselves "other" in an attempt to free ourselves from the culture's phobia of the other, we face an insuperable contradiction: "The contradiction between the ethical inspiration of the project (a critique of Western ethnocentrism) and the final result—the disbanding of a single code of ethics in favor of a kind of generalized relativism. In other words, no one set of obligations applies any longer in a world now defined as a multitude of irreducible peoples who proliferate and confront one another."[72]

It is here that Finkielkraut reintroduces Lévinas' distinction between difference and otherness. While Lévinas condemns those who promote a philosophy of hatred of the other, he warns against merging otherness and difference. European disdain for the other has little to do with whether a particular individual or group eats or dresses exotically, but rather with the "nakedness of the other's face," with the resistance I feel to assuming my responsibility for this being who intrudes on my space and who reminds me that I am not alone. Those who call for the right to be different in the name of respecting the rights of others have not only misunderstood the roots of the problem, but have actually contributed to the general confusion by relieving Europeans of any obligation to aspire to a higher moral standard, to an authority that rises above competing value systems. Lévinas himself makes the point clearly, when he expresses his concern about those who claim that one civilization is as good as the next. "Modern atheism," Lévinas warns, "is not the negation of God. It is the total indifference of [Lévi-Strauss'] *Tristes Tropiques*."[73]

An obscure philosophical debate? For Finkielkraut, these issues have very serious political and moral implications in today's world, where cultural fanaticism destroys entire populations and raging nihilism denies the possibility of establishing an ethical system. At the present, he argues, we find ourselves forced to show our respect for all peoples, even if they commit acts we find abhorrent (female circumcision, infanticide, etc.) and to judge all forms of human activity as having the same cultural worth: a pair of boots equals a play by Shakespeare.[74] Alarmed by what he sees as the absence of any hierarchy of values, Finkielkraut calls for a return to the principles of the French Enlightenment and a reevaluation of the concept of a universal culture. This leads him to review the history of ideas of the late-eighteenth and early-nineteenth centuries and to contrast the French philosophical tradition of creating a nation made up of abstract individuals who come together as equals before the law with that of the German romantics who evoked the idea of a *Volksgeist,* of a nation made up of people who were all born with the same national spirit or culture:

> The Enlightenment philosophers defined themselves as the "peaceful legislators of reason." Masters of truth and justice, they opposed despotism and abuses of the natural rights of man. They defended what they called the ideal law. In contrast to them, representatives of German romanticism, reversed the priorities. Privileged guardians of the *Volksgeist,* lawyers and writers who identi-

fied with this movement, fought against the ideas of universal reason and the ideal law. Speaking in the name of culture, they no longer worried about eliminating prejudice and ignorance, but looked for ways to express the unique soul of the people they watched over, to describe the invincible *singularity* of their folk.[75]

Finkielkraut attributes the concept of Volksgeist to the eighteenth-century German philosopher Herder. Careful not to fall into the trap of reducing a people to a single national spirit, he quickly contrasts the ideas of this Prussian romantic with those of another German, namely Goethe, who devoted his great literary gifts to the ideal of creating a universal culture. Critical himself of those who celebrated the Volksgeist, Goethe believed that Germans should take every opportunity to open themselves up to influences beyond their frontiers and read the works of writers from other traditions.[76]

The Germans had their universalists and the French their Volksgeist-nationalists, the latter gaining strength in France during the last quarter of the nineteenth century, after the Franco-Prussian War of 1870–71: A curious response to a humiliating defeat that cost France those provinces in which large segments of the population spoke a German dialect! Finkielkraut describes how the French ended up embracing the very ideology that justified the unfavorable resolution to the war.[77] This change of mood set the shabby stage for the Dreyfus Affair.

As he moves into the modern period, Finkielkraut identifies national liberation movements with Herder's theory of the Volksgeist and the West's blanket endorsement of cultural diversity with a "generous betrayal" of the humanistic principles of the Enlightenment. He directs his attack against social scientists in general, and anthropologists in particular, against those who support the notion of cultural relativism. Historians of anthropology usually associate the perspective with Franz Boas and his disciples in the United States, who made their case in the early 1920s in order to challenge theories of race supremacy that were gaining prominence at the time on both sides of the Atlantic.[78] Finkielkraut, however, identifies cultural relativism with French structuralism, basing most of his argument on an essay Lévi-Strauss wrote for UNESCO (United Nations Educational, Scientific, and Cultural Organization) in the early 1950s (*Race et histoire*).

As the world was trying to pull itself together after the Second World War, traumatized by the horrors of National Socialism, government representatives and intellectuals gathered in London to form an organization that would provide educational and cultural opportunities for all peoples of the world. Espousing the values of the Enlightenment, they hoped to protect the international community from the rise of fascistic movements in the future. Finkielkraut summarizes UNESCO's original intention in the following way:

> They made connections between the moral and intellectual progress of humanity and set out to achieve a double goal, with political and cultural objectives: to defend human freedom and to provide education for all people. By defining their project in these terms, government representatives and important intellectual authorities spontaneously endorsed the spirit of the Enlightenment. As they planned the new era at the gathering in London, they rooted themselves philosophically in the eighteenth century and placed UNESCO under the patronage of Diderot, Condorcet and Voltaire, under the ideas of people who taught us that if freedom is a universal right, only the enlightened can be said to be free. It was these thinkers who came up with the formula . . . : respect the autonomy of individuals and offer them, through instruction, the means to be autonomous.[79]

But UNESCO's agenda rapidly changed, Finkielkraut continues, at first in imperceptible ways, from an educational campaign against forms of fanaticism to a critique of the ideals of the Enlightenment. Lévi-Strauss provided the arguments necessary for this ideological shift by making an apology for cultural relativism. Interpreting the anthropologist's efforts in the following way, Finkielkraut observes: "Enlighten humanity to prevent the possibility of falling back into barbarism: Lévi-Strauss endorses the solemn goal of the founders of UNESCO, but he turns it against the philosophy that guided the organizers of this international project. . . . The objective remains the same: destroy prejudice, but in order to do so, we do not have to open up others to reason, but open ourselves to the reason of others."[80]

Finkielkraut defends the principles of the Enlightenment against people who blame these ideas for bringing about the end of cultural diversity in Western Europe. In a nation like France, he maintains, nothing prevents the government from respecting the traditions of its minority peoples, at least up to a point. Citizens of a democratic nation-state do not have to assimilate into one hegemonic culture, but they do have to accept a common set of laws that favors the rights of individuals over all other rights. No matter who they are, all ethnic groups must agree to obey the rules imposed equally on every participating member of the contract-nation, even if some of these obligations defy the beliefs practiced by their people.[81]

With no apologies, Finkielkraut asserts the superiority of a cultural and political system, like the democratic nation-state, which protects the rights of the individual. What is more, he implies that ethnic minorities only come into conflict with the policies of this state when they do not respect the freedom of individual members of their group. Democracy, he agrees, will threaten the ways of people whose customs resist treating everybody equally before the law.

Traditional cultures, it is true, frequently protect the interests of the group at the expense of the individual, abusing in the process rights that Europeans consider inalienable. But Finkielkraut leaves himself open to criticism when he frames the problem in these terms and then does not challenge the contradictions that exist in almost every democratic nation-state. Praising the virtues of the kind of society envisioned by Diderot, Voltaire, and Condorcet, he does not examine the problems encountered by many citizens living in less idealized versions of the eighteenth-century dream: in contemporary France, for example, or the United States, where many do not yet enjoy the privileges promised to abstract individuals. Although the situation has improved in recent years, Finkielkraut's description of the enlightened West does not account for the abuses experienced daily by members of the working class, women, blacks, North Africans, and other minority groups.

Nevertheless, Finkielkraut has raised some fundamental questions about the politics of culture and has done so in terms reminiscent of those voiced by Jewish minority nationalists earlier in this century. His defense of the Enlightenment and universalism recalls the ideals of Yiddishists who struggled for political and cultural emancipation from the oppression of Jewish Orthodoxy and the czar. While he has broken with Le Cercle Gaston Crémieux and criticized the celebration of difference espoused by minority movements in France, he remains faithful to the goals of Jewish writers from the East, to those of people who tried to produce a literature in Yiddish and Hebrew that met the standards of a universal culture.

Immigrants living in the Yiddish-speaking community of Paris openly identify with Finkielkraut's views. Litvine, for one, endorses the young man's position with enthusiasm. So do many others, according to a recent study of landsmanschaftn in France.[82]

Finkielkraut also reflects the concerns of the Russian Jewish historian

Simon Dubnow, whose ideas on minority nationalism influenced Richard Marienstras. In Dubnow's essay on the philosophy of Jewish history, the great spokesman for diaspora Jewry draws the following "final lesson":

> In the sunny days of mankind's history, in which reason, justice, and philanthropic instinct had the upper hand, the Jews steadfastly made common cause with other nations. Hand in hand with them, they trod the path leading to perfection. But in the dark days, during the reign of rude force, prejudice and passion, of which they were the first victims, the Jews retired from the world, withdrew into their shell to await better days. Union with mankind at large, on the basis of the spiritual and the intellectual, the goal set up by the Jewish Prophets in their sublime vision of the future (Isaiah, ch. ii and Micah, ch. iv) is the ultimate ideal of Judaism's noblest votaries.[83]

Dubnow embraced those enlightened moments in history when Jews lived happily among other peoples and worked with them to develop a set of universal values that everyone could share. Such periods, Dubnow maintained, did not necessarily threaten the cultural specificity of Jews either. For, to use Lévinas' words on the same subject, "Jewish universalism always manifested itself in its particularism."[84]

But why do Jews bother to remain different at all? Lévinas contends that they do so to uphold the universalistic teachings of the Torah, not because there is anything inherently sacred about keeping oneself apart. Following his mentor, Finkielkraut goes a step further and warns against singling out cultural diversity as a good in itself:

> Jews did not accept the yoke of the Torah in order to set themselves apart. They set themselves apart in order to bear witness to the Torah, to the Revelation that humanity is one across time and space and that man himself is only human when he channels the spontaneous energy of his life force into taking responsibility for the other. Now, if we confine people to their differences, systematically reducing them to a product of their community, and if we also take the humanist idea of culture, defined as a product of the mind, and attach it to a concept of culture described as a unique way of being and thinking that reflects the specific qualities of individual groups, we impoverish communication among peoples and even go so far as to endanger the very idea of humanity.[85]

Occasionally Finkielkraut makes reference to the Torah, but he remains outside the realm of religious scholarship. When he received the award from the Fondation du Judaïsme, he humbly confessed that he was raised on the debates between Corneille and Racine, not on those between Hillel and Shammai. He has virtually no background in Judaic studies. Recently, however, through his reading of Emmanuel Lévinas, Finkielkraut has begun to see how the Torah and commentaries might enrich his appreciation of the ethical issues that concerned the great writers and thinkers of his own French tradition. And with this new insight he stands tentatively on the threshold of the Talmud. But he has still not "knocked at the door," as some disciples of Lévinas have gone on to do.

Other students of the generation of 1968 have not only knocked at the door, but have literally moved into the world of Talmudic studies. In the process, they have abandoned Lévinas' goal of engaging European philosophy and religious scholarship in a common search for universal ethics. They have closed themselves off in yeshiva communities, modeled on the ones that existed previously in Lithuania. But before we turn to the concerns of these newly converted Orthodox Jews, let us remain a while longer with the ideals of maskilim and consider the life and work of a second philosopher from Lite who came to France before the Second World War and who also looked for ways to engage Judaic scholarship and European philosophy.

In the last few years, those interested in the study of religious texts have rediscovered Jacob Gordin, a man who had an important following during the Second World War and in the early postwar years, until his death in 1947. Known for his teaching more than for his published work, Gordin was responsible for establishing a style of Jewish study in France that continued for many years after he died.

Like Litvine and Lévinas, Gordin was born into a family of enlightened Jews from Lite. Although his father gave him little formal religious training as a child, he still made sure Gordin received lessons in modern and ancient Hebrew, Aramaic, and a number of other classical languages—excellent preparation for someone who went on to specialize in medieval philosophy and the Kabbalah. Slightly older than Litvine and Lévinas, Gordin was in his early twenties in 1917, and he volunteered enthusiastically to fight in the Russian Revolution. But a few years later he grew disillusioned with Soviet communism. Leaving the country, he went to Germany to study the philosophy of the neo-Kantian Hermann Cohen and to join the circle of scholars affiliated with the Academy for Scientific Research on Judaism.

In the next chapter, we turn to the story of Jacob Gordin and his wife Rachel Zaber Gordin, told largely from the perspective of the philosopher's widow and from a few published sketches of the man. Although their families came originally from Lite, both sets of parents belonged to that privileged class of Jews whose economic and professional status gave them the right to live in Saint Petersburg. They grew up, therefore, in a more cosmopolitan world than did Litvine and Lévinas.

Still, as Rachel Gordin describes life in the two households, her portrait is reminiscent of the enlightened homes we saw in Shavli and Kovno. She too stresses how the children received an education that combined Judaism and European culture. Even in the case of Jacob Gordin, where his father did not bother to take his son to synagogue, the boy received regular lessons in Hebrew and the sacred texts.

In the end, Jacob and Rachel Gordin made choices similar to those of many other Jewish intellectuals from the Baltic states. Despite having the rare opportunity to attend Russian universities, after the Revolution they went to Berlin to study: psychology and education for her; philosophy for him. Then, in the 1930s they moved to France, where Jacob Gordin became a librarian and archivist at the Alliance Israélite Universelle, and his wife opened a Montessori school.

During the war, the Gordins helped run a refuge home for children, in the southwest of France, that was sponsored by the French Jewish Scouts (Eclaireurs Israélites de France). In the home, tucked away in a small hamlet, Jacob Gordin gave classes in Judaism to resident scout leaders and to those who regularly passed through as messengers, keeping the isolated homes in contact with one another. Given Gordin's extraordinary erudition in both Jewish and European philosophy, he quickly developed a passionate following.

As Rachel Gordin recalls the war years, she reveals some of the tensions —frequently referred to in the literature—that existed between immigrant and native-born French Jews. But most of her stories deal with the courageous ways scouts and French Christians cooperated, risking their lives to save Jewish children, the majority of whom were the sons and daughters of deported immigrants. The Gentiles who helped out were the inhabitants of small villages: policeman, peasants, directors of schools, and the well-known network of Protestants who took many risks on behalf of the Jews.

As this biographical sketch wanders through some of the personal details of the Gordins' life, we have the opportunity to meet a man whose "openness to human beings went beyond his taste for study and that is no small matter."[86] Although Jacob Gordin did not publish much during his lifetime, he left a great legacy for future generations of French Jews through his teaching and the model he offered for returning to Judaism. This maskil, revolutionary, and philosopher made his teshuvah first by the books, then in his practical life, just as some of his disciples have done in the years following 1968.

FIGURE 1. Rachel Ertel, 1970s. Photo by Marcel Ertel.

FIGURE 2.
Richard Marienstras, 1980s.
Photo courtesy of
Richard Marienstras.

FIGURE 3. Alain Finkielkraut, 1980s.
Photo by Deschamps, Agence Vu.

FIGURE 4. Elisabeth de Fontenay, *ca.* 1968.
Photo courtesy of Elisabeth de Fontenay.

FIGURE 5. Dominique Schnapper, 1980s.
Photo courtesy of Dominique Schnapper.

FIGURE 6. Benny Lévy, 1980s.
Photo by Deschamps, Agence Vu.

FIGURE 7. Shmuel Trigano, 1980s. Photo by Deschamps, Agence Vu.

FIGURE 8. Mordecai Litvine, 1980s. Portrait by M. Milberger.

FIGURE 9. Emmanuel Lévinas, 1970s. Photo by Jean-Luc Olivié. Courtesy of *L'Arche*.

FIGURE 10. Jacob Gordin, 1925.
Photo courtesy of *La Tribune juive*.

FIGURE 11. Olga Katunal, 1980s. Photo by Alain Kleinmann.

FIGURE 12. Oskar Goldberg,
interwar years.
Photo courtesy of
Manfred Voigts.

6

The Lithuanian Jewish Enlightenment in French Translation, Continued: Jacob Gordin

Jacob Gordin was born in 1896 in Dvinsk (Daugavpils), a small city in eastern Latvia near the Lithuanian border (see map 3).[1] His ancestors settled in this part of Lite in the eighteenth century, establishing themselves as flour merchants in the area. While the early history of the family is hazy, we do know that the Gordins enjoyed good social standing by the beginning of the nineteenth century. Everybody in town knew them. Distinguished visitors did business with them, even Napoleon: According to family legend, when the French emperor marched through Dvinsk in 1812, he bought flour from Jacob Gordin's great grandfather for his hungry soldiers' bread.

The Gordins were observant Jews who encouraged gifted sons to devote their lives to religious learning. As a young boy, Jacob Gordin's father showed great promise. He knew Talmud so well he could recite any passage by heart. The family, therefore, expected him to enter the rabbinate. But soon after his seventeenth birthday, the youth's father died, and the young scholar had to abandon his studies to help his mother carry on the business.

The real problem, the major difficulty for Jews living in the Diaspora, is the conflict between particularism and universalism. Gordin once said that this was the continuing paradox: Jews in the Diaspora have a universalistic calling and a particularistic way of life. While they stand together with the seventy other peoples of the universe, they remain separated from them all.

—WLADIMIR RABI

Actually, Jacob Gordin's father had secretly rejected the idea of becoming a rabbi even before he had stopped his formal education. Like many other young Jews of his generation, the boy had embraced the Haskalah and developed a passion for secular learning. Whenever possible, he stole time in the yeshiva to teach himself Russian and French from books he kept carefully hidden under heavy volumes of Talmud and commentaries. For him, modern languages had replaced ancient Hebrew and Aramaic; they were the keys to an emancipated culture.

In the mid-1890s Gordin's father married. Eager to raise a family in a more cosmopolitan setting, and wealthy enough to gain permission to do so, he moved to Saint Petersburg in 1899, where he gave his three children the education they needed to assimilate into the world around them. From the beginning Jacob, together with his younger brother and sister, went to school with the sons and daughters of Russian aristocrats.

At home, the Gordins mixed European culture with the emerging secular—but not Yiddish—traditions of emancipated Jews. While Gordin's father, for example, hired a tutor to give his children lessons in Hebrew, he did not take them to synagogue. The boy attended services for the first time when he was ten and went with the Zabers, the family of his childhood friend and future wife.

Rachel Zaber's parents had moved to Saint Petersburg from Shavli at about the same time the Gordins arrived from Dvinsk. Although they too were Russian-speaking, emancipated Jews, the Zabers maintained active ties to the city's Jewish community. They attended synagogue regularly, supported Jewish settlements in Palestine, and owned many Hebrew books and brochures that had been published in the Holy Land. In fact, their excellent library brought Jacob and Rachel together, for the boy's Hebrew teacher knew about the Zabers' collection and wanted his gifted pupil to make frequent use of it.

Gordin did not have the rigorous training his father had received in ḥeder and the yeshiva, but the child inherited the man's prodigious memory and love for learning. Recalling Jacob Gordin as a young boy, Rachel Zaber Gordin observed: "My husband, who was a little older than I, was ten years ahead in his studies. When we were young, he used to tell me about the stories he was reading. First it was Jules Verne, then works by Russians and the other classics."

At fifteen and a half, Gordin passed his baccalaureate brilliantly and received a silver medal. His performance, however, was not good enough to be admitted to the University of Saint Petersburg, which routinely excluded

Jewish students under the terms of the *numerus clausus*. Unwilling to inter-rupt his son's education and bow to discrimination, Gordin's father hired the "best professors" to give him private lessons in philosophy, Aramaic, and Arabic—the boy already knew Hebrew, Greek, and Latin. Three years later, Gordin entered the university,[2] where he received a degree in Semitic languages at the Faculty of Oriental Languages in 1915.[3] But World War I had begun by that time, and the Russian Revolution erupted soon after, forcing him to postpone plans for further study: "Like most students at the time, he was actively involved in politics. A disciple of Ahad Ha-Am and then a Bundist, by 1917, he identified with the Anarchists. Speaking out in demonstrations, Gordin was among those who convinced 10,000 sailors of the Russian Navy to join the Revolution."[4]

When the revolution broke out, Rachel Zaber was attending university at the Bestuzhevskye Kursy, an institution of higher learning for women. The war, however, interrupted her studies, and she fled Petrograd, as Saint Petersburg was now called, with her family. The Zabers decided to go to Odessa in the Ukraine. Jacob Gordin also left Petrograd and joined his parents and sister in the Crimean city of Yalta, where his enterprising father had managed to start a wholesale shoe business (see map 3).

To travel twenty-five hundred kilometers through Russia during the Bolshevik Revolution took more than a month. At times the train stopped in heavily forested areas, and passengers got out to help chop down trees to provide fuel for the locomotive. When they arrived in a town of some importance, they remained for days. Travelers ended up knocking on doors of complete strangers, offering their meager provisions in exchange for a place to stay. Over one such delay in the Ukraine, Jacob Gordin convinced a group of Kabbalists to take him in: "At first these Jewish mystics were wary of the young man who dressed in the European style and wore no side-locks. . . . They quickly realized, however, that Gordin had a solid ground-ing in Judaism and, more precisely, in the Kabbalah. Finally, they even agreed to give the young student three books on Jewish mysticism in ex-change for flour, sugar, tea, and salt."[5]

In Yalta, Jacob Gordin spent months reading the Kabbalah by himself and taking copious notes. Having studied ancient Semitic languages, Chris-tian mysticism, and the Koran, he had excellent preparation for analyzing these texts according to the standards of academic scholarship. He lacked, however, the rigorous training he would have received had he been raised in an Orthodox Jewish community, where gifted students worked closely with teachers steeped in Jewish learning.

Before either she or Gordin had left Petrograd, Rachel Zaber tried to end their relationship. As she explained it many years later, her childhood sweetheart was ready to marry, but she was not, particularly with a man she had known since she was nine years old. Instead of settling down immediately, the young woman wanted to live on her own for a while and meet new people. But chance brought them together again in Yalta.

Rachel Zaber's mother had a nervous breakdown in 1919 and needed medical attention immediately. With her father's permission, Rachel brought the ailing woman to Yalta, where she knew nobody, she thought, but where she had heard of an excellent sanatorium. A few days later, as the young woman was walking alone through the streets of the city, she ran into Jacob Gordin's father. The good man insisted that she take her mother out of the hospital and come live with him and his family. There was plenty of room.

The Gordins had rented a dacha that had once belonged to Chekhov. At the end of the garden there was a separate cottage, where Rachel Zaber could care for her mother in peace. Since the psychiatrist agreed that Mrs. Zaber did not have to remain in the sanatorium—all she needed was isolation and quiet—Rachel Zaber accepted the invitation and moved in.

Jacob Gordin and Rachel Zaber grew close once again. The young man came daily to take over the watch and let his friend go to the main house for meals and company, giving her breaks from her deeply disturbed mother. Even when the Gordins changed residences, which they did several times, they made room for Rachel Zaber and her mother. But finally the young woman decided that it was time to separate: Gordin had been pressuring her to marry him, and she was still not ready to do so.

In 1920 the rejected suitor returned to Petrograd to finish a second degree at the university, this time in philosophy, from the Faculty of Social Sciences.[6] During his studies, Gordin discovered the work of the German Jewish philosopher Hermann Cohen and the neo-Kantian school.[7] Cohen's approach to Judaism would have a profound influence on Gordin's future work.

Rachel Zaber returned to Petrograd with her family a few months later. Although her mother was still not well, she could travel, and the Zabers decided to move back home, at least for a while, long enough for Rachel to finish a degree in history. The young woman saw Gordin again, but when she left Petrograd two years later, she was sure things had finally ended.

Like many progressive, middle-class Jews, the Zabers had sympathized with the Mensheviks, not the Bolsheviks, and lost a lot of money during the Russian Revolution. Feeling threatened by Soviet communism, they abandoned their clothing business and left the country. In 1922, the Zabers returned to Shavli (now called Šiauliai), in the newly constituted independent Republic of Lithuania, leaving behind their younger daughter, who had decided to marry a Russian surgeon.

After three months in Lithuania, Rachel Zaber went to Berlin to continue studying history. She rapidly discovered, however, that the program was inferior to the one she had already finished in Petrograd. So she switched fields, concentrating in psychology and childhood education instead, areas in which the Germans were far ahead of the Russians.

During her first year in Berlin, Rachel Zaber received word from Gordin that he needed her help to secure a visa for a Russian professor who wanted to come to Germany with a team of students. Gordin would be among them. Things had taken a dangerous turn back home, the young man explained. In 1923 the Bolsheviks had fired eighty scholars from the University of Petrograd, accusing them of engaging in counterrevolutionary activities and of having a bad influence on the students. Removed from their posts, many gifted professors had to leave the country immediately, hence the request for a German visa. Rachel Zaber did as she was told and obtained the necessary papers.

When Gordin arrived in September, he insisted that they marry. This time the young woman accepted, and the childhood friends became husband and wife on December 8, 1923. The only member of their families present at the ceremony was a much improved Mrs. Zaber, who had come to Berlin to visit her daughter.

Gordin attached himself almost immediately to the disciples of Hermann Cohen—the philosopher himself had died in 1918—and to the Academy for Scientific Research on Judaism (Akademie für Wissenschaft des Judentums). Founded by Eugen Täubler in 1919, the academy trained students in Jewish history and philosophy, subjects not available in German universities. It provided them, as well, with the opportunity to specialize in a wide range of topics previously neglected by nineteenth-century scholars of Judaism, such as the Kabbalah.[8] While studying at the academy, Jacob Gordin received invitations to write articles on Jewish philosophical subjects for the *Encyclopaedia Judaica*. He also finished his doctoral dissertation and published it in German in 1929, under the title (in translation) *Investiga-*

tions on the Theory of Infinite Judgment.[9] Emmanuel Lévinas summarized the importance of Gordin's thesis in the following way:

> Writing with unrelenting discipline, in the last pages of his book Gordin compares the philosophy of Hegel with that of Hermann Cohen, revealing in the process certain incompatibilities that are hardly noticeable between the two dialectics. Gordin demonstrates how Hegel describes antithetical terms as reciprocal, giving priority to none of them, while Cohen presents the terms in a hierarchical order, indicating that there is a *beginning*.
>
> Was the great neo-Kantian inspired here by Jewish thought? Gordin does not ask the question. But he reveals the richness of a tradition by identifying a crack in the foundation of the rational system. . . . Gordin's strength lay in his ability to recognize subtle differences.[10]

During the years they lived in Germany, Rachel Gordin gave birth to a girl, whom they called Noémi. After weaning the child, she left her husband in Berlin and their daughter in Shavli with her parents, while she went to Rome for eight months to study at Maria Montessori's Institute. The Italian's radical approach to childhood education had become very popular in Germany, and Rachel Gordin wanted to open a kindergarten in that tradition.

Rachel Gordin finally started her own school in autumn of 1932. By the following spring, however, she and her husband realized how serious the Nazi threat had become, and they quickly left the country, hiding most of their belongings in a cellar. Rachel Gordin went to Shavli with Noémi, where the couple thought Jews would be safer and where she already had the necessary connections to open another Montessori school. Her husband, however, went to Paris to continue working in one of the great centers of European learning.

Jacob Gordin was unprepared for how difficult life in Paris would be, especially alone. Despite the disruptions of World War I and the Russian Revolution, he had never worried about money. As a married man, he continued to have security—his large inheritance took care of his family while he devoted himself to scholarly pursuits. In Germany they lived off the interest of 40,000 gold rubles that he had deposited in a bank in Berlin during the 1920s. But when they left the country in 1933, all he received for his considerable savings were sixty German marks. Jacob Gordin arrived in Paris with little money and no practical skills. His most valuable possession was a valise filled with notes on the Kabbalah that he had made during the long months he had spent in the Crimea.

When she heard how miserable her husband was, Rachel Gordin closed the Shavli school, left Noémi in the care of her parents, and came to Paris to join Gordin in an unheated hotel room on the rue Corneille. He had found these lodgings thanks to the help of the Comité de Bienfaisance Israélite de Paris. The French Jewish charity had also provided him, and now them, with meal tickets for the kosher students' restaurant on the rue de Médicis.

For months, they looked for work. Jacob Gordin went from philosopher to philosopher, seeking a post in the university. Famous professors received him graciously, complimented him on his erudition, and sent him on his way with a recommendation to go see another. Finally the French Jewish community came through with an invitation for him to give a series of lectures on medieval Judaism at the Ecole Rabbinique de France.[11] By 1934 he was also writing articles for *Cahiers juifs* on such subjects as Maimonides, Spinoza, and Dubnow.[12] For his contributions, he received a modest fee from the editor, an Egyptian Jew by the name of Maxime Piha. Soon he also got a regular, if poorly paying job, as librarian at the Alliance Israélite Universelle.

Rachel Gordin found work in a secular school directed by a Jewish woman, where she could use her Montessori training, even though the place did not strictly follow the method. A year later she opened up her own nondenominational Montessori kindergarden, which attracted the children of French, Russian, and Jewish families. With both of them working, life certainly became easier, but they still had difficulty making ends meet.

The Gordins left their dreary hotel on rue Corneille in 1934 and moved in with two friends who had French citizenship and did not have to pay an enormous deposit, the way foreigners did. Although this new arrangement was far better than the damp room they had had before, the husband of the couple did not like children and refused to let Noémi live with them.

The child, however, insisted on leaving Shavli in 1935 and coming to Paris to be with her parents. Seeing no other solution, Rachel Gordin put Noémi in a German-language boarding school nearby, where at least her daughter could speak to the teachers and other children. But the little girl hated it and came down with one illness after another. Then Rachel Gordin placed her in a Montessori school located on the outskirts of Paris, where the atmosphere was more congenial, but this was small comfort to the child. All Noémi wanted was to live with her parents—a simple request, but one the Gordins could not grant her for years.

Before the war, Jacob Gordin had not been a religious man and his wife only casually so. When Olga Katunal first met the philosopher in Berlin in the 1920s he was like other assimilated Russian Jews of the period.[13] Similarly, when they saw each other again in Paris in the 1930s, she remembered reciting Russian poetry with him and participating in the usual activities of secular Jewish intellectuals.

Then, during the first weeks of the German occupation, Olga Katunal bumped into him in Toulouse (Haute-Garonne). He was wearing a skullcap and had become, like herself, a practicing Jew. Gordin had just reached the Free Zone and was on his way to join his wife, who was working in the Department of Corrèze for the Jewish Scouts (map 4).

Even before the occupation began, the Eclaireurs Israélites de France had established homes for Jewish children in the south of the country, in what came to be known as the Free Zone. Encouraging parents to send their daughters and sons out to the cities before it was too late, they offered educational and camping experiences for girls and boys, with a decidedly Zionist slant, hoping in the process to prepare a new generation to emigrate to Palestine.[14] By the time the Germans arrived a year later, several houses were already in place to receive the youngsters. Of the five hundred children who found refuge with the scouts, all of them survived, except for one little boy, whose parents insisted on taking him back home.[15]

During the early years of the occupation, the Eclaireurs decided to cooperate with the Union Générale des Israélites de France, the equivalent of a French Judenrat. In doing so, the Eclaireurs agreed not to go underground and hide children from the Nazis, but to keep them in establishments registered with the police. Then, even after Darquier de Pellepoix declared the scouts illegal in 1941, the Eclaireurs continued to work openly in the Free Zone. They did not change their policy until the end of 1943 when the Nazi campaign against Jews and resisters had reached its peak, even in the South.[16] Only at this late date did they disband the homes.

When the Eclaireurs asked Rachel Gordin to help them in autumn of 1939, she took Noémi with her and left Paris for the southwest of France. Given her training in childhood education, she felt that the Eclaireurs should have put her in charge of a group from the beginning. But because she was a foreigner, they made her an assistant, placing her under the direction of a young scout by the name of Liselotte Gorlin. As Rachel Gordin tells the story, the less experienced woman brought the group to La Braye, in the Department of Lot, where she took over a rundown chateau, a shell of a building with boards missing and weak rafters. When Rachel

Gordin saw the condition of the house, she insisted that they move the children to a safer place in town.

Since her husband had remained in Paris to continue working at the Alliance Israélite Universelle, Rachel Gordin returned as often as possible to see him. On one of these visits, she heard from the Eclaireurs that Liselotte Gorlin had left the country and gone to the United States with her husband and baby. The scout leader had put her mother—a well-meaning woman with no training for the job—in charge of the house. Now the Eclaireurs needed Rachel Gordin more than ever, but they still only offered to make her an assistant.

This time she refused. If they wanted her professional help, they would have to recognize her properly. The Eclaireurs finally agreed to her terms, and Rachel Gordin returned and took over a home for girls in Beaulieu-sur-Dordogne, located in the Department of Corrèze. Two years later, in this same place, Jacob Gordin taught the work of European philosophers and Jewish thinkers to the young scout leaders based in Beaulieu and in the surrounding area.

Jacob Gordin left Paris in June 1940, just as the Germans were entering the gates of the city. He had stayed behind until the very last minute to help load a truck with the archives of the Alliance Israélite Universelle, in the vain hope of saving the library from the hands of the Germans. Now eager to join his wife in Beaulieu, he accepted a lift to Vichy (Allier) with an officer of the alliance who was on his way to North Africa, where the organization had a ready network to receive refugees from France.

After separating, Gordin did most of the remaining two hundred kilometers on foot, though he occasionally received rides from French soldiers—a mixed blessing. The commander of one military truck arrested Gordin and accused him of being a spy. Why else would a foreigner be wandering around like this by himself? The penalty for his alleged crime was death.

On the morning Gordin expected to die, some policemen arrived at the soldiers' camp to see what was going on. The military did not have the authority, Rachel Gordin explained, to stop people on the roads. This was the job of the police, and they objected strongly when the soldiers interfered:

> The police said, "Have you arrested anyone"?
> "Yes, we have a prisoner."
> "Bring him out."

When my husband appeared, they said, "Show us your papers." My husband gave his papers to them. "Where are you
going"?

"I am going to join by wife who runs a home for children."

"Can you prove it"? Luckily, my husband had receipts in his
wallet of money orders he had sent to me. The postal slips had the
address of the home written on them. At the time, I was working
for nothing, and my husband sent money to pay for my living
expenses. After seeing the receipts, the police said to the soldiers,
"What do you want with him? The man is on his way to join his
wife!"

When he finally reached Beaulieu, Jacob Gordin was a sick man, suffering from the arterial condition that eventually killed him. The long days of
hiking and damp nights in ravines had been too much for this fragile man,
who had never regained his health after he contracted typhus in the last days
of the Russian Revolution. In the early 1920s, Gordin had made a second
visit to the Crimea to study with a group of Kabbalists, during which time
he became deathly ill.

Rachel Gordin remained the head of Beaulieu until 1942, the year the
Gestapo began massive roundups of Jews in occupied France and expanded
their activities to the Free Zone, as well. Many of the homes sponsored by
the Eclaireurs responded to the new emergency by trying to take in more
children. At Beaulieu the all-girls' refuge now opened its doors to boys.

As the situation worsened, the Eclaireurs returned to their earlier policy of employing only native French Jews to direct the homes, assuming that
citizens would be safer than foreigners in such visible positions. They therefore asked Rachel Gordin to step down and assigned Georges and Julienne
Hertz from Strasbourg to take over. Although the couple had no previous
connection to the scout movement, they had good training for the job. Mr.
Hertz came from an Orthodox family and had studied the Torah and Talmud seriously. He also had experience as an administrator. Mrs. Hertz was a
practicing nurse, an artist, and a former president of the Strasbourg branch
of the Women's International Zionist Organization (WIZO), hence an important personality in the Jewish community.[17] While it was difficult for
Rachel Gordin to accept the change, the four became close friends, and the
Gordins maintained many of their responsibilities: she, as coordinator of
the educational programs for young children, and he, as the accountant.

Given his Orthodox background, Georges Hertz assumed that he was the one best qualified to give a course on Jewish thought to the young scout leaders who lived at the home, most of whom were teenagers or in their early twenties. He soon learned he was wrong and turned the class over to Gordin: "He [Gordin] was so modest that the casual observer did not even take notice of him. Once he requested to attend the course I was giving for the young scout leaders—there were about ten of them—who were helping with the 115 children assigned to us. But after he asked two or three questions, I realized whom I was dealing with and changed places. He went to the front of the room, and I sat on the benches with the students."[18]

Gordin's reputation grew rapidly, and the quiet man soon had a large following. Stories about his extraordinary learning reached Moissac in the Tarn-et-Garonne Department. Then, as scouts traveled from home to home, serving as messengers, they spread the word even farther. In no time young couriers were trying to arrange a stopover in Beaulieu in order to have time to study with Gordin for a while.

In October 1943 the Gestapo arrested the scout leader Claude Guttmann. Before they sent him north to the French internment camp in Drancy, a suburb of Paris, and then on to Auschwitz, Guttmann managed to get word to the Eclaireurs that the movement was truly in danger, a fact many leaders up until then had still refused to accept. Finally, the national committee responded. The scouts closed their homes and went underground.[19] From then on, the Eclaireurs helped to hide children in a wide network of French boarding schools where Gentile directors had agreed to take the risk of enrolling Jewish students with false identification papers.

When Beaulieu shut its doors, Georges Hertz joined the maquis, and his wife and their children went into hiding in the department of Lot, where Julienne Hertz did resistance work as well.[20] The Gordins remained in town as long as they could, in order to watch over their daughter and the other boys and girls from the home who had been placed in schools in the area. When they heard that someone had leaked information to the Gestapo, they moved the children quickly to another school on the precious list Jacob Gordin kept with him at all times.

Within a few months the Gordins were forced to leave Beaulieu too and join the Eclaireurs in their mountain hideout located in Chaumargeais, a small village near Chambon-sur-Lignon (Haute-Loire, see map 4), in the Massif Central, a major center of Protestant resistance in France during the Second World War. As Rachel Gordin described their escape, she spoke warmly about people from Chambon who had taken care of the couple during the last leg of the trip and brought them safely to the scouts' secret retreat. But they would never have made it to Chaumargeais at all had it not been for the help they received from the residents of Beaulieu, in particular from the chief of police, who had warned them in time that they had to leave:

> In the little village [Beaulieu], the Germans came looking for the maquis to avenge the death of two French collaborators killed there by members of the Resistance. As it happened, the Chief of Police was a good friend of mine. Everybody respected us because we worked for other people's children. And so the policeman came to see me and said: "Madame Gordin, you know how much I like you and respect you and how I have always done what you wished. But now I must ask you to leave. They are going to burn the house you live in and arrest me for protecting a Jewish couple. They will take you, as well.
>
> As it happened, a young scout leader was with us at the time. One of many miracles. She or somebody else came every week to get instructions from my husband. Her totem [scout nickname] was Honeysuckle. I said to her: "Honeysuckle, you must come with us. We both have accents, and my husband looks like a member of the Russian intelligentsia—Russian and Jewish. You must accompany us and speak in our place."

In Chaumargeais, the Gordins joined a community of scout leaders, including Georges Lévitte, the former director of the house in Moissac. For months the group there had been asking the philosopher to leave Beaulieu and establish a "school of prophets" with them. Now, finally, Gordin had arrived, and he worked with these young people, to prepare them to preserve Jewish learning and values for the period of reconstruction after Liberation. In his memoirs, the scout leader Hammel observed that "this undertaking was one of the most original, the most pure and the most Jewish of all our efforts during the time we were in hiding."[21]

After the war, Jacob Gordin returned to his job as librarian at the Alliance Israélite Universelle, but he remained closely tied to the intellectual activities of the Eclaireurs as well. In 1946 he gave a series of lectures and seminars at the first national gathering of the scouts after the war. Robert Gamzon, the founder of the Jewish Scouts of France, chose the Chambon region for the camp site as a way of expressing thanks to members of the Protestant resistance movement for the courageous way they had helped Jews during the occupation.[22]

Gordin also taught at the Ecole d'Orsay, the school Gamzon established after the war to train new scout leaders. Officially known as the Ecole Gilbert Bloch, it was located just outside Paris, in the town of Orsay. Léon Askenazi (Manitou), a major figure in the North African scout movement and the son of the chief rabbi of Oran, became the director of the school and one of Gordin's most devoted admirers.

As Emmanuel Lévinas explained, for more than twenty years, the Ecole d'Orsay dominated the spiritual life of young French Jews "attached to an ambitious Judaism." And until his death in 1947, Jacob Gordin was the school's shining light: "As [Gordin] dipped into the treasures of the Midrash and Jewish mysticism, he drew on his remarkable background in philosophy. The resulting courses established a tradition at this school that Léon Askenazi and his disciples continued, defining an entire style of Jewish studies."[23]

Jews in France remember Gordin for reasons beyond the considerable contributions he made there during the Second World War and the years immediately following Liberation. He remains important because he applied the rationalism of Hermann Cohen to the secrets of Jewish mysticism. Few others have ever attempted to do the same.

Gordin, of course, was hardly the first to look at Jewish mysticism as a rationalist; the Gaon of Vilna was himself a great scholar of the subject and studied Kabbalistic texts according to the analytic tradition of Lithuania. But Gordin's project evolved out of modern philosophical issues hotly debated in Germany in the interwar years. While he may have found comfort in identifying his efforts with his Jewish heritage from Lite, he framed his questions in terms familiar to European scholars, as he tried to make connections between a body of religious thought that many claimed defied rational analysis and the philosophical approach of Hermann Cohen. Lévinas explained it this way: "Despite the differences in register, he combined his strong attachment to the neo-Kantism of Marburg with an exploration of Israel's mystical heritage in the literature of the Kabbalah. Interested in the Concept and the Mystery, he brought the two together in his teaching later on, where his discussion of *logos,* clearly influenced by Cohen, supported the boldness of the visionary."[24]

With few exceptions, Jewish philosophers writing in German in the early twentieth century had little interest in trying to explain mysticism in terms of the European philosophical tradition of eighteenth-century rationalism.[25] Thinkers like Gershom Scholem and Martin Buber, for example, two of the most prominent contributors to the field, broke with the neo-Kantians and with what they considered to be Cohen's assimilationist interpretation of Judaism. When they turned to the Kabbalah, they did so, says Michael Löwy, with the fervor of "religious anarchists" attracted by "the magical, irrational, 'anti-bourgeois' aspect of Jewish mysticism."[26]

But if Scholem and Buber approached the Kabbalah as religious anarchists, they challenged Hermann Cohen's German nationalism as Zionists, not as people opposed to the formation of all nation-states. Eventually, they both abandoned Europe and moved to Palestine—Scholem in 1923, and Buber in 1938. Jacob Gordin, on the other hand, remained true to his anarchist past and took a stand against Zionism as a diaspora Jew, preferring to live among many different peoples.

While Gordin joined Cohen in refusing to endorse the creation of a political homeland for Jews, he must have had difficulty reconciling his ideas about the Diaspora with those often attributed to Cohen. Perhaps he never did. Or perhaps he interpreted Cohen's position the way Rabbi Meyer Waxman did, in terms very different from the ones suggested by the neo-Kantian's critics. According to Waxman, the German Jewish philosopher believed in a kind of stateless nationality for the Jews, a spiritual nationalism for the People of the Book.[27] Seen in this light, Cohen's ideas were entirely compatible with Gordin's own views on the subject: "In our exile [Gordin once said to his students], we have been mixed together with the peoples of many states and we participate in their struggles. But as a Holy Community, as the center of the world, we cannot and should not have a state of our own . . . ; we have been stripped of that possession precisely in order for us to represent the world to come, the kingdom on high."[28] Finally, while Scholem and Buber associated Cohen's rationalist approach to philosophy with his willingness to accept the German Jewish Enlightenment, Jacob Gordin did not necessarily do the same. As a Jew from Lite, he had other models to draw on. For him, rationalism had as much to do with Lithuanian Talmudic studies as it did with Western European thought.

During the last years of his life, Gordin gave up writing, preferring to transmit his teachings orally, in the tradition of the great masters of Jewish mysticism. We therefore have few traces of his later work, save a few notes made by people who studied with him during the war and immediately thereafter. In the obituary Georges Hertz wrote for Gordin, he said that he regretted his friend's decision to stop publishing. But even without much recent material, Hertz felt he could give a sense of the man he had known in the 1940s by quoting at length from the end of Gordin's 1934 article on Maimonides.[29]

In this essay Gordin suggested that the teachings of the medieval philosopher had much to offer Jews in the twentieth century. Making these observations the year after Hitler took power, Gordin worried about Jews in the Diaspora wandering about "with no direction or goal." They needed to read Maimonides' *Guide to the Perplexed,* he said, for it would help them find their way back to Judaism. Composed in the late 1100s, Maimonides' work was profoundly religious without being separatist. It did not encourage Jews to isolate themselves from the ideas of the people around them, Gordin continued, but demonstrated instead how Jewish thought might engage the scientific philosophy of the Greeks, in particular that of Aristotle.

Gordin, like Lévinas, looked for ways to build on the philosophical project medieval philosophers had initiated centuries before. But Gordin's work with Jewish mysticism also led him to worry about the possible limitations of modern attempts to create an ethical Judaism in which God came to play a minor role. In a paper entitled "The Impossible Synthesis between Jewish and Secular Culture," Gordin summarized the problem with an anecdote he had once heard about Hermann Cohen:

> One day he was giving a lecture and speaking with eloquence and profundity about the moral value of religious Judaism, describing the biblical God as the only guarantor of moral progress and peace among men, as the one who would bring to pass the messianic era that the prophets spoke about. He delivered his talk in an organized fashion, balancing everything: the Bible and Greek philosophy, the Talmud and Kant or Hegel. After this magnificent, if long-winded performance, somebody in the audience asked an innocent question: "But where does the Creator fit into your philosophy? Is He the principle you mentioned earlier that will bring about the messianic era?"
>
> As he tried to respond, this founder of a philosophy, this man of international reputation, this famous author of an entire library of books, found no other way to answer the question than to break down and cry.[30]

As Jacob Gordin struggled to reconcile Jewish mysticism with Hermann Cohen's approach to Judaism, he reinterpreted without ever abandoning the guiding principles of the neo-Kantian's work. His students, however, were less faithful. By the time the Ecole d'Orsay closed its doors in 1970, the teachings of Hermann Cohen no longer concerned many students of Judaism in France.[31] The ideas of Gordin threatened to disappear as well, until very recently, when a handful of Jews of the generation of 1968 rediscovered the philosophy of this maskil from Lite through graduates of the Ecole d'Orsay. Now some of them express interest in studying what can be salvaged of his published and unpublished work.

Léon Askenazi's students have been a link between the tradition of Jewish scholarship Gordin established in France and the religious renewal presently going on. Among them, there is Jean Zacklad. Teacher of philosophy in Paris at the Jewish Lycée Abneh, Zacklad has also directed a university seminar in the 1980s at the International School of Philosophy with a group of scientists—Jews and Gentiles—interested in comparing methods of reasoning in science and Talmud. Zacklad seeks ways of building a bridge between two systems of thought—one Gentile, the other Jewish; one scientific, the other nonscientific. The author of several challenging volumes on a range of ethical and theological subjects, in the late 1980s Zacklad was working on the covenants God made first with Noah and then with the Hebrews.[32]

Jean Zacklad did not want to talk about his family's history, but he did mention that his father came to France from Lithuania as a boy, in the early 1900s.[33] Settling down in Paris, the immigrant youth attended the Ecole Rabbinique de Jean Jaurès. And that was about all the philosopher felt like sharing. The past was not important, he explained, only the future. He wanted us to think about the year 2010, when, he believed, Jews would play a significant role in the world, more so than Christians or Marxists.

In the end, Zacklad did provide a few more details: He was born in France and raised, more or less, as a secular Jew, despite his father's early training in rabbinical Judaism. When the Germans entered Paris in 1940, Zacklad, who was still quite young, left the city with his family and spent the war in hiding in the Free Zone of France. After Liberation, he returned home and continued his studies. Like many intellectuals of his generation, he decided to major in philosophy, but he did not share the passion of his contemporaries for the work of "Rabbi" Sartre. Zacklad chose to study the phenomenology of Husserl instead.

In the late 1940s, Zacklad found his way to the Ecole d'Orsay. Gordin was dead by then, but Léon Askenazi took an interest in the young philosopher and invited him to join a small group of students he had selected to carry on the mission of the "school of prophets" by becoming teachers of Judaism for future generations. A few years later, Askenazi sent Zacklad to Morocco to work for the Eclaireurs, during which time the young man attended a rabbinical seminary in Rabat and became the disciple of a Moroccan "master."

After spending several years in Morocco, he returned to France and discovered the rationalistic Lithuanian approach to sacred texts. He also went back to university to do a doctorate degree in philosophy with Paul Ricoeur and André Neher. By the 1960s he was teaching at the Lycée Abneh.

In the mid-1970s Zacklad ran a seminar with Sartre's intellectual companion Benny Lévy, the political radical who was seeking a way to return to Judaism. Attracting many former Maoists of the student movement, the group continued for several years until Lévy left Zacklad and went off to study with the Moroccan rabbi Eliahou Abitbol, first in Paris and then in new teacher's yeshiva in Strasbourg. The few who remained with Zacklad were, for the most part, physicists and mathematicians, and they decided to turn the seminar into a forum for comparing scientific and religious thought.

Jean Zacklad is not the only student of the Ecole d'Orsay who has played a role in the present Jewish revival. Eliahou Abitbol also studied at the school briefly in the 1950s. So did Aaron Fraenckel, the Alsatian Jew who eventually assumed direction of the Ecole in the late 1960s. Today, Fraenckel, like Abitbol, lives in Strasbourg, where he runs a Jewish bookstore and enjoys the respect of members of La Yéchiva des Etudiants. In recent years he has also developed a small following in Paris through the courses he gives at the new "Beit Hamidrach" that Shmuel Trigano has opened at the Alliance Israélite Universelle.

As we turn now to examine the ideas and experiences of members of generation of 1968 who have converted to Orthodox Judaism, we begin with a biographical sketch of Benny Lévy, the best known representative of the group. Lévy's story takes us through important moments in the history of the Maoists in France in the late 1960s and early 1970s. It also touches on the influence Jean-Paul Sartre has had on Lévy and on other gauchistes, as the distinguished philosopher fought for the rights of radical journalists and helped reintegrate young leftists into the intellectual community of France. Most important, Sartre brought Lévy back to philosophy and prepared the way for the young radical to discover Emmanuel Lévinas, whose work led Lévy to study the sacred texts and eventually join a community devoted to the tradition of Lithuanian Talmudic scholarship.

Lévy, like Gordin, made his teshuvah via the books. But the young man had virtually no background to draw on when he decided to devote himself to Jewish texts. He started from scratch and acquired basic skills in Hebrew and Aramaic, skills that Gordin, the son of a maskil, had mastered as a boy.

7

From Mao to Moses (via Lithuania): The Return to Orthodox Judaism by Intellectuals Identified with May 1968

Benny Lévy left Paris with his family in 1983 to join an Orthodox Jewish community in the Alsatian city of Strasbourg (Bas-Rhin).[1] Nearly a year later, *Libération* published a lengthy article about him, characterizing his move as symptomatic of the times. Better known by his alias, Pierre Victor, Lévy had been a disciple of the Marxist-Leninist philosopher Louis Althusser at the Ecole Normale Supérieure in the mid-1960s. He had also been the clandestine leader of La Gauche Prolétarienne, a Maoist faction of the French student left, and the secretary of Jean-Paul Sartre, from 1973 until the philosopher died seven years later. When Lévy embraced Orthodox Judaism in the early 1980s, other young radicals did the same, following their charismatic leader into the yeshiva.

Journalist Alain Garric took the assignment for *Libération* hoping to find reasons why a growing number of Jews in the generation of 1968 had recently gone from "Mao to Moses." While the resulting article left many questions unanswered, it gave Lévy the chance to correct the record and defend himself against those wishing to reduce his conversion to one more case of an identity

I didn't turn to Jewish texts, because I was having an identity crisis. . . . I turned to Jewish texts for intellectual reasons. To be more precise, philosophical issues led me to the Jewish texts.

—BENNY LEVY

crisis. Philosophical questions, the former Maoist explained, not a longing for roots, had led him to the sacred texts.

Although he no longer lives in Paris, Lévy still holds a position as adjunct professor (chargé de cours) at the University of Paris VII, and in that capacity he continues to give a weekly seminar in philosophy.[2] Topics vary, ranging from Plato to Lévinas, depending on the semester. After teaching, Lévy returns to Strasbourg, where he spends the rest of his time at the Yéchiva des Etudiants, studying Talmud with Rabbi Eliahou Abitbol.

Born in Cairo in 1946, Benny Lévy is the third of three children, all of them boys. In Egypt, his father made a living in the import-export business, and the family belonged to Cairo's middle-class community of French-speaking, assimilated Jews. Like many others in their circle, Lévy's parents were not religious people, but they identified strongly with their heritage. At home, for example, while they paid little attention to ritual detail, the family celebrated the Sabbath and holidays as ways of expressing their national loyalty to the Jewish people. Still, Lévy's parents remained uninterested in the teachings of the sacred law and did not bother to give their sons a Jewish education.[3]

The Lévy boys inherited a love for revolution, not Judaism. As they grew up, they heard stories about their uncle Hillel Schwartz, the founder of the Egyptian Communist party, whose radical activities led to his arrest. Carrying forward the family's political tradition, Lévy's oldest brother, Bobby, joined the Union of Workers, Peasants and Students—one of several parties identifying with communism that existed in Egypt in the early 1950s, and he solemnly assumed the responsibility of educating his siblings about the evils of capitalism.[4] But tensions in the Middle East separated teacher and students, putting an end to these lessons.

When the British lost control of the Suez Canal in 1956, most Jews living in Egypt at the time decided to leave the country, the Lévys included. Within a few months, the family had completed the necessary arrangements to move to Brussels, but Bobby, all of eighteen years old, refused to go. He insisted on staying behind to continue his political work. Although the Lévys were unhappy about it, Bobby got his way and remained in Cairo, where he was eventually arrested and sent to prison.

In Belgium, "Benny didn't understand where he was and the feeling never left him. This sense he had of being in exile defined him from then on in."[5] Lévy saw himself as "a man from nowhere and for that reason, perhaps, [he became] a formidable Sartrean."[6] Despite his sense of existential despair, his belief that he would never belong, Lévy found a place for himself in school and quickly rose to the top of his class: "In Brussels, Lévy did brilliantly in high school, and his professors did not hide their great admiration for such a gifted adolescent, who could not stand being anything but first, no matter what the subject. Lévy dominated the class, but he did so gracefully, without the plodding dedication typical of competitive students. On the contrary, he never hesitated to be provocative, to twirl around unexpectedly, to be witty and incisive, to use words with an implacable, poetic precision—he spoke the way people wrote and he wrote the way he spoke."[7]

In autumn of 1963, Lévy came to France to study philosophy and entered a two-year college program (hypokhâgne and khâgne) that would prepare him to take the highly competitive qualifying exam for the Ecole Normale Supérieure. By the end of the first year, he had distinguished himself and gained admission to the prestigious Lycée Louis-le-Grand, where he spent another twelve months studying for the difficult exam with some of France's most gifted students. He passed the test and began classes at the Ecole Normale in 1965.

Lévy also came to France to participate in the political life of French university students whose activities he had been following closely in Belgium, thanks to his brother's reports. Tony Lévy had moved to Paris a couple of years before Benny to take a degree in mathematics. In no time he had joined the Union des Etudiants Communistes (UEC) and was supporting the Algerian liberation struggle. Following his brother, Benny Lévy became a member of the UEC, and through Tony he met a number of people who subsequently rose to prominence in the student movement. Pierre Goldman was among them. Twelve years later, the celebrated radical of Polish Jewish origin reminisced about Benny Lévy in his memoirs, recalling the literary and philosophical interests of this recent addition to the UEC. "I got to know this rigid Marxist-Leninist at a time when a passage by Eluard, Emmanuel Lévinas, and the young Marx, would cause him to sob with ecstasy. . . . He was Jewish, and I always felt that he was a Talmudist who had lost his way and ended up doing doctrinal interpretations of Maoist texts."[8]

But Lévy's most important friend before 1968 was the *normalien* Jacques Broyelle, who introduced the newcomer to a select group of students at the école: the disciples of Louis Althusser. Among them was Robert Linhart, a brilliant dialectician and the leader of the Althusser faction of the UEC. Impressed by Lévy's intelligence and sense of politics, Linhart invited this young Egyptian Jew—whose credentials included a Communist brother in prison—to serve on the executive committee of the group.

By 1966 the Union of Communist Students was having trouble holding its various factions together. Linhart and his followers criticized the movement for continuing to support the Soviet Union and called on its members to endorse the Cultural Revolution that Mao had just introduced in China. Eventually, the group split apart. In December of that same year, at a meeting held in the auditorium of the Ecole Normale Superiéure (rue d'Ulm), more than a hundred students, the Lévy brothers among them, joined Linhart to form the Union des Jeunesses Communistes (marxistes-léninistes) (UJC[ml]). Someone suggested that they call themselves the French Union of Young Communists, but Linhart rejected the idea: "We are internationalists, we have no country!" Within a few weeks, the new group had won the support of 95 percent of all the Communist students in Paris and the majority of those in the provinces.[9] Benny Lévy rose to second in command, and Jacques Broyelle became number three.

Determined to keep the revolution with the working class, Linhart refused to let the UJC(ml) participate in the early days of May 1968. As thousands of students poured into the Latin Quarter and occupied the Sorbonne, he spoke with disdain about the historic revolt, dismissing it as a childish outburst of the bourgeoisie: "Linhart, who dreamed of joining the proletariat, who wanted the students to move to the suburbs where the workers lived and labored, he did not understand, nor did he tolerate, this infantile fixation on the Sorbonne."[10] At a heated meeting of the UJC(ml) Linhart argued his point against some opposition, managing, in the end, to convince the large gathering to accept the logic of his position. But after winning the debate, he collapsed from exhaustion and had to leave Paris to get some rest. This put Lévy temporarily in charge of the group.

By mid-May, French workers throughout the country had responded to the students' call for a general strike. On May 16, the radio announced that 60,000 people had walked off their jobs. The next afternoon, reports put the number at 300,000.[11] Now, the UJC(ml) had the excuse they needed to join the demonstrations as well.

When 4,000 employees occupied the Renault car factory in Billancourt, a suburb of Paris, Benny Lévy decided that the time had come for the UJC(ml) to send students out to support the striking workers. Unlike most other groups of young radicals, his movement, he claimed, was clearly identified with the proletariat. They were the ones who should help form a new Popular Front in France, the way Léon Blum briefly did in the mid-1930s, and bring workers and progressive members of the bourgeoisie together.

The UJC(ml) quickly gathered its forces and went down to the Sorbonne. From there, several hundred students marched over to Billancourt to demonstrate their solidarity with the strikers. Those in the front ranks carried a large banner that read: "The workers will take from the fragile hands of the students the flag marking the struggle against a regime that opposes the people." Stalin had written these prophetic words, hardly the author one would expect to inspire a group of anti-Soviet Marxist-Leninists who had just started siding with China. But since most of the marchers had no idea whom they were quoting, the irony of the moment escaped them.[12]

The students' sense of euphoria and optimism did not last for long. On June 12, de Gaulle declared a number of their groups illegal, including the UJC(ml). A few days later, most of the strikes had come to an end. Then, on June 30, after the second round of legislative elections, de Gaulle won 358 of the 465 seats in the National Assembly, gaining back his authority with a resounding vote of confidence (but only for a while—the following spring he was forced to resign).

In July and August of 1968, virtually everything came to a halt. Demoralized, but determined not to give up, students left Paris, as they traditionally did for their summer vacation, to recuperate from the past two months and give some thought to what they should do next. De Gaulle may have outlawed the UJC(ml) and other student groups, but the young revolutionaries had no intention of abandoning their political struggle. As Jacques Broyelle looked toward the future, he concluded that their movement needed to change leaders: the three top men—Linhart, Lévy, and himself—should relinquish their power and let others take over. Writing and circulating a piece of self-criticism, Broyelle claimed: "We based our leadership style on the authority of the bourgeois intellectual: I was in charge because I had good training in theory."[13] To single out people for their intellectual prowess went against the ideals of Mao, Broyelle continued. Those in command should resign, call for new elections, and let the party choose a different committee, one that would be more in keeping with the nonelitist ideology of the Chinese Revolution.

At the end of August, members of the UJC(ml) held a meeting to discuss Broyelle's criticisms, and it rapidly deteriorated into a free for all. Months of frustration erupted into cruel accusations against Linhart and Lévy, who were branded "revisionists." Stunned by the verbal abuse, Linhart took the blows in silence. Lévy, however, responded in kind. At a second hearing, he staged a counterattack, blaming his enemies, whom he called "*liquidos*" (exterminators), for destroying the party and preventing students from transforming their revolt into revolution. When he finished speaking, he invited those who supported his position to leave with him: "In one leap, Benny, the juggler of ideas, the master of theory, mobilized his handful of hardline supporters with a primal scream: those who've had it, follow me. 'Shit-assed terrorism [Terrorisme des couilles au cul],' sneered Roland Castro. Perhaps, but this 'terrorism' attracted the Ecole Normale's most abstract thinkers, their most subtle dialecticians."[14]

Lévy then stormed out of the theater with a small group of followers, perhaps fifty. A few months later, he had enough backing to form a new party, La Gauche Prolétarienne (GP), whose platform called on students to leave the protected walls of the university and ally themselves with the proletariat, with the people destined to make the revolution. Defying the image Broyelle had imposed on him, Lévy claimed that he and his intellectual comrades should seek instruction about life from the workers, from those who really knew something about hardship and exploitation. The time had come for students to stop isolating themselves behind the ideas of abstract theorists. Althusser had to go, so did much of Lenin: "To cut a long story short, Marxism-Leninism was no longer in fashion. . . . They used to be 'Leninists.' They called themselves 'pro-Chinese.' Now they were 'Maoists.'"[15]

Renouncing his allegiance to the world of theory, Lévy took the revolution out of the library and into the streets, abandoning books in the name of direct, violent action. His movement, however, did not give up on the written word entirely. Taking over the newspaper *La Cause du peuple,* previously the organ of the UJC(ml), the GP presented their political analysis in print, distinguishing themselves clearly from the humanistic spirit of early Marx and from the Jewish revolutionary tradition with which some of them had grown up at home:[16]

> Hate is the clearest expression of a revolutionary consciousness. . . . But this sentiment can be found nowhere in the strategy of the social petite bourgeoisie. Hate is foreign to them. Historically, the proletariat has taught them about it. Left to themselves the social petite bourgeoisie celebrate their false victories, arm themselves with flowers instead of Molotov cocktails or guns. A class with ambitions, they have internalized the Judeo-Christain mentality that members of the bourgeoisie have professed as a universal morality. . . . The ideology of the proletariat not only recognizes the class struggle as the driving force of history, but

reflects the practice and concrete knowledge of that struggle which the bourgeoisie and the proletariat are engaged in to the bitter end. It provides a way to live *while fighting:* it is a *code of ethics* in the strict sense of the term.[17]

Despite the combative tone, La Gauche Prolétarienne put limits on how and when they would use violence. They did not promote random acts of aggression and turned down Pierre Goldman, for example, when he offered his expertise as a guerilla fighter, proposing to train members of La Gauche Prolétarienne to kidnap famous personalities and attack police stations. Holdups were not what they had in mind. They wanted to see the working class rise up in armed rebellion.[18] Defining their position publicly, the GP took a formal stand against terrorism three years later when gunmen attacked Israeli athletes at the Munich Olympics. Their statement, however, did not question the legitimacy of the PLO's struggle, which they continued to support with enthusiasm.[19]

The three Lévy children had identified with the plight of poor Arabs from an early age, despite their mother's firm commitment to Zionism. Bobby had even converted to Islam and changed his name, as all non-Moslems did when they joined the Union of Workers, Peasants and Students, a party founded, incidentally, by a Jew (Marcel Israel-Sherezli). First he called himself Adel Rifaat, then he and a friend decided to take the same name, Mahmmoud Hussein.[20] When the former Bobby Lévy got out of prison and came to Paris, he resumed his role as guide and teacher, continuing to instruct his younger siblings in the subtleties of the Middle East crisis. As early as 1967, Tony Lévy was applying his older brother's lessons by helping to organize the Committee of anti-Zionist Jewish Students at the Cité Universitaire, the big dormitory complex in Paris.[21]

When Yasir Arafat became head of the PLO in 1969, Mahmmoud Hussein (Lévy) allied himself closely with the organization's Parisian ambassadors and presented his brothers to some of the leading personalities of the movement.[22] Shortly thereafter La Gauche Prolétarienne received an invitation to visit a PLO camp and evaluate the situation for themselves. The group agreed to send a small delegation to the Middle East to spend the month of August with the Palestinian rebels, and they appointed Alain Geismar and Benny Lévy's wife, Léo, to represent them—two major figures in the party, both Jews. Joined by leftist students from several other European nations, Geismar and Léo Lévy camped out in the village Karamé (near the Jordaian border). There, they had the opportunity to talk to high-level leaders of the PLO and learn how French radicals might help the Palestinian struggle back home: "As time went on, their nightly discussions clarified people's questions. The Palestinians wanted to understand how someone like Sartre, whose support for the Algerian insurrection never faltered, could openly express sympathy for Zionism."[23]

The two GP representatives had mixed feelings about some of the people they met, but they left firmly committed to the Palestinian cause. Among the many promises they made, they assured their hosts that they would speak to Sartre on behalf of the PLO.[24] The Palestinians, however, never had the satisfaction of winning the French philosopher over to their side. In 1979, a year before he died, Sartre spoke at a gathering in Paris of Israeli and Palestinian intellectuals, organized by Benny Lévy and sponsored by *Les Temps modernes*. But even then his comments lacked conviction. According to the Palestinian literary critic Edward Said, Sartre's remarks were disappointing: "His speech was full of platitudes: ritualistic formulas, without any emotion. . . . Later, I went over to Sartre and knelt down beside him so that he could hear me well. Once again he told me how much he respected Sadat, and that was all. The colloquium left me with bad memories."[25]

Sartre may never have lent his name to the PLO, but he enthusiastically came to the defense of La Gauche Prolétarienne when the French government declared the group illegal and tried to close down their newspaper. In March 1970, the police arrested Jean-Pierre Le Dantec, the director of *La Cause du peuple*. The GP replaced him with Michel Le Bris, but ten days later he was sent to prison, as well.

The Maoists quickly realized that they would survive only if they found a way to beat the French government at its own game. So they decided to ask Sartre to front for the paper, assuming, correctly, that President Pompidou and his minister of the interior would rather put up with *La Cause du peuple* than arrest the philosopher and risk international scandal. The GP chose Sartre because he had a big name, but also because they had recently revised their position on abstract theorists and were seeking ways to initiate dialogues with individuals, like Sartre, whom they now classified as "new intellectuals": philosophers and critics who were activists as well.[26]

When the GP approached Sartre, he was delighted, for he had been feeling rejected by the student movement. Happy to be of some use, he agreed to become the paper's titular director, a position, he understood, that gave him no authority to influence editorial policy. As he announced his decision to the public on the first of May, he chose his words carefully, endorsing the Maoists' right to publish their articles, while he also made clear that he frequently did not support the group's political actions.[27]

Despite his continuing reservations, Sartre often joined the Maoists when they marched on factories and staged demonstrations. He enjoyed spending time with them, he explained, for they communicated a kind of human warmth he had never seen among activists before:

> I've spent time with Communists and Trotskyists, but have never felt any sense of comradery. We spoke about politics and then went our separate ways. With the Maoists, however, there was real rapport. When we met, we talked like old buddies who had come together to go to the movies or whatever, but decided instead to do something important. I never stopped talking philosophy with Benny. . . . I was attracted to their moral conception of action and to the way they related to one another as human beings. Before anything else, that's what the Maoists meant to me.[28]

In the early 1970s, Sartre also gave his name to two other papers representing small groups. The solidarity he expressed in this way to extremist publications helped the student left survive for a few more years, but Sartre made an even greater contribution to radical journalism when he endorsed *Libération*. In January 1973, the GP asked the philosopher to help them launch their first daily paper.

This time Sartre insisted on doing more than merely serving as a shield against the government. Truly interested in the idea, he wanted the GP to let him help determine editorial policy and make this *the* paper of the left, the one people read if they wanted to consider a wide range of progressive and radical ideas, not just those representing the position of a single group. While Lévy agreed, in general, to accept Sartre's terms, he claimed the right to create a "Maoist cell" on the editorial board and to appoint Serge July, a member of the GP, as editor-in-chief.[29] Sartre went along with Lévy's demands, and on February 5, the first issue of *Libération* appeared on the stands.

In the summer of 1973, the Maoists dissolved their editorial board cell, but July remained editor-in-chief, a position he has continued to hold, despite several organizational and ideological shifts that have taken place at the paper over the years.[30] Sartre had to give up his active role almost immediately, because he became virtually blind and could no longer assume any responsibility that required a lot of reading and writing.[31]

Then, in autumn of 1973, La Gauche Prolétarienne disbanded all political activities. Lévy and other leaders of the group had decided to do so because the military arm of their movement had grown dangerously violent.[32] What is more, they had come to the conclusion that the GP had served its historical purpose. The working class no longer needed them.

In April 1973, employees of Lip's watches liberated their factory in the city of Besançon (Doubs), taking over operations entirely. Their extraordinary action convinced members of the GP that the proletariat was now assuming its revolutionary role in society. Workers had finally achieved what the Maoists had hoped they would do since the early days of the movement. Furthermore, they had accomplished this feat in the most important center of watch manufacturing in the country, after having marshaled the enthusiastic support of the local inhabitants and of much of the nation.

When the workers at Lip learned that the company had plans to fire 480 individuals, they mobilized the people of Besançon to challenge the decision. The Socialist mayor and a local priest were among those who joined efforts to support the strike. Within days of the announcement, employees had taken over the factory and begun producing and selling Lip's watches themselves, charging 40 percent less than the retail price. From the beginning, Benny Lévy and other members of the GP participated in this historic, if only temporary, victory, assisting the action in every way they could.[33]

Analyzing the significance of the event for La Gauche Prolétarienne, Lévy concluded: "With Lip we see . . . the progress made by the new left since 1968. The ideological revolution had moved to the world of the workers: imagination was no longer only at the Sorbonne. This shift was necessary, this proletarianization of protest had to occur. Now it had."[34] Satisfied with the role they had played in raising the revolutionary consciousness of the working class, members of the group now went their separate ways, returning to the life they had planned for themselves before the events of 1968. Tony Lévy, for example, prepared for the national exam that would qualify him to teach math. Alain Geismar went back to university to take a degree in engineering.

Benny Lévy could make no plans for the future, until he had regularized his immigration status. Although his brother had become a citizen several years earlier, Benny had not yet acquired French nationality, a situation that made him extremely vulnerable, given his political activities. Before pursuing other projects, he therefore had to get his papers in order.

Once again Sartre, who was virtually blind by this time, came to the rescue, first by giving Lévy a job—"You'll help me finish my *Flaubert*"[35]—then by writing a letter to Valéry Giscard d'Estaing in 1974 to ask the newly elected conservative president to give citizenship to a notorious political radical. Reminiscing about Sartre's request, Giscard d'Estaing observed to the philosopher's biographer, Annie Cohen-Solal:

> Sartre wrote . . . to ask me to do this favor for him. He explained that his sight was getting progressively worse and that he could no longer read or write; he therefore needed this boy in order to finish his work. I do not hide from you that the case was difficult to plead; it involved a former militant extremist. Nevertheless, it was out of the question that I not do everything possible to help Sartre. There were two reasons for this: first of all, because he agreed to take full responsibility for the boy, whom he said would become a useful member of society from now on in, but mostly because he insisted that he needed him to finish his work. I therefore handled the matter as discreetly as possible and I think Sartre was grateful. True, we did not share the same convictions or beliefs, but I have always had the greatest respect for the French tradition that [Sartre] represented.[36]

Benny Lévy remained in France, where he took his place alongside other veterans of the student movement who were rapidly creating a new generation of leftist intellectuals in the country. In doing so, the former Maoist faced a number of contradictions. For example, his request for citizenship had given Giscard the opportunity to make a brilliant case for French democracy, for the very form of government the young man's group had hoped to destroy. When the president gave Sartre his wish and granted Lévy citizenship, he honored a request made by the opposition and demonstrated in the process the vitality and moral strength of France's political heritage.

Before Lévy started working for Sartre in an official capacity, he and the journalist Philippe Gavi had been interviewing the philosopher in preparation for a book that eventually came out in 1974 bearing the title *On a raison de se révolter.*[37] A more moderate gauchiste than Lévy, Philippe Gavi belonged to Vive la Révolution, a group with anarchist leanings, whose newspaper *Tout* had received Sartre's protection as *La Cause du peuple* had. Gavi was also a contributor to *Les Temps modernes* and one of the founders of *Libération.* Together, the three men traced Sartre's political itinerary and analyzed the thinking of the new left, as it had developed in France since 1968. The resulting volume was Lévy's first publication with Sartre.

Once employed, Lévy came every morning to Sartre's home in the fifth arrondissement, on the rue Edgar-Quinet, and spent several hours reading to a depressed old many who could no longer see and had, so it seemed, lost interest in living. Lévy remembered these days as very difficult:

> The hardest period in our relationship was at the very beginning. . . . In fact it got so difficult at times I felt like quitting. I'd arrive, ring the bell, and sometimes Sartre wouldn't even hear me. He'd be in there by himself, dozing off in his big armchair. From the other side of the door, I could hear the radio, tuned to France Musique. Simone de Beauvoir used to turn it on for him before she left, so that he wouldn't get too bored. To be frank, it was a struggle between life and death. I felt as if I were fighting against the powers of sleep, lack of interest, or, more simply, a nodding head. . . . At first, it was really like doing mouth-to-mouth resuscitation.[38]

But within a few months, Lévy had successfully revived Sartre. They worked on the philosopher's *Flaubert,* read about the French Revolution, religious heresies, the Gnostics and, finally, about purely ontological problems. The discussions they had delighted Sartre, who reported to the publisher Robert Gallimard, "I like working with Victor. He amuses me. We really know how to give it to one another."[39]

When Gallimard saw the two together, however, he was shocked. So were many other old friends. Lévy looked like a kid next to the old man, Gallimard remarked, and an arrogant one at that, who addressed Sartre with the familiar pronoun, *tu* as if this were the most natural thing in the world, which it was not.[40]

Still, whether the old guard liked it or not, the philosopher enjoyed working and arguing with Lévy, as well as socializing with him and his friends. They frequently dined together at Lévy's commune in Eaubonne, where the young man lived with his wife Léo and another couple, just on the outskirts of Paris.[41] Sartre also liked having Lévy along when he went on fact-finding trips.

In December 1974, the two of them went to Stuttgart, with another student activist Jean-Marcel Bourguereau, to talk to the terrorist Andreas Baader, who had recently been arrested and thrown into jail. A few years earlier, Baader had come to Paris eager to make contact with the GP. Daniel

Cohn-Bendit, persona non grata in France since 1968, joined them in Germany and served as Sartre's interpreter.[42] In the spring of 1975, Sartre and Lévy traveled to Lisbon, this time with Simone de Beauvoir and Serge July, to celebrate the first anniversary of the downfall of fascism in Portugal.[43] They also went to Israel in February 1978, four months after Egypt's President Anwar al-Sadat had made his historic trip to Jerusalem, to interview Israelis and Palestinians about their hopes for the future. Arlette Elkaïm-Sartre, the philosopher's adopted daughter, of Algerian-Jewish origin, joined the two men on this trip.[44]

Soon after they returned from Israel, Lévy submitted an article about the visit to *Le Nouvel observateur,* signed by Sartre and himself. As Simone de Beauvoir tells the story, Jacques-Laurent Bost, editor-in-chief of the magazine at the time, phoned to ask her to step in and prevent a terrible embarrassment: "It's horribly bad. Everyone at the journal is dismayed. Do persuade Sartre to withdraw it."[45] Beauvoir was sure that the article was Lévy's idea—Sartre would never have written a report based on such a brief trip. As if to prove her point, she demonstrated in her memoirs that she had no trouble convincing Sartre to withdraw the irresponsible manuscript.[46]

When Benny Lévy heard what had happened, he was furious. After an initial outburst, he managed all the same to keep reasonably civil, until the matter came up in an editorial board meeting at *Les Temps modernes*. Sartre, significantly, was absent. As members of the committee offered their opinions about the article, Lévy exploded, insulted people right and left, and stormed out. The former Maoist never attended another gathering of the board, announcing in this abrupt fashion that he had resigned his privileged position as one of the editors of a major journal in France, an honor many coveted and one that he had enjoyed since the autumn of 1976, when *Les Temps modernes* had appointed him, together with the recently freed Pierre Goldman.[47] From that moment on, Lévy and Beauvoir never spoke to each other again.

In *La Cérémonie des adieux,* Beauvoir described Lévy in harsh terms, charging him with having the mentality of a two-bit leader of a sectarian party. She also claimed that he moved freely from one conviction to another, embracing new causes with the same impassioned intensity he had expressed for the old. While some people, including Sartre, seemed to find his style compelling, she did not.[48]

Between vituperative remarks, Beauvoir admitted she was sorry all the same that things had ended this way:

Up until then, Sartre's close friends had always been mine too. Victor was the only exception. I did not question his affection for Sartre nor Sartre's for him. In an interview with Contat, Sartre explained himself clearly: "All I wish is that my work should be taken up by others. I hope, for example, that Pierre Victor will do the work he wants to do, which is that of an intellectual and a political activist. . . . From that point of view, of all the people I have known he is the only one who has given me complete satisfaction." He appreciated in Victor the radical nature of his ambitions and the fact that he, like Sartre himself, wanted everything. "Obviously you don't get everything, but you must want everything." Perhaps Sartre was wrong about Victor, but it doesn't really matter. That was how he saw him.[49]

The falling out between Beauvoir and Lévy reflected more than temperamental differences. It had to do with major philosophical and ideological disagreements, as well. During these same years, Lévy was changing rapidly, moving away from politics and toward Judaism. Beauvoir had little sympathy for his new interests. She worried, what is more, that he, together with Arlette Elkaïm-Sartre, who was undergoing a similar transformation, would take advantage of Sartre and convince the philosopher, old and ailing as he was, to reconsider his position on a number of issues, including the Jewish question. Sartre, however, dismissed Beauvoir's concerns and engaged his two young companions in lengthy discussions about their new work. In the process, he began to appreciate, at least vicariously, the importance of studying the Torah and Talmud.

When Lévy first left the GP, he began reading again—with Sartre, on his own, and in a philosophy group he had organized called Le Cercle Socrate. Through these scholarly activities he soon developed an interest in Jewish texts, he explained, for "rigorously metaphysical" reasons.[50] Before turning to Judaism, Lévy continued, he tried everything else, slowly and methodically, as he studied philosophy and history with Sartre in preparation for the book they had hoped to publish together (*Pouvoir et liberté*).

I tried everything within the realm of the Western philosophical tradition, which was the common foundation that Sartre and I had. Sartre and I spoke of all this together. . . . What strikes me is the extent to which, while working with Sartre, I was still attached to the idea of a common access to the word. The Christian metaphysical schema was extremely strong, extremely tenacious. It's not that we were interested in Christian texts as such, but the texts of Western civilization were themselves steeped in Christian schema. Take Sartre's own texts, for example, which have spectacularly Christological elements.[51]

What, then, made him turn to Jewish texts?

The name of one person is important, a person to whom I must confess my indebtedness, Emmanuel Lévinas. Here is someone who had the very same philosophical training as Sartre, the same roots in phenomenology and humanism. He was someone who was very close to Sartre in his philosophical language, and yet profoundly different, because he had roots in the Talmud. This was extraordinary to me. I had two great philosophical moments in my life: in my youth it was Sartre, and then Lévinas, when I came away from the Left in 1973–1975.

[Actually,] I am reminded by Pierre Goldman that I had discovered Lévinas earlier, and with ecstasy. I had completely forgotten. It was before I became totally involved in politics. Goldman and I were good friends in the Latin Quarter when I began my philosophical studies. It seems it was in a preparatory class for the Ecole Normale Supérieure, around that time, that I discovered some texts of Lévinas on the Other. I don't know which ones. That probably left a considerable mark on me, very largely without my knowing it. He must have had a subterranean effect on me. I couldn't notice this influence at first because when you're involved in politics there isn't so much time to talk about the Other. To talk about the masses, that's all right, that comes off better.

When I finally extricated myself from politics, when I got my head above water, when I got back to philosophy in its original purity, I resumed everything, systematically, methodically, with ecstasy and extreme happiness. I turned to the philosophy of Plato on the one hand, and my dialogues with Sartre on the other. After a long series of unfruitful attempts to articulate the questions raised by my political experience, including a rereading with Sartre of all his works—after all that, thanks to encountering the texts of Lévinas, I began to suspect that here was something decisive, something which also related to my existential constitution as a Jew.[52]

This same Lévinas who provided Finkielkraut with new ways to think about the French Enlightenment and European humanism, gave Lévy reason to study Hebrew and discover the wisdom of religious learning. And as he began reading the sacred texts and commentaries, Lévy came upon astounding statements that set his mind on fire as he tried to understand what they meant. In the Kabbalah, for example, a passage proclaimed that the world was created with letters. What an extraordinary image for a student of philosophy. Lévy approached these texts intellectually, he explained, but before long, they "ravaged" him.[53]

In 1978 Lévy started studying Hebrew with his new friend Shmuel Trigano. The two men met earlier that year at *Les Temps modernes,* before Lévy resigned, when Trigano approached the journal about doing a special issue on Sephardic Jewry.[54] At the time, Trigano was also writing his controversial book about Jewish identity, *La Nouvelle question juive,* an attack on Western models of Judaism and a call for Jewish renewal through an exploration of the traditions of Sephardic Jews, women of all nations, and young people.[55] Ten years before, Lévy and Trigano would have had nothing to do with each other, but now they were drawn together through a common interest in studying religious texts.

SHMUEL TRIGANO

Shmuel Trigano was born in 1948 in Blida, a small town near Algiers.[56] His father, like Lévy's, was in the import-export business. Although the family observed the Jewish holidays at home, the children received virtually no Jewish education. It was too dangerous to do so, Trigano explained. Growing up during the Algerian War, he attended a French lycée where he studied Greek and Latin, not Hebrew.

In 1962, when Trigano was fourteen, his family left Blida for Vichy, in theory for a cure, but they settled permanently in la métropole, and eventually moved to Paris. For Trigano, the adjustment was not easy. He described his first years in France as his "Camus period," during which time he felt deeply alienated and uprooted. By the mid-1960s, Trigano had exchanged his sense of existential despair for a deep feeling of belonging to the Jewish people. In search of others like himself, he started to attend the Colloque des Intellectuels Juifs and to write about the Jewish condition.

As Trigano met Jewish intellectuals and read their works, he found answers for himself in the ideals of Zionism and planned to move to Israel after he was graduated from high school in 1967. Absorbed, by his new ambitions, however, he found it difficult to study for his baccalaureate exam once the Six-Day War broke out in early June. He was forced, therefore, to take an extra year at the Lycée Buffon and was still in Paris for May 1968.

When the students demonstrated in the streets and occupied the Sorbonne, Trigano did not join in. He felt that the uprising offered just one more example of how Western solutions to humanity's problems were morally and ethically bankrupt. After having studied European philosophy in his last years at school, he reached the conclusion that even the West's revolutionary tradition held few answers for the future. All he wanted to do was to go to Israel, where he hoped to find another way of thinking about the world. He finally went in 1969, after spending one more year in Paris studying Hebrew at INALCO.

In Jerusalem, Trigano began classes at Hebrew University, where he hoped to major in both political science and Jewish philosophy. Both departments disappointed him, however—the first because it borrowed heavily from European and American notions about politics and government, speaking not at all about Jewish law, and the second because it tried to establish a science of Judaism. He eventually switched fields, choosing a double major in political science and international relations.

The four years Trigano spent in Israel were critical in determining the choices he subsequently made. As he reflected on this period nearly two decades later, he saw how his experiences there had given meaning to his life in ways that France could never have done. Still, he was deeply troubled by what was going on in Israel, and to this day he maintains that he had to leave the country in order not to grow cynical and lose faith in Zionism.

Trigano completed his bachelor's degree and returned to France in autumn of 1973, one month before the Yom Kippur War. The political situation in Israel at the time was already very tense. During his last weeks in Jerusalem, he expressed his concern for the future of the country, telling anyone who would listen that Jews needed to redefine their understanding of the Zionist mission and develop an ideology that no longer imitated Western ideas about the nation-state.

Back in Paris, Trigano became the administrative secretary in 1974 of the socialist Zionist group Le Cercle Bernard Lazarre. He also began to write. By 1977 he had published his first book, *Le Récit de la disparue,* a plea for creating a society based on Jewish ethical values, which he believed were incompatible with many of the ideals espoused by the European Enlightenment.[57] He would develop this theme more fully in his next book, *La Nouvelle question juive.*

At the time he met Benny Lévy in 1978, Trigano was back in school, taking courses at the University of Paris II in political science and reading Aḥad Ha-Am on his own. By then he had also registered to write a doctoral thesis on the religious genesis of Jewish politics. In the course of his research, he explored, as well, the possibility of developing an "epistemology" of Jewish studies. He defended his dissertation successfully in 1981 and published the work three years later (*La Demeure oubliée*).[58] In 1985, together with his teacher, the political sociologist Annie Kriegel, Trigano started a scholarly journal in Jewish studies called *Pardès*. A year later he also became director of a *Beit Hamidrach* at the Alliance Israélite Universelle, a university-level program for people who had little background in Judaism but wanted to learn to read Jewish texts.[59]

When Trigano agreed to give Benny Lévy lessons in Hebrew, others joined the class, too, including Arlette Elkaïm-Sartre, who several years later became proficient enough in Hebrew and Aramaic to translate a portion of the Babylonian Talmud (the Aggadah) into French. Her ambitious endeavor appeared in 1987, published by Verdier, the group of former Maoists who had moved back to the land to join the struggle of the Corbières wine producers in the early 1970s and had subsequently turned to publishing.[60] At the suggestion of Benny Lévy, the Verdier collective has brought out a series of highly regarded French editions of erudite Jewish texts under the direction of Charles Mopsik, a former student of Jean Zacklad and an ultra-Orthodox Jew. Lévy met Mopsik through Trigano.

Among the other participants in Trigano's class was Francis Gribe, a former Maoist, whose parents were of Polish Jewish origin. In the early 1970s, Gribe joined Le Cercle Gaston Crémieux, where he caused a scandal in 1976 by inviting the Moroccan rabbi Eliahou Abitbol to speak at a meeting of the group. The young man left the Cercle soon after the uproar and became one of the founding editors of *Traces* in 1980.[61]

The Hebrew class met twice a week for about two years, not long enough, Trigano admitted, for any of his students to accomplish very much. Still, the course served as a good beginning. Trigano started with modern Hebrew and moved quickly to the biblical language, giving Lévy and his friends carefully chosen selections of sacred texts, through which he introduced them to a philosophical universe entirely different from the one they had learned about in the West. For most of his students, this was the first time they had read the Torah in Hebrew.

The course also provided a forum for the ongoing debate about how to be a Jew in the modern world. As Trigano remembers it, he took his usual position against the nation-state, arguing that this political system, with its commitment to creating a universal culture, had led to the spiritual disintegration of the Jews. Lévy, on the other hand, perhaps influenced by Sartre, disagreed. At the time, says Trigano, Lévy supported the principles of the French Revolution. The former radical challenged those who preached separatism by developing the ideas of Philo, the Greek Jewish philosopher who had lived in Alexandria during the first century of the common era and had claimed that Jews and Romans should eat at the same table. In the late 1980s, as Trigano looked back on those discussions, it made him laugh to think about how he defended the importance of kashrut against a still unconverted Benny Lévy.

Trigano's course and Lévy's Socratic Circle disbanded at about the same time. But Lévy continued studying Hebrew and Jewish philosophy in Jean Zacklad's seminar. For several years already, Zacklad had been holding a weekly study group in his home, located, appropriately, on the rue de Dieu. After meeting Zacklad through Trigano, Lévy convinced the philosopher to expand his seminar to include the former Maoist and his friends.

During the two years that Lévy participated in the group, about thirty people would crowd into Zacklad's apartment each week to hear the philosopher read and translate a biblical passage, then analyze the text from the perspective of Jewish law and Western philosophy. As Zacklad led the discussion, he would draw on what he had learned from Léon Askenazi at the Ecole d'Orsay, from his rabbinical "master" in Morocco, and from his university mentors: André Neher and Paul Ricouer.

In 1979, Zacklad was writing a book on Cain and Abel, in collaboration with Claude Birman and Charles Mopsik, who also attended the seminar. The weekly gatherings provided the authors with an excellent opportunity to present their ideas and to benefit from the observations of others in the group. Lévy prepared seriously for these meetings and shared what he had learned with Sartre: "During the last eighteen months I worked with Sartre, I used to tell him in the morning about what I had learned the night before about Cain and Abel. I was discovering the power of these writings, the incredible power that they gave me to express clearly the desire we had within us and to explain how this desire got distracted by politics."[62] As Lévy pored over the Torah and commentaries, Sartre asked Simone de Beauvoir to read to him from Salo Baron's multivolume work *The Social and Religious History of the Jews*.[63] He also had Arlette Elkaïm-Sartre review with him the selections from the Talmud she was translating for Verdier. During this time, Sartre and Lévy began recording, as well, a series of interviews that would appear in three consecutive issues of *Le Nouvel observateur*, just weeks before the philosopher died.[64]

Simone de Beauvoir read the three articles a few days before they were to be published and discovered that Sartre had revised his argument on a number of major philosophical issues. Upset by the changes he had made, she blamed Lévy for wearing her old friend down and convincing him to reject much of what he had maintained for years. In *La Cérémonie des adieux*, she reported that, during the last months of his life, Sartre complained bitterly about the arguments he was having with Lévy, who, he told her, was determined to have him believe that all forms of morality emanated from the Torah. While Sartre never accepted the authority of the Five Books of Moses in print, the resulting interviews suggested to Beauvoir that Lévy had still won. Sartre, she felt, had given in to the former Maoist and had stopped defending the integrity of his earlier ideas. Instead of enriching the thought of a philosopher who was in his waning years—she felt—Lévy had led Sartre to distort much of his work. Infuriated by what she had read, Beauvoir tried to persuade Sartre not to publish the interviews, but this time he refused to listen.[65]

Sartre revised his position on the Jewish question, among other issues. Reconsidering his controversial work on the matter in the third interview, he began by explaining that at the time he wrote *Anti-Semite and Jew* he had intended readers to interpret it as a philosophical attack on anti-Semites, not as a treatise on Jews. In the process of making his argument, however, he had dismissed the possibility that a Jewish reality existed beyond the restrictions placed on Jews by anti-Semites. "Clearly, the Jew is the victim of the anti-Semite. But I used to limit the existence of the Jew only to that. I now think there is a Jewish reality that transcends the devastation inflicted on Jews by acts of anti-Semitism. There is a profound Jewish reality, as there is a Christian reality."[66]

Sartre admitted that he had written the essay without ever referring to a single book about Jews. What is more, he had had little interest then in trying to understand the idea of Jewish messianism, the belief held by many Jews that their people had a destiny. In recent years, however, with the help of some Jewish friends whom he met after the war, the philosopher realized that he had misrepresented the very people whose cause he had tried to defend.

In the interview, Sartre explained that three individuals had helped him to recognize what he now called, "the Jewish reality": Claude Lanzmann, Arlette Elkaïm-Sartre, and Benny Lévy himself. In different ways, they had each taught him something about what it meant to be Jewish, leading him to see how the victims of anti-Semitism could define their experiences in terms that went far beyond the limitations placed on them by their enemies.

Through these postwar friendships, Sartre gradually grew to accept that the Jewish people had a history, something he had categorically denied in his book. This was no minor concession, for to revise his position on that point he had to reject Hegel's definition of history, the terms of which had dominated European thought for more than a century. According to the German philosopher, a people had a history only if they lived together on their own land, as a sovereign political entity, clearly recognized as such by other similarly organized states. When Hegel proclaimed that the Jews had no history, he was speaking about a people who had not lived together on a territory of their own for nearly two thousand years.

Sartre finally freed himself from Hegel and began reading about the history of Jews in the Diaspora. In the process he learned to recognize a certain "unity of dispersed Jews," a people scattered all over the world who had nevertheless remained culturally and spiritually connected.[67] Jews managed this extraordinary feat, Sartre concluded, not by living together, but by continuing to read the same body of texts and by maintaining the same relationship to YHWH.

Other peoples had developed important ties to their deities too, but what happened here was different: "God speaks to the Jew, the Jew hears His word, and through this exchange what emerges as real is the creation of a primary relationship between the Jewish man with the infinite. That, I believe, is the first definition of the ancient Jew, the man who somehow has his whole life determined and ruled by his connection to God. The entire history of the Jews consists precisely in this primary relationship. . . .

The name [YHWH] itself means nothing to me. What is important is that the Jew has lived and continues to live, metaphysically."[68]

Had Lévy used Sartre in these interviews to mouth his own words, like the dybbuk in Ansky's play? Many felt he had, in effect, done exactly that, and they questioned the authenticity of the philosopher's voice. Others, however, believed that Sartre had freely revised his ideas after discussing them at length with his young friend who knew the philosopher's work better than almost anybody else.

While people have come to different conclusions about the meaning of these interviews, almost everyone agrees that they attest to Sartre's interest in the changes occurring in the intellectual life of his young friend. Sartre may have objected at times to Lévy's ideas in private, but he apparently remained curious and reasonably lighthearted about the direction the former Maoist was taking. One day, for example, the philosopher laughed affectionately and asked Arlette Elkaïm-Sartre, "He's not going to turn into a rabbi, is he?"[69] Had Sartre lived long enough to see Lévy move to Strasbourg and join the yeshiva, he might have felt a little less jovial, but he did not. Instead, he spent the last months of his life accompanying the young man in his intellectual journey, playing the role of a fellow traveler—a part he had taken with Lévy before, when he had lent his name to the Maoists. And as his friend delved deeper and deeper into Judaism, Sartre saw his adopted daughter doing the same.

Through Lévy and Elkaïm-Sartre, the philosopher grew to appreciate, in abstract terms, the vitality of the culture of religious Jews, of a way of life that had survived for two thousand years in small communities scattered all over the world. With his newly acquired insight about Jews in the Diaspora, Sartre finally joined members of the generation of 1968 in challenging his earlier assumptions about the culture and history of a people who did not live together under a single flag. In collaboration with Lévy, he accepted a position that went beyond that held by other critics of the French nation-state—one that justified, ironically, the former Maoist's eventual decision to become an Orthodox Jew.

Before Lévy challenged the hegemony of French culture with his version of the "right to be different," Jews of the generation of 1968 had two main strategies to oppose assimilation. Shmuel Trigano represented one of them, Richard Marienstras the other. Trigano, as we have seen, borrowed many of his ideas from Aḥad Ha-Am and proposed to save Jews from disappearing in the West by creating a spiritual center for them in Israel. His vision of a Jewish homeland had little in common with the present-day state of Israel, which he considered to be a disappointing imitation of a European nation-state. What he proposed, nevertheless, still involved forming an ethnically unified soverign entity. Marienstras, on the other hand, drew his inspiration from diaspora secularists like Simon Dubnow and the Bundists. While he firmly rejected the nation-state and called for a political structure that promoted cultural pluralism, he continued to hold on to the Enlightenment's vision of what constituted the national traditions of a people. In other words, as members of both groups tried to distance themselves from Western political and cultural forms, Trigano presented a model of a nation-state infused with Jewish ethics, whereas Marienstras introduced an Eastern European version of the cultural ideals of the French Enlightenment.

Now Lévy offered a third position. Insisting on the right of his people to cultural autonomy in the Diaspora, he, like Marienstras, rejected all forms of territorially based cultures, including Trigano's more benign model of spiritual Zionism. But he also challenged the secularism of the French Enlightenment and chose to live as an ultra-Orthodox Jew.

When Lévy joined the Yéchiva des Etudiants, he became a member of an autonomous Jewish community that has, in effect, recreated some of the very conditions Clermont-Tonnerre and the Abbé Grégoire opposed in the late eighteenth century when they made their celebrated case for emancipating the Jews and integrating them into French society. The yeshiva, of course, does not threaten the political structure of the state, for it exists as part of the private sector, like any other personal interest group. Still, the followers of Eliahou Abitbol have dropped out of French culture and recreated firm ethnic boundaries in ways reminiscent of the days when Jews still lived as a "nation within a nation."

Together with other groups of Orthodox Jews, members of the yeshiva have made a commitment to follow customs and values that set them apart from the wider society. Having taken a radical step backward, they challenge the hegemony of French culture in ways far more threatening than spiritual Zionists who hope to liberate Israel or Yiddishists who have devoted themselves to translating secular Jewish writers from Eastern Europe into French. While many practicing Jews forcefully argue that Orthodox Judaism is compatible with European culture, people like Lévy claim that their way of life is fundamentally antithetical to the West: "Is wearing *tephillin*, phylacteries, within the reach of Western man? I don't believe so. Is refraining from mixing wool and linen in one's clothes something available to Western man?"[70]

It took Lévy several years to decide to leave the secular world and enter the Yéchiva des Etudiants. Even after Sartre's death in 1980, Lévy continued participating regularly in activities that engaged European philosophy and Jewish thought. Most important, he remained in Zacklad's seminar for nearly another year. By this time the two men had become partners, and they shared an enthusiastic following among students of the generation of 1968.

Still, Zacklad remained the teacher and Lévy the student. They may have run the seminar together and exchanged ideas as if they were equals, but during this period, Zacklad, not Lévy, was writing books about Judaism. Not until several years later did the former Maoist publish his personal reflections on Jewish thought and European philosophy, first in a work that grew out of the dialogues he had engaged in with Sartre,[71] then in a more recent volume in which he rejected the efforts of Philo and Lévinas, to engage Greek philosophy and Jewish thought.[72] In this earlier period, however, Lévy's contributions appeared most prominently in Zacklad's acknowledgments. In *Pour une éthique: L'Etre au féminin,* for example, the philosopher wrote: "I express my deep gratitude to Mr. Benny Lévy, whose corrections and advice helped me a great deal."[73] And as Lévy studied with Zacklad and read the man's work, he learned about the Talmudic tradition of Lithuania.

L'Etre au féminin is the second volume in a series on ethics. In this work, Zacklad examines the question of a Jewish moral system by analyzing the ways Judaism has treated women. Reviewing the lives of biblical heroines and the laws imposed on female members of the faith, Zacklad interprets selections from the Bible and the Kabbalah in the Talmudic tradition of the celebrated School of Vilna. In the process he introduces a number of aphorisms attributed to the Gaon of Vilna and recorded by the Gaon's disciple Rabbi Isaac Eizik Haver. As Zacklad describes the Vilna School, he notes:

> Like the Essenes of long ago, but in a far more radical way, the scholars of Vilna chose as their culture the very core of the covenant. And as they did this, they sadly believed that their contemporaries would not follow them. At the same moment in time when the French Revolution was inscribing in history the spirit of the Enlightenment, those working in Hebrew, in all its purity, were cutting themselves off from the ancient system of beliefs and from all new ideas. While they waited, no doubt, for the final coming, they offered an unconditional and disembodied position between the best that could spring forth from history and the most precise games of language that had no historical content. For better or for worse, Western and Eastern rationalists would live in total isolation from each other for two centuries.[74]

Lévy heard about the Vilna School from other scholars as well. In 1978 Lévinas published the first article ever written in French on Litvine's ancestor, Chaim of Volozhin, the man who founded the Volozhin Yeshiva in 1802 and wrote *The Soul of Life (Nefesh Ha-Chaim).* Known as the Gaon of Vilna's most gifted disciple, Chaim of Volozhin decided to preserve his master's method of teaching for future generations. Since 1978, Lévinas has written two more articles on the Gaon's disciple, as well as a brief preface to Benjamin Gross' French translation of *The Soul of Life,* which Verdier published in 1986.[75]

Finally, Lévy has also learned about Lithuanian Jewry from his new mentor, Eliahou Abitbol, who offers a very different picture of the community from those of the others. Whereas Zacklad and Lévinas have compared the Talmudic tradition of the Vilna School to Western European philosophy in ways that draw out the universalistic themes in them both, Abitbol describes the two systems as diametrically opposed. In his eyes, the Gaon of Vilna and his devoted disciples offer French students a viable alternative to the values of modernity and the West.

In the late 1970s the Moroccan rabbi began making frequent trips to Paris to work with former radicals who now expressed an interest in studying Jewish texts. On some of these visits, he showed up at the Zacklad/Lévy seminar, where he invariably provoked heated arguments and threatened the future of the group. Ideological differences grew rapidly, and in 1981 Lévy and his friends left Zacklad for Abitbol, who had agreed to meet with them regularly. Two years later the Lévy family packed their bags, left Paris, and joined the growing community of young Jews who had settled in Strasbourg, within walking distance of the Yéchiva des Etudiants. Located on the rue Spach, the school occupies a large two-story house, just across the street from one of Strasbourg's many lovely parks.

LA YECHIVA DES ETUDIANTS AND ITS STUDENTS

About sixty men and seven women attended Sabbath services at the Yéchiva des Etudiants, one Saturday morning in June 1986.[76] Men and women prayed separately in two adjoining rooms upstairs, divided by a partition. Although the women could not see their husbands or the Holy Ark, they heard the men praying and participated actively from their side of the divide, paying little attention to the children who ran in and out freely.

Every week a different man in the community leads the assembled in prayer. No cantor chants medieval verses in operatic tones, no rabbi gives a sermon. Eliahou Abitbol attends the services as a regular member of the congregation; he is not a clergyman in the Western sense of the term, but a *rav*, or teacher, responsible for running study groups and for the administration of the school.

Most of the men have full beards, but they do not dress in the style of Ḥasidim. Instead of the characteristic long cloaks and fur-trimmed *shtraymls*, they sport modern black suits and small fedora hats. Although they wear the prescribed fringes, they do not display them in public the way Ḥasidim do. The women dress conservatively, in skirts well below their knees and in blouses with sleeves that cover their elbows. Then, following the Commandment, wives hide their hair, some with kerchiefs, others with wigs. There is nothing distinctive about the dress of little girls, but boys wear skullcaps, held in place with bobby pins attached to their sidelocks. Here again, custom separates the sons of these ultra-Orthodox Jews from those of the Hasidim, for parents of the former do not draw attention to their children's sidelocks by shaving the rest of the head, as the Hasidim do.

By the mid-1980s, Eliahou Abitbol had gathered more than one hundred families to his community. Most of these people had little prior education in traditional Judaism. As they joined the group, they embraced Orthodoxy and tried to fulfill as many of the 613 Commandments as they could, including the one calling upon Jews to "be fruitful and multiply." Setting a good example for his followers, the Moroccan rav has had eleven children.

Among Abitbol's serious students is Jean-Michel Tolédano, a former member of Le Cercle Gaston Crémieux and a North African Jew. Joining the yeshiva in the late 1970s, he became a devoted disciple of the rav and subsequently married into the family. By 1986 Tolédano had become an accomplished scholar and received permission to open a school of his own in Créteil, near Paris.[77]

Another student of the rav is Alain Lévy.[78] Raised in Alsace, he came from a family with only casual ties to Judaism. Eager for more, he joined the Strasbourg yeshiva in 1967, when it first opened, and has become an enthusiastic student of the sacred law. In 1981, Lévy moved his family to Toulouse to assume the direction of the Collège Ozar Hatorah, a Jewish day school located near the train station. There were forty children attending the school in 1986, two of whom were Ashkenazim, the rest Sephardim. Although the collège did not yet cover the final grades of high school, the staff had plans to expand its curriculum.

In 1986, Lévy's wife, Claudine, the mother of six, was in charge of the administration of the collège, thereby freeing her husband to devote all his time to study and teaching. In addition to giving lessons in the sacred books to the older students, the rav held classes for interested adults living in and around Toulouse. In his courses, Lévy occasionally introduced passages from the Kabbalah, but he approached these texts in the Lithuanian tradition. The Gaon of Vilna, after all, had also been a celebrated scholar of Jewish mysticism.

Alain Lévy firmly distanced himself from the Hasidim and expressed his concern about the success they were having in France. According to the rav, the Lubavitcher sect, more than any of the others, has attracted many

Jews of the generation of 1968 who have recently returned to Judiasm. These Ḥasidim, he continued, have had their greatest influence with those lacking background in philosophy. Intellectuals like himself, Lévy continued, preferred the rationalism of the Vilna School and followed the teachings of Eliahou Abitbol and the Yéchiva des Etudiants.

In Toulouse, Rav Lévy's most accomplished student was Monique-Lise (Lilou) Cohen, a native of the city who had recently returned from Paris to accept a research position in the municipal library.[79] She had left home in the mid-1960s to study philosophy at the Sorbonne and she went on to participate enthusiastically in the student uprising, allying herself with the Trotskyists. Recalling her days as an activist, Cohen observed that somebody like her would never have sat down with someone like Benny Lévy. By the late 1970s, however, it was normal to find former Trotskyists and Maoists studying Talmud together, and she was among them. When Benny Lévy joined the Yéchiva des Etudiants, Cohen moved to Toulouse and attended classes at the Collège Ozar Hatorah, working closely there with Alain Lévy until her teacher moved to Paris in 1987 to start another school.

Although her parents were born in France, Monique-Lise Cohen identified herself as a Jew of Eastern European descent. One grandparent came from Russia and two from Poland. Growing up in the fifties, she learned virtually nothing about the meaning of Judaism and received mixed messages about the importance of practicing the Commandments. Her father, for example, laid tefillin and said the morning prayers, but her mother did not keep a kosher home. As a family, they fasted on Yom Kippur and ran seders on Passover, but that was about all.

Cohen's father was a committed Zionist who devoted much of his time to pro-Israeli activities in Toulouse. Hoping to pass down his political convictions, he educated his daughter in the Zionist tradition by sending her to the local branch of the Ha-Shomer Ha-Za'ir, a group affiliated with Israel's Labour party. There, Cohen learned to think of herself nationally, not religiously, as a Jew.

When she went to Paris, Cohen quickly replaced her Zionist leanings with the internationalism of the Ligue Communiste. She chose a Trotskyist group, she explained, because they were "making the revolution with the written word." Identifying herself with the teachings of a Russian Jewish Communist, she had the sense of remaining true to her people and to their ancient tradition of study. While a member of the Ligue, Cohen became a feminist and joined the fight against France's antiabortion law. This led her to work with MLAC (Mouvement pour la Liberté de l'Avortement et pour la

Contraception) in the early 1970s, the radical grass-roots organization that went into working-class neighborhoods to help women secure illegal abortions and safe means of contraception. She and her feminist comrades also challenged Trotskyist men on a wide range of issues, disrupting meetings and then marching out.

In 1978 Cohen suddenly abandoned the extreme left. She now realizes that she had been looking for months for an excuse to break with radical politics. When she did it, however, she thought she had made the decision spontaneously, after seeing how badly the left had done in the legislative elections.

At about the same time, Cohen began studying Jewish philosophy with Henri Meschonnic, a well-known poet, linguist, and translator of biblical texts, who teaches at the University of Paris VIII and directs a team of scholars at the CNRS that specializes in the analysis of literary texts. In the late 1970s he started to attract a strong following among former Jewish activists who had recently taken an interest in diaspora Jewry. Although Meschonnic usually works with students of literature, he also agreed to direct Cohen's doctoral research on a historical and philosophical subject.

In June 1989, Monique-Lise Cohen successfully defended her dissertation, "The Theme of the Emancipation of the Jews: The Archeology of Anti-Semitism" (in translation), before a most distinguished jury: Henri Meschonnic, René Samuel Sirat, the former chief rabbi of France, and the historian Gérard Nahon. Cohen argues in her thesis that those who supported the emancipation of Jews in late eighteenth-century France proposed a plan that would destroy Judaism and turn the Jewish people into assimilated members of the French nation-state. Inspired by her reading of Salo Baron, she takes us back to the Middle Ages, when European kings, she explains, had not yet tried to create culturally unified territories. During this period, Jews had to endure the humiliation of anti-Semitic decrees, but they still enjoyed a certain degree of cultural autonomy.

When kings began to pursue policies of national unification, Jews lost the right, she continues, to live as Jews in Europe. First came the expulsions in the late Middle Ages and Renaissance: England in 1290; France in 1306; and Spain in 1492, to name only the most famous. Then came the more benign method of eliminating Jewish culture from Europe in late eighteenth-century France, when progressive leaders of the French Revolution forced Jews to give up their own way of life in exchange for the right to belong to the newly emerging democratic republic. Like many other Jewish activists of her generation, Cohen challenges the philosophical assumptions that led to the formation of the French nation-state, blaming those who supported the new political experiment for the destruction of Jewish culture in Western Europe. In her case she focuses on the loss of Talmudic learning and Orthodox Judaism.[80] When she began studying Jewish philosophy and history, Monique-Lise Cohen had had no religious aspirations. Her interest, like that of Benny Lévy, had been purely intellectual. As time went on, however, she considered the possibility of observing the Jewish Commandments. First, she returned to her family's practice of celebrating Yom Kippur and Passover. Then, in 1983 she became kosher and shortly thereafter an ultra-Orthodox Jew.

While some people may wonder how a left-wing feminist intellectual could have made a choice like this, Cohen dismisses the apparent contradictions. Remaining true to her love of books, she decided to change her life, she explains, after reading Trigano's *La République et les Juifs,* a work concerned with many of the themes she treats in her thesis.[81] Now that she has made the commitment, she looks forward to fulfilling the Commandments of her sex by marrying and raising a family.

Former radicals like herself do not fear Orthodoxy, Cohen explains, because they have extraordinary people to pattern themselves on, mentors who also embraced the left before turning to Judaism. As she tells the story, many of her teachers became politicized as teenagers, during the Second World War. In some cases they joined the Resistance with the Eclaireurs and met the ideal model for them all—Jacob Gordin. When the war ended, a privileged few continued studying with the legendary revolutionary and scholar, with this Russian Jew who "knew everything."

Actually, most of the people Cohen has in mind went to the Ecole d'Orsay after Gordin had died. Nevertheless, they still came under the philosopher's influence, for his approach to learning lived on thanks to Léon Askenazi, who continued Gordin's method of teaching for another twenty years. Cohen, therefore, is right when she traces her intellectual legacy to this former anarchist who subsequently became an observant, if not ultra-Orthodox, Jew.

Monique-Lise Cohen counts Jean Zacklad among her teachers trained in the Gordin tradition. She studied with him briefly during the time he and Benny Lévy ran their seminar jointly, but when the two men split up, she sided with Lévy and chose to continue her studies with Eliahou Abitbol, a man who had also attended the Ecole d'Orsay for a short time, before he abandoned the school's more ecclectic method of teaching Judaism in favor of the rigorous approach offered by Lithuanian-style yeshivas.

Eliahou Abitbol was born in the 1930s in Casablanca, where he grew up in poverty.[82] His father was a carpenter and a religious man who raised his son in the tradition common to working-class Orthodox Jews in Morocco. As a child, Abitbol was often sick, with one disease or another, but despite his health problems, he remained a good student and received permission to leave home and continue his studies in France. Arriving in Aix-les-Bains (Savoie), he attended lycée and dutifully passed his baccalaureate exam in 1956. Abitbol did not choose Aix-les-Bains for the quality of its French schools, but in order to study at the only Lithuanian-style yeshiva that existed in the country. The history of this establishment goes back to the interwar period.

In 1936, Ernest Weil, the chief rabbi of Colmar (Haut-Rhin), invited two scholars from Lithuania to France to set up a yeshiva in the Talmudic tradition of Eastern Europe. One of the two men was the son of the distinguished Lithuanian rabbi Elḥanan Wasserman. He died during the war. The other was a disciple of Ḥafeẓ-Chaim, the scholar with whom Litvine's father had studied, as well. His name was Chaim Chaikin, and he survived the war.

Established, first, in a suburb of Strasbourg, the yeshiva began with fifteen students. In 1939, the members dispersed, and rav Chaikin joined the Polish army exiled in France. Captured by the Germans, he subsequently spent five years in captivity.

In 1945, Ernest Weil was more determined than ever to preserve the Lithuanian Talmudic tradition. He therefore reconstituted the yeshiva, this time in Aix-les-Bains, appointing Chaim Chaikin to direct the institution once again, a position the Lithuanian rabbi has continued to hold into the 1980s. Beginning with thirty-five students, the yeshiva rapidly became a place of refuge during the early postwar years for hundreds of orphaned children who had been sent there by an American organization of religious Jews. Then, between 1955 and 1975, the yeshiva grew in importance. Soon it ranked among the top schools of Jewish learning in Europe, a reputation it maintains today.[83]

In addition to the yeshiva in Aix-les-Bains, Eliahou Abitbol attended the Ecole d'Orsay, for a brief period in the 1950s. Jacob Gordin was already dead by then, but the Moroccan knew all about him and regretted that he never had the chance to study with the Russian scholar. Abitbol did take classes with Léon Askenazi, however, and spoke with admiration of the important contribution his former teacher has made to Jewish studies in the country.

According to Abitbol, students at the Ecole d'Orsay expressed great interest in the rationalistic approach of Jewish scholars from Lite, but they shied away from the Lithuanian yeshivas. He alone decided to leave the Ecole d'Orsay and pursue his education with the "black hats" in Israel, at the ultra-Orthodox schools in and around Tel-Aviv (Bene Berak and Be'er Ya'akov) that were keeping the Lithuanian tradition alive after the Second World War.

In 1967, after Abitbol was ordained, he returned to France to open a school for Jews who had little or no background in Judaism. Establishing himself in Strasbourg, he immediately set out to attract gifted students with a solid background in philosophy. In the early years, this involved making regular trips to Paris, where he gave seminars and invited people back to Strasbourg to visit the yeshiva. And as he looked for recruits, the rav wasted no time teaching Hebrew with aimless exercises meant for beginners. From their earliest lessons, he showed those who gathered around him why great minds have been studying the Torah and Talmud for centuries.

Abitbol presents the texts in the rationalistic tradition associated with the Gaon of Vilna, challenging students trained in European philosophy to ask complex metaphysical questions. Those who know no Hebrew learn the letters of the alphabet off the pages of Talmud Abitbol gives them to read as he lectures. As they stumble through a passage, the rav translates it, providing them with interpretations from other religious texts as well.

Abitbol attributes his appeal to the decline of ideologies. While many Jews of the generation of 1968 remain critical of Western values, they have recently lost faith, in the alternatives provided to replace them. Responding to their profound sense of intellectual and political loss, Abitbol has provided these former activists with a new way to refuse the nation-state and the ideals of the Enlightenment.

Comparing the situation today to that of the nineteenth century, Abitbol said he could understand why Jews in the past had embraced the Haskalah and welcomed the promises held out to them by those committed to their emancipation. Had he been living in Eastern Europe, for example, in the late 1800s, he might easily have joined movements dedicated to bringing about cultural and political change. But now, things were different. Dismissing secular ideologies in general, Abitbol singled out Zionism for special criticism.

According to the rav, many Jews have wasted their lives with the "Zionist adventure," an effort, he said, that legitimized some of man's basest interests—nationalism and the nation-state. It upset him, he explained, to think that people continued to renounce the texts to pursue lowly matters of no enduring significance. Not surprisingly, Abitbol has alienated many members of the Strasbourg community who believe deeply in the importance of taking political stands as Jews on Israel and other issues.

Freddy Raphaël, for one, has expressed some concern about Abitbol and his yeshiva. A distinguished professor of sociology at the University of Strasbourg, Raphaël has written extensively on the Jews of Alsace, an interest that extends beyond his academic activities.[84] In contrast to Abitbol and his followers, Raphaël is an observant Jew in the French tradition and identifies proudly with the political and cultural heritage of France.

Like many other scholars of Jewish culture in his generation, Freddy Raphaël studied briefly at the Ecole d'Orsay in the 1950s. For him this experience complemented his secular education, furthering his belief in the compatibility of Jewish thought and the ideals of the French Enlightenment. True to his double heritage, Raphaël actively supports the efforts of human rights groups.

In 1983, for example, he and other Jews in Strasbourg organized a demonstration in support of Soviet Jewry. Seeking the participation of a wide range of groups, they asked Abitbol and members of the yeshiva to study outside on the appointed day, so that passersby might see the kind of activity that was banned in Russia. The yeshiva turned them down, even though the request required nothing of them other than to do what they always did in the open air. As Raphaël remembers their excuse, they refused to cooperate because they did not have an opinion on what was best for Jews in Russia today.

The group's unwillingness to lend their support to this particular event reflects their stand on worldly issues in general. As Benny Lévy explains it, the texts have led him to develop "a critique of politics": "When I speak of a critique of politics, you must understand that it is a critique of the *pretension* of politics, the idea that politics is adequate to respond in terms of the destiny of man. It is this pretension, this arrogance of politics in all its visions, whether the highest forms of German idealism or the more ideological forms of today, that the Jewish texts help me to criticize."[85]

Members of the yeshiva may not take part in joint activities, but they remain dependent on the infrastructure of the wider Jewish community, a fact that contributes to feelings of bitterness on the part of many in Strasbourg. Some point out that Abitbol's followers would never be able to lead the life of ultra-Orthodox Jews were it not for the city's mikveh, kosher butcher shops, and Jewish school system. While the yeshiva has recently opened a primary school, they have no high school and cannot, therefore, even provide their children with a complete education. Given their reliance on Strasbourg's Jewish community, many feel they should be more generous about participating in events sponsored by other groups of Jews in the city.

Some people have managed to overlook the problems and become good friends of Rav Abitbol and his students, among them Aaron Fraenckel, who comes from a very old Alsatian Jewish family.[86] Over the years, Fraenckel has played the part of elder statesman for the group, the person students go to when they want another scholarly opinion.

Fraenckel was born in the late 1920s in a small village in Alsace. His ancestors on his mother's side have been in Alsace since the 1600s; on his father's, since the early 1700s. Fraenckel grew up in an assimilated household in which his family merely paid lip service to Jewish traditions and law. The men, for example, could read the letters of the Hebrew alphabet and pronounce the words, but they did not know what they were saying when they recited the prayers. Once, when he was a young boy, Fraenckel challenged an uncle about the family's tradition of ignorance and was told that it was better this way—if they understood what they were reading, they would probably stop praying. At home, his parents obeyed the dietary restrictions, but they did so without religious conviction—rather out of loyalty to a cousin who owned a kosher butcher shop.

When the Germans occupied France, the Fraenckels moved to Brive (Corrèze) in the Free Zone, not far from Beaulieu, where the Gordins were running a home for children. Before 1939, the small city had had no Jewish inhabitants. Then a thousand families arrived, hoping to escape the Nazis. Although the Fraenckels were part of a massive invasion, the highly assimilated family never had to hide. During his years in Brive, Aaron Fraenckel joined the Eclaireurs Israélites de France, participated in their resistance efforts, and became an observant Jew.

Fraenckel never studied with Gordin in Beaulieu, but he did hear him speak in 1946 in Chambon, when Robert Gamzon gathered several thousand Jewish youths for a retreat immediately after the war. He was about sixteen at the time. When Fraenckel attended classes at the Ecole d'Orsay two years later, Gordin had already died.

In the early 1950s Fraenckel tried to study with the legendary Shushani, but this was not very easy. Once, he remembers, the man made a date to meet him and four others at 3:00 P.M. on the platform of the Balard Métro Station. After keeping them waiting for over an hour, he finally arrived, greeting them with harsh words: he had no idea why he wasted valuable time to be with dullards like them. But seeing that he had, he might as well give them a lesson. Shushani instructed them to board the next métro, go back to the other side of Paris, and get off at Saint Paul. When they climbed out of the underground in the heart of the Marais, the man walked the bewildered students through the winding streets of the Jewish quarter until they reached somebody's apartment, Fraenckel never knew whose. Opening the door with a key, Shushani invited everybody in, spoke brilliantly for ten minutes, and then told them to leave.

In 1954 Fraenckel became assistant director of the Ecole d'Orsay. The following year he left for Morocco, where he spent eleven years, helping the American Joint Organization set up Jewish schools throughout the country. Finally, in 1966 he came back to France and assumed the direction of the Ecole d'Orsay for two semesters. By that time, however, the school was having serious administrative difficulties, and it eventually closed down in 1970.

Fraenckel returned to Alsace in the late 1960s, together with his wife Hayah, whom he had met at the Ecole d'Orsay, and their seven children. Settling in Strasbourg, he accepted a job teaching Jewish thought to older students at the Ecole Aquiba, the main Jewish school in the city. Today, Fraenckel and his wife run a Jewish bookstore (La Librairie Hébraïque), which they opened in Strasbourg in the intervening years. Still highly regarded as a teacher, Fraenckel also gives seminars at La Yéchiva des Etudiants, where he has a devoted following, and an occasional course in Paris in Shmuel Trigano's Beit Hamidrach at the Alliance Israélite Universelle.

Sam Gottfarstein is one of Aaron Fraenckel's many admirers and was among the first people to join Rav Abitbol's yeshiva. He is also one of the few members of the group to have family ties to Lite and to the Lithuanian Jewish tradition. His father, Joseph Gottfarstein, was a major figure in the Paris Yiddishist community.

THE GOTTFARSTEIN FAMILY

Joseph Gottfarstein was born in the small town of Pren (Prienai) in the early 1900s and raised in Mariampol (Marijampole) and Kovno (see map 3).[87] His father worked in fruit orchards in the spring and summer and peddled fruit in the winter, hence he was away from the family much of the time. When Joseph Gottfarstein was thirteen, he left home himself to attend yeshiva in Slobodka, but after World War I he abandoned the rigorous life of a Talmudic scholar. He finished high school in a Hebrew gymnasium and continued his studies in Kovno's Yiddish teaching seminary.

Although Joseph Gottfarstein never belonged to a political party, he sympathized with the anarchists and left Lithuania in 1923 for political reasons. Gottfarstein went to Berlin, where he planned to study philosophy and the violin. Soon after he arrived, however, he joined a circle of literary anarchists, moved to their commune, and became the editor of a German-language magazine called *Die Tsvelve* (*The Twelve*).

Litvine met Gottfarstein in Berlin during these years and remembers reading works of his in the Yiddish journal *Di Vispe* (*Island*). Among other things, Gottfarstein had made an excellent translation of a Russian poem by Sergey Yesenin, for which he received considerable praise. People even started calling him the Yesenin of the Yiddish language.

Gottfarstein moved to Paris in the late 1920s. Making contact with the Yiddish community there, he settled down to the same kind of life he had been living in Germany, writing fiction and poetry and doing translations. By the time the Germans invaded France, Gottfarstein was married and a father.

Gottfarstein spent the war in Switzerland with his wife, Sophie, and an infant son, Sam. After Liberation, he returned to Paris, where, like many other survivors of Eastern European origin, he decided to devote his life to the preservation of what was left of Jewish culture. In the years following the war, he organized a university-level program at the Fédération des Sociétés Juives de France to train teachers of Yiddish. He also published a book on how Germany's educational system prepared its young for National Socialism.[88]

Today, people remember Gottfarstein best for his many translations of Yiddish and Hebrew literature. Often collaborating with others, in the postwar years he brought out French versions of stories by Sholem Aleichem and I. L. Peretz. He also translated the tales of the Ḥasidic Rabbi Naḥman of Bratslav. When he died in the early 1980s, he was in the middle of preparing the French version of the *Bahir*. Sam Gottfarstein completed his father's work and saw it through to publication with Verdier. Written in Hebrew and Aramaic in twelfth-century France, scholars consider the first part of the *Bahir* to be the earliest of the classical Kabbalistic texts.[89]

Although Joseph Gottfarstein stopped practicing Judaism in Kovno in the early 1920s, he never lost interest in studying religious texts. His Lithuanian background had taught him, he said, that one did not have to obey the law to study Talmud seriously. As time went on, almost all of his friends and students were secular Yiddishists, but he still cultivated close ties with marginal scholars of Judaism—people like Shushani, for example, who stayed regularly in his home, and the "mystical rationalist" Oskar Goldberg, the German Jewish philosopher who provoked much debate in Berlin during the interwar years.

Gottfarstein also took an interest in the young Yiddishist community. Supporting the activities of Richard Marienstras and Rachel Ertel, he willingly gave lectures at events sponsored by Le Cercle Gaston Crémieux. Still, he remained an outsider to the politics of the group, preferring to serve as an example of the Lithuanian Haskalah, rather than a spokesman for a particular ideology. And Gottfarstein did indeed represent the typical Jewish scholar for the new generation of Yiddishists. Richard Marienstras, for example, used Gottfarstein as the model for the Jewish intellectual he portrayed in "Le Golem," a short story he published in the early 1960s.[90] Calling Gottfarstein, "Edelstein," Marienstras had the narrator describe him in the following way: "Edelstein peppered his conversation with extremely erudite comments and he did so to such an extent that I was stunned by the breadth of his knowledge, which, it seemed to me, covered every possible domain, including those mysterious and somewhat magical traditions of the Zohar, the two Talmuds, Hasidism and the doctrine of the Gnostics."[91]

Until the day he died, Joseph Gottfarstein balanced his interest in the commentaries with secular intellectual pursuits. His son, however, decided to devote himself fully to Orthodoxy and religious study. Sam Gottfarstein announced his intentions while he was still in high school. His father was not enthusiastic about it, but his mother gave her support and agreed to keep the house kosher.

Born in 1940, Sam Gottfarstein attended a French public school in the early years after the war. One day, when he was still a young boy, a few of his classmates called him a "dirty Jew." The child told his parents about the incident, and the Gottfarsteins immediately withdrew their son from the school and enrolled him in the Ecole Maïmonide. During his years as a student in this Jewish lycée, the boy studied English with Richard Marienstras.

After high school, Sam Gottfarstein went to university to prepare for a degree in mathematics. In 1967, when he was still a student in Paris, he heard about Eliahou Abitbol and the rabbi's plan to open a yeshiva in Strasbourg. Eager to join such a community, Gottfarstein left Paris to help set up the school. Then, in 1970 he married his wife, Vicki, a Moroccan Jew, who came from a religious family that had moved to Lyon in 1964. Although she never completed her education, before she met Sam, Vicki spent a few months studying at the yeshiva at Aix-les-Bains in their modified program for women.

Soon after they married, the couple went to Israel, where they stayed for a couple of years. When they returned to Strasbourg, Sam Gottfarstein took a job teaching math at the Ecole Aquiba, and since then he has divided his time between his work and his studies at the Yéchiva des Etudiants. His wife remains at home to care for their rapidly growing family, occasionally stealing a few hours to attend special classes held at the yeshiva especially for women. By June 1986, the Gottfarsteins had six children, and another one was on the way. In July of that year their second son celebrated his Bar Mitzvah.

The summer of 1986 marked another memorable event for Sam Gottfarstein and the yeshiva community—the visit of Rabbi Shulman from Israel. A highly respected Talmudist, Shulman is the grandson of the last rabbi of Slobodka. Since Sam Gottfarstein's father had attended yeshiva in this celebrated suburb of Kovno, he had personal reasons for being excited. But these family connections were only incidental. For Sam Gottfarstein and the others, Rabbi Shulman represented the Musar tradition of Lithuanian learning, an ethical movement that had taken root in Slobodka in the midnineteenth century and now fascinated many people at the Yéchiva des Etudiants.[92]

Sam Gottfarstein may live in the world of the ultra-Orthodox, but he continues to share his father's wide intellectual interests. And like Joseph Gottfarstein, he is fascinated by ecclectic Jewish thinkers who defy classification, such as Oskar Goldberg, the German philosopher whose work has been virtually forgotten today. While Sam Gottfarstein was growing up, he heard a great deal about the curious Oskar Goldberg, but he does not read German and therefore has access to very little of what this "mystical rationalist" wrote.

With the exception of a couple of articles, Goldberg's work has never been translated into any other language. Interestingly enough, among the few samples of his work available in French, there is a small selection in Edmond Fleg's celebrated *Anthologie juive,* a work edited by an eminent Jewish scholar fully committed to the French Enlightenment and to the nation's brand of assimilated Judaism.[93] But Goldberg's main work is the controversial *Die Wirklichkeit der Hebräer* (The Reality of the Hebrews), and at one point there was talk of bringing out a French edition.[94] The person chosen for the task was Olga Katunal, a good friend of the Gottfarstein family.

Olga Katunal was also from Lite. Coming from an assimilated middle-class family, she, like Litvine, the Gordins, and Gottfarstein, went to Berlin to study after the First World War. It was there that she first met Oskar Goldberg and other members of his group. Years later, when she was settled in Paris, the philosopher gave her the rights to make the authorized French translation of *Die Wirklichkeit der Hebräer*. Olga Katunal never managed to do it, however, for a set of complicated reasons.

In 1988, Olga Katunal passed away. With her death, the fate of Oskar Goldberg's work has fallen into the hands of the next generation. Given Sam Gottfarstein's close association with Benny Lévy and Editions Verdier, perhaps he will take over the project and arrange for the French edition of a book that caused scandal in Germany and captured the imagination of a small group of Jewish intellectuals, a number of whom identified themselves with the rationalistic Lithuanian tradition.

In the next chapter, we turn to Olga Katunal, a political activist who eventually left the Communist party and returned to Judaism via German philosophy. Lévinas and Gordin also found their way back by means of the same European tradition, but these men remained closely tied to the intellectual and cultural world around them, both in their work and in their personal lives. Olga Katunal, on the other hand, made more radical choices when she abandoned Trotsky for Moses in the interwar years.

8

From Trotsky to Moses: The Return to Orthodox Judaism by an Intellectual Identified with October 1917—Olga Katunal

Olga Katunal was born in 1900 in the Latvian port city of Libau (Liepaja) (see map 3).[1] Her parents had recently moved there from Lithuania for reasons of business, never intending to blend in with the German-speaking Courland (Kurland) Jews of the area. Joining the community of their fellow expatriates, the Katunals raised their two children, a boy and a girl, to take pride in the family's heritage. And with their daughter they succeeded. Olga Katunal saw herself as a Lithuanian Jew with ties to the province of Kovno. When it came to her father's side of the family, she had stories going back to the early 1800s, to the days of her paternal great grandparents.

One great grandfather came from Subocz (Subačius), a small village northeast of Kovno.[2] A respected scholar, this ancestor spent most of his time deep in study, leaving the burden of supporting the family to his wife, who made a pitiful living as a locksmith.

Everybody expected Olga Katunal's grandfather to follow in the footsteps of his father and become a great Talmudic scholar. One day, however, at the age of eighteen, he announced he would go into business. Rejecting the poverty he had grown up with at home, he devoted his life to lumber, not Torah, a good choice for someone eager to grow rich, for Lithuania had abundant forests.

By the time Olga's father was born, his father was a wealthy man and a nonobservant Jew. Raising his son in comfort and ignorance, what little the boy learned about Judaism came from his grandparents, whom he saw frequently as a child, often going to their home to spend a few days with the religious couple. During these visits, his grandmother used to wake him at dawn and take him to his grandfather's study, so that he could observe the old man reciting his morning prayers, wrapped up in the customary phylacteries and shawl.

Although Olga's grandfather raised her father in a nonreligious home, he remained inconsistent in his secularism. Every Sabbath, for example, he yielded to tradition and spent a few hours reading the Talmud (Gemara). But he did so defiantly, ignoring the prohibition against smoking on the day of rest and lighting up a cigar. People admired the man for his knowledge all the same and consulted him on aspects of religious law, visiting the erudite rebel at his house in Ponevezh (Panevezys), a town famous for its Orthodox yeshiva.[3]

Despite their break with religion, Olga's grandparents kept their home kosher, for merely "aesthetic" reasons, they claimed, so that her grandmother could use her fine culinary skills. That was not the only reason, however. They did so for the sake of their parents, as well, something their children would not have to do. When Olga's father married, his parents looked forward to visiting him and his wife and having the opportunity to eat a little *treyf* (nonkosher food).

Although Olga's grandfather was no longer observant, two matters of law remained important to him: His children, he insisted, had to marry Jews and, he continued, to circumcise their sons. Olga's father respected these requests, but her uncle was less compliant, challenging the contradictions they had grown up with at home. First, he fell in love with the daughter of a Danish sailor and threatened to run off with the Gentile woman. Eventually, her uncle did marry a Jew, but soon after the wedding, he and his wife moved to London where they converted to Christianity and raised their children in the High Church of England. Her uncle became a successful doctor, and his children assimilated into English society.

Olga's father had no interest in a medical career, but he purchased a diploma in dentistry, an intelligent thing to do in czarist Russia, for Jews with professional titles could leave the Pale of Settlement. Her mother, however, wanted to be a dentist and went to university in Estonia to prepare for the degree. Then, in the late 1890s, soon after the couple had married, her parents moved to Libau. Her father set up a maritime business to help Jews and political refugees leave Russia, and her mother worked as a dentist.

Neither parent wished to maintain a religious home. Although Olga's mother had been raised as a practicing Jew, she still shared her husband's negative views about following the tradition. Nevertheless, despite their secular convictions, both wanted their children to have a strong sense of belonging to the Jewish people, something, they felt, they would not have if they lost all ties to the religion. Yiddish culture, they believed, was simply not enough. The couple, therefore, asked Olga's renegade grandfather to help the family observe modified versions of the major Jewish holidays.

With such limited exposure to Judaism, Olga Katunal gained only a superficial understanding of her people's religion. In contrast, she grew up deeply immersed in the dominant cultures of Europe. Although her parents were not scholars, they read several languages fluently and made sure that their children could do the same. Olga's father, for example, knew Russian literature well, and both parents read widely in Yiddish and German.

Olga Katunal learned to speak and read five languages fluently, excellent training for her later work as a translator: Russian, Yiddish, English, Polish, and German. She acquired a familiarity with Hebrew and a good working knowledge of French. At home, the family spoke Russian and Yiddish to each other. Whereas most Jewish families in Latvia who could afford it had German or French governesses, her father preferred women from England, so that the children could communicate with their cousins in London. To the day she died, Olga Katunal spoke and wrote perfect English, even though she never lived in a country where people used the language. For a short while the family had a Russian governess as well, the daughter of a colonel from St. Petersburg.

The Katunals also spoke Polish at home to the servants, domestics from Lithuania brought to Latvia by Olga's parents.[4] When she was a child, the family's staff included a cook and two maids. Olga Katunal continued to use Polish as an adult with Stanislas Belinsky, a man of Polish working-class origins who was her companion for many years. German, she learned with friends in the street, for the middle classes of Libau communicated in that language. Hebrew, she studied with a tutor her mother had hired for her and her brother. Finally, Olga Katunal decided on her own to learn French, and she did so by exchanging English lessons for French with a Polish aristocrat friend of the family.

Missing from this impressive list of languages are Latvian and Lithuanian, for in this world of polyglots, where the Jewish middle classes spoke five and six tongues, nobody but philologists bothered to learn the "dialects" of peasants. Not until after the First World War, when Latvia and Lithuania gained their independence, did these languages receive official status and become part of the required curriculum that every child followed at school.

As a middle-class Jew of Lithuanian parents, Olga went to a Russian-language gymnasium, instead of the German schools attended by Courland Jews. The director of the gymnasium was her mother's sister, and Olga Katunal expected to graduate from there and go on to a Russian university. But soon after World War I broke out, the Germans occupied Libau and forced all Russian-language schools to close down. Olga was transferred to a German gymnasium.

Freed from czarist oppression, the Jews and German-speaking Latvians of Libau welcomed the German invasion with enthusiasm. Already fluent in the language and culture, Olga Katunal joined the general celebration and had little difficulty making the transition. A teenager by this time, she fell in love with a young man of German extraction. The boyfriend was drafted into the German army and left Libau to fight in the war, but Olga remained attached to him. In 1921 she left Libau for Berlin in the hopes of taking up again with the young soldier.

The affair ended sadly. Rejected by her first love, she followed the advice of her emancipated father and scorned bourgeois conventions. With that end in mind, she remained in Berlin, attended university, and engaged in a number of liaisons—like a man, she said bitterly, trying not to fall victim to sentimental feelings. To live this way was not always easy.

For the most part, Olga Katunal found classes disappointing. But she did take a course in philosophy outside the university that excited her. Her teacher, Erich Unger, was a colleague and friend of Oskar Goldberg, the German Jewish philosopher who would play a major role in the young woman's life.

In the early 1920s Olga Katunal spent much of her time with a group of marginal intellectuals and artists who gathered at the Cafe des Westens, located at the corner of Joachimstalerstrasse and the Kurfurstendamm. The place had a reputation for attracting prostitutes who read Kant. When the Cafe des Westens closed down for repairs, the group moved to another popular spot, the Romanische Cafe, across the street from the Gedächtniss Church.[5]

In Katunal's crowd was a young man by the name of Simon Guttmann.

He had belonged to the revolutionary German youth movement before the First World War and played a major role in the Neopathetisches Kabarett, as well as in other groups of expressionist artists. Guttmann was also a member of a circle later known as the Philosophische Gruppe, which had formed around Oskar Goldberg.[6] A self-taught man, he had many interests, including a passion for theater and poetry. Guttmann eventually devoted his life to political photography and film.

In the early 1920s Guttmann started a press and photo agency that provided material for leftist newspapers. He used Berlin as his base until 1933, then continued clandestine operations from Zurich for a while, making the Swiss city his home as he traveled back and forth to Germany. In 1940, he went to France and joined the Resistance.[7] When the Second World War ended, Guttmann moved to London and founded the photographic agency The Report, which remained in existence through the late 1980s.

But back in Berlin in the early 1920s Guttmann fell in love with Katunal, who accepted his advances. She was charmed, she said, by the way he described himself as the handsomest of ugly men. During the time she was seeing Guttmann, Olga had no interest in Judaism and was rather impatient with the mystery that surrounded Oskar Goldberg's group. The philosopher, she remembered, always worried that somebody would steal his ideas. He did not even like people to take notes when he delivered a lecture. Only after he published *Die Wirklichkeit der Hebräer* did he relax a little, but even then he remained very difficult.

Despite her lack of interest and his paranoia, Katunal met Goldberg several times, at weekly gatherings in the philosopher's home, to which attractive young women were invited. Rumor had it that Goldberg held orgies at these parties, but Katunal never saw anything of the kind. Still, she admitted, the circle had unconventional ideas about sex. Accompanied by Simon Guttmann, Olga Katunal said she had been a great success with Goldberg and his friends on the few occasions she joined them for the evening.

In 1923, Katunal broke up with Guttmann. According to her, he wanted to marry and she did not. Eager to escape his constant pleas, she moved to Paris. Still, she continued to visit Berlin regularly and even tried living there once again for several months in 1932, together with her parents.

In the early interwar years, the family's maritime business in Libau began to fail. By 1925, Olga Katunal's father had declared himself bankrupt and accepted a job with the British Mails Shipping Company, which transferred him almost immediately to Argentina. He expected his wife to join him there after he got settled, but she had no intention of doing so. She went to Paris instead and moved in with her daughter, forcing her husband to resign from his job and come to France, where the man never adjusted. To please her unhappy father, in 1932 Olga agreed to move to Berlin with her parents. They stayed there until Hitler came to power the following year.

In 1933, Olga Katunal's father died. Soon after, her mother became senile. Unable to bear watching the old woman deteriorate, Olga Katunal sadly took her back to Latvia to live with a sister in Riga. She remained there until her death in 1939.

Like his sister, Olga Katunal's brother had moved to Berlin after the First World War. When she went to Paris, he left for the Soviet Union. By 1937, the two had lost touch. Thirty years later, Olga Katunal confirmed what she had suspected for a long time: her brother had been killed in the Stalinist purges.

When she arrived in Paris in the early 1920s, Olga Katunal looked for work as a translator and multilingual secretary. Among her more interesting jobs, she spent several months at the International Institute for Intellectual Cooperation, the UNESCO of the League of Nations. The offices were located in the Palais Royal. On her first day of work, she met the departing secretary, who warned that she would need the patience of a saint to survive the boss, a German writer by the name of Werner Picht. Although the man was difficult, Katunal did extremely well. She also managed to befriend her fired predecessor, a Jewish woman who had converted to Catholicism. It was through this new acquaintance that she first learned about the publication of Oskar Goldberg's *Die Wirklichkeit der Hebräer*—her friend had found the book in the institute's library and brought it to her to read.

Olga Katunal embraced life in Paris in the 1920s with enthusiasm, frequenting the cafés of Montparnasse and enjoying the company of luminaries of the period. In later years, she dismissed her youthful fascination for famous people, but she still enjoyed telling stories about those she had known. Among her acquaintances was Raymond Duncan—she happened to be at a party in his home the night he learned that his sister Isadora had been killed in Nice. During those years, she also joined the Communist party (CP) and had an affair with a major figure in the French CP.

Katunal did propaganda work for the Communists on international matters. Given the nature of her assignment and her fluency in Russian, she reported directly to Moscow, and this threatened some of her comrades. Independent of French hostility, she quit the party in 1927, the year it expelled Trotsky. She also left her Communist lover when he refused to take a stand against Moscow. For Katunal, the party had become too authoritarian; it was not living up to the ideals of socialism. Years later, when she reviewed her life as a political activist, she regretted having dedicated so much time to the revolution. She felt that she should have gone to medical school instead.

Olga Katunal's ideas about medicine were deeply influenced by Lenin's doctor, whose picture stood on a chest in her flat. And she was not alone. In the interwar period, Russian Jews in Paris swore by the exiled Dr. Salmonoff, a man noted for his success in treating tuberculosis. Among his many admiring patients was Wladimir Rabi's sister, Sonia Grinberg. As Salmonoff explained it in his book, *Secrets et sagesse du corps,* he healed a person through a holistic approach to medicine, by looking at the entire body, not just at one organ.[8]

Olga Katunal did not spend all her time with famous people. Her circle of friends included members of the underworld as well, some of whom she met under precarious circumstances, not entirely of her own choosing: One evening, late, as she was crossing the isolated Esplanade des Invalides, a man accosted her and asked menacingly if she were alone. Realizing that nobody would hear if she screamed, Olga Katunal replied sadly that she was; her man, she explained, was in prison. Taken in by her story, the *voyou* changed his tone and accompanied her home, admonishing her like a big brother for wandering around by herself at night. After the encounter, the thief kept in touch, and they continued to see one another occasionally.

When it came to friends, Olga Katunal took care not to lock herself in with one class of people and one set of ideas, but exposed herself to others as well. Critical of intellectuals who isolated themselves, she enjoyed having friends who were manual laborers. She also made sure to read the popular press to see what their newspapers were telling them. If bourgeois Jews in the 1930s had followed her example and looked occasionally at what the tabloids were printing, they would not have been so poorly prepared for the turn of events.

Two nights before the Germans entered Paris, Olga Katunal caught the train to Bordeaux. Embarrassed for the French who had refused to fight, she could not bear to see the Nazis march into the city. The trip south took four days. In the Free Zone, Olga Katunal was still not safe. As a Jew and an activist identified with the left she had a police record. She knew she should leave the country. But go where? A cousin living in Pittsburg had already made the necessary arrangements for her to join him and his family. She could leave by boat immediately. But Katunal had little sympathy for American capitalism or for the United States' refusal, at this stage of the war, to send troops to help its allies. More important, as a politically engaged person, she did not want to abandon Europe when its future was in danger.

Olga Katunal also had the option of going to London on a submarine and joining the Resistance there, but in the end she decided to stay in France, and she soon settled down with Stanislas Belinsky. In later years, she described her Polish friend as a "part-time intellectual," member of the "aristocracy of the working class." A house painter by trade, Belinsky remained with her until he died in 1970.

Stanislas Belinsky had joined the French army in 1939. Disappointed with France for having surrendered so quickly, he returned to Paris to do resistance work there. Katunal went with him, reasoning that it was just a matter of time before the Free Zone became occupied as well.

And so, a few months after the German invasion, Katunal and Belinsky took the train back to Paris. When they crossed into occupied France, they had the ironic pleasure of passing the border with ease. At this point in her life, Katunal held a Soviet passport that did not mark ethnicity. It merely identified her as an ally of the Reich. Belinsky cleared quickly too, for he was a former soldier in the French army who now chose to return to occupied France. Still, they were in enemy territory, and Olga Katunal felt vulnerable. She was relieved to be traveling with a Gentile whose looks fit the Aryan ideal.

When they reached Paris, Katunal went to see some Jewish friends who had stayed behind. Much to her surprise, they told her to rush right down to police headquarters to register. The Germans were taking a census of all foreign Jews and had already passed the letter *k*. Although they warned her that she would get ten years in prison for disobeying orders, she decided she preferred a jail sentence to what she believed awaited Jews who complied. Encouraged by non-Jewish friends to avoid the police, Katunal took her chances with the Soviet passport, at least for a while. By the time Hitler invaded Russia, she had taken another identity.

Belinsky and Katunal joined a small group of resisters who called themselves, "France, Liberté, Fédération." Although there was no single political line, the group leaned to the left. In all they were thirty, ten of them foreigners. Olga Katunal was the only Jew, and she kept this a secret from almost everyone. The group used to meet on the Boulevard St. Michel at the home of a lawyer and Freemason by the name of Lucien Barquisot.

Involved as it was in a wide range of political activities, France, Liberté, Fédération was eventually denounced in 1943. Olga Katunal remembered it happened on a Friday evening. When she arrived in front of the apartment house where the Barquisots lived, a strange intuition prevented her from climbing the stairs. Her legs simply refused to obey. She turned around and went home.

The police barged in shortly after 6:00 P.M. with warrants for Katunal and Barquisot. Olga Katunal was not there, and they found Lucien Barquisot doubled over in pain, suffering from an acute attack of an intestinal ulcer. Pleading with the officers to leave her husband alone, Barquisot's wife said he was dying of cancer. Believing her story, they generously said the lawyer could turn himself in on Monday. Then they went off, presumably to look for their other prisoner. Barquisot felt he should report to the police, but he eventually listened to reason and went into hiding in a house located fifty kilometers from Paris. Hating the isolation, he was back again in a few days to carry on his clandestine activities.

When the group dissolved, Katunal, too, continued her work of drawing up false papers for Jews and political activists. She herself had a fake identity card, first from the Ile de la Réunion, which was not very safe, then from a small village in the Nièvre. If she had ever needed to use the Island papers, the police would have had little difficulty in calling her bluff. Nobody there would have covered for her. In the Nièvre, however, the mayor of the little town could be counted on. What is more, she noted proudly, people often said she spoke French with the accent of the region.

Olga Katunal had many stories about hiding out in Paris. For months at a time, she slept in a different place every night. Finally, thanks to Belinsky, she found a room near the rue Soufflot that had a secret door leading into a courtyard. Food, as well as lodging, was a daily problem for resisters like herself, who had no ration cards and had to depend on a network of trustworthy shopkeepers to sell them provisions on the black market.

Olga Katunal's stories about the war frequently described Jews who turned themselves in. She even knew a black fellow who claimed he was Jewish and went to register with the police. The Germans refused to believe him and hired the man to be their chauffeur instead, a job he gladly accepted, for it permitted him to steal cars and obtain secret information for the Resistance. This black comrade had married a Polish Jewish woman, whom he kept successfully hidden for the duration of the war.

Then there was Frau Dr. Marmoreck, the wife of an Austrian physician and Zionist, who had been a good friend of Herzl. The Marmorecks had served in the medical corps of the Austrian army during World War I and received medals for their courage. By the time Olga Katunal knew the Frau Doktor, she was a widow, about seventy years old, and she lived by herself in a rooming house on the rue de Nevers, near the Pont Neuf. Although the old woman had means, she rejected bourgeois luxury, preferring a one-room flat on the eighth floor of a pension where students took lodgings. The kitchen was just a nook in the wall, and she had no private bathroom—communal facilities were down the hall. On her landing alone were twelve separate units, and Frau Dr. Mamoreck enjoyed playing the role of an emancipated grandmother. If a young man started an affair and needed a bigger bad, she found one for him.

When the Germans invaded Paris, the students fled the city, leaving Frau Dr. Mamoreck all alone on the eighth floor of the pension. Some of them gave her keys to their rooms so that she could look after their belongings, which she did religiously. The old woman not only dusted the individual units, but washed down the steps in the hall—her medical training and Austrian culture made her critical of the job done by the French concierge.

Since Frau Dr. Marmoreck was all by herself, Olga Katunal asked if she could sleep in one of the empty rooms. Although she enjoyed the company, the old woman finally asked Olga to leave, because she refused to register with the police. In the eyes of Frau Dr. Marmoreck, Olga Katunal was a fugitive from the law. No matter how hard the younger woman tried to explain, the Frau Doktor refused to listen.

One day, Olga Katunal arrived at the pension and found Frau Dr. Marmoreck busily writing a letter to Hitler. She had taken out all her medals and papers and was describing to her fellow Austrian how she had fought on his side during the First World War. The old woman apologized to Hitler for writing exclusively in her own self-interest—clearly the Führer would be moved and spare her—but she hoped her case would help Hitler realize that all Jews were not enemies of the Reich. What is more, she would be happy tell him about many others like herself. When Olga Katunal argued that to send the letter would hasten the doctor's arrest, the old woman called her a paranoid.

In desperation, Olga Katunal brought a German friend to the pension to speak to her stubborn friend. Bauerwind, a painter, knew what was happening, for he had served in the S.A. (Sturmabteilung) before abandoning National Socialism and escaping to France. Only after the Frau Doktor heard him describe what he had seen, did she agree to tear up the letter.

As Katunal and Bauerwind left the Frau Doktor's flat, they crossed the Pont Neuf and walked into a surprise check of identity papers. Not daring to turn around, Bauerwind took Katunal's arm and started speaking loudly in German. Fortunately they were stopped by members of the French police, not by Nazi officers, who saw that Bauerwind was German and accepted that Katunal was with him. At this point, Olga Katunal carried papers from the Ile de la Réunion, and she did not want put them to the test.

Olga Katunal had many close calls, but she firmly believed she would not have ended up in a concentration camp. Like many other politically active Jews, she had decided from the beginning that the Nazis would never take her alive. This confidence in her own willingness to fight made her impatient with those who obeyed passively and, in her eyes, assisted the Germans in their murderous task.

After the war, Olga Katunal was not interested in applying for reparations from the Germans. The loss of so many lives could not be exchanged for money. But friends soon convinced her that she and others had lost property too, and this could be compensated for. Having spent four years in occupied Paris, in hiding and unable to make a living, Katunal had a clear-cut case—she was the victim of psychological and economic hardships. She had medical complaints, as well: During the Occupation, she developed cardiac complications.

As Olga Katunal described how one applied for reparations, she returned to the theme of misguided, even complicitous, Jews. This time she spoke of French Jewish doctors who agreed to examine victims of National Socialism for the German embassy and diagnose the seriousness of their ailments. One of these doctors gave Katunal a hard time, and she had to appeal her case before a tribunal in Düsseldorf. In the end she won almost all the money she had asked for, and to the day she died, she lived largely off the monthly payments she received from the Germans.

After the war, Olga Katunal moved into a student pension on the rue St. Jacques. Belinsky had taken separate lodgings for himself, but he almost always stayed with his companion, sharing her one large room and small kitchen. The place resembled the flat Frau Dr. Marmoreck had rented on the rue de Nevers. Like the Austrian woman, Olga Katunal made friends with many of the students and artists who had taken rooms there.

The door to Olga Katunal's apartment was always open to a stream of young people who came to talk to her about philosophy, art, and politics. While their discussions covered a wide number of subjects, they frequently returned to Jewish thought and history. Among those who visited her were André Schwarz-Bart, the future author of *The Last of the Just*,[9] and Richard Marienstras. The psychoanalyst Jacques Lacan also found his way to Katunal's flat in the late 1950s in order to read her copies of Oskar Goldberg's work.

During the last forty years of her life, Olga Katunal maintained close ties to an anarchist group based in Israel that published a Yiddish journal called *Problemen*. She also read extensively about the prophet Elijah and began writing about him. When she died in April 1988, Katunal's cousin, the painter Alain Kleinmann, found the manuscript, still unfinished, composed in her characteristically clear and flawless French.

Until the very end, Olga Katunal continued to live in the same flat on the top floor of the same pension. In later years, she rarely left home, but students of Judaism and philosophy continued to climb the four flights of stairs to spend hours talking to this erudite old woman. Occasionally she found someone eager to learn about the obscure, but fascinating figure of Oskar Goldberg.

THE INFLUENCE OF OSKAR GOLDBERG

When Olga Katunal decided to return to religion, Oskar Goldberg offered a reasonable path. Given her background, it made sense to embrace Judaism through the work of a philosopher grounded in the German tradition, But why return to religion in the first place?

Having come from a family that had broken with the Jewish tradition one full generation before she was born, she had no personal gripes to settle with religion or, for that matter, with the usual restrictions imposed on young women of the privileged classes. Unlike contemporaries of hers one reads so much about, Olga Katunal *remained* the dutiful daughter by joining the international struggle for political and social change. It was her father, not comrades, who first taught her about emancipation and free love.

Olga Katunal rebelled by returning to Judaism. However, even though she embraced the religion, she did not take the vows of a traditional Jewish woman. Over the years, she had developed a passion for living in the world of ideas—a world, she acknowledged, inhabited almost only by men. Unwilling to give up this life, her return to Judaism would have to be on her own terms. Oskar Goldberg's approach made this easier to do than did conventional Judaism.

Olga Katunal succeeded, even in traditional Orthodox circles, finding ways to study Torah and Talmud with important rabbis who usually refused to work with members of her sex. The greatest teacher she ever had, she claimed, was Zalman Schneurson, a man many expected to inherit the position of chief rabbi of the Lubavitcher Ḥasidim, but he never did. A formidable scholar, Schneurson attracted a large following of intellectual

Jews in Paris during the early postwar years. And during her close association with him, Schneurson too became interested in Goldberg.

Olga Katunal first read *Die Wirklichkeit der Hebräer* in the late 1920s, when she was a member of the Communist party and had little interest in Judaism. The book, however, startled her so, that it changed her life, forcing her to reconsider the choices she had made. Actually, the work was just the first part of a far more ambitious philosophical project that Goldberg had promised to reveal in a second volume, but he never did, sorely disappointing Olga Katunal, Simon Guttmann, and other impassioned followers.

Still, the first volume had great power, appealing to Katunal's rational mind. It also satisfied her mystical yearnings, providing her with an explanation for some disturbing events that had recently taken her by surprise. Before reading the book, she had just been through a difficult period of mysterious illness, accidents, and psychological pain. Now, as she studied Goldberg's complex discussion of the magical connection of the Jews to their God, she realized that her recent encounters with misfortune had always occurred on Jewish holidays. The regularity of the pattern must have meaning, she concluded, and she decided she had best start observing the Jewish holidays religiously and following the ancient rituals of her people.

Upon finishing the book, Olga Katunal wrote Oskar Goldberg, asking him to clarify a few points. He telegrammed back immediately, announcing that a letter would follow. And so began their lengthy correspondence and collaboration. On her trips to Berlin in the intervening years, Katunal stopped to see Goldberg and to study with him. In 1932, Goldberg left Germany for Italy, Switzerland, and France before quitting Europe entirely to wait out the war in the United States. When visiting Paris in the 1930s, Goldberg gave a number of lectures.

To introduce the French public to the work of her mentor, Olga Katunal wrote a short article in 1935 for the Reform Jewish journal *Le Rayon*. Called, in translation, "Towards the Solution of the Problem of Judaism," her piece demonstrates how Goldberg's work engages creatively the European philosophical tradition out of which it comes. Following the interpretation of her former teacher Erich Unger, she refers obliquely to the way Goldberg developed Leibnitz's ideas about the real and the possible: if it can logically be imagined, it can also exist.[10] Given this line of reasoning, the argument goes, one can prove philosophically that God wrote the biblical account. And Goldberg, says Katunal, did just that, through his method of "rational mysticism." Here, then is Olga Katunal's summary of the importance of Goldberg's work:

There exists a spiritual movement in Judaism which remains virtually unknown in France. Its central text is a book by the philosopher Oskar Goldberg, *Die Wirklichkeit der Hebräer*. Published in Berlin in 1925, it is the first volume of a larger project, the second volume of which has still not appeared. In intellectual circles, *Die Wirklichkeit der Hebräer* has been read and commented upon by Jewish and Christian thinkers—the Orthodox and the Reform—by philosophers, theologians, scientists and scholars of literature; by all those who are interested either in Semitic languages, mythology, or the philosophy of religion. One of the author's collaborators, Erich Unger, himself a writer whose work is well known—*Gegen die Dichtung* (*Against Poetry*), *Wirklichkeit, Mythos, Erkenntnis* (*Reality, Myth, Knowledge*), etc.—has published an introductory essay which summarizes admirably Goldberg's doctrine.[11]

We do not intend to examine today the work of Goldberg in all its complexities. We will limit ourselves instead to defining his subject and method. As the subtitle to *The Reality of the Hebrews* indicates, his book is an *Introduction to the System of the Pentateuch*. It does not claim to interpret the Five Books of Moses in a unilateral fashion, but to penetrate these books in the sense of the very universality of the human spirit.

This work interprets without translating—without distorting the strict meaning of the words, without weakening the primitive strength of the text by offering conventional explanations. Goldberg asks us to reject symbolic interpretations, the involuntary and the voluntary, for they are unable to clarify certain texts and become suddenly silent, powerless, cautious. But then, how do we find the real meaning of these ancient texts, the value and scope of words and phrases that have undergone considerable changes since biblical times? The state of things that is the object of these writings, no longer exists. What is more, our relationship to life is different from what it was then. Our own ideas about reality keep us from grasping this distant way of thinking. In spite of ourselves, either we tend to reduce biblical texts to conform to the typical prejudices of science, of our sense of morality and of our practical experiences; or, like our ancestors, we simply accept the wisdom of tradition, even if blind faith blocks the possibility of serious research.

Now the work of Goldberg opens an entirely new way for us. To follow him successfully, the attentive reader must rid himself of all preconceived notions: his critical judgment, his believing soul, and his active will must be free of those static ideals that obscure the truth.

We must move forward, motivated by the highest goal— creative knowledge—and be guided by a clear and intransigent conscience: by reason in the broadest sense of the word. The vastness of human thought must let what we see now as only a conceivable possibility become as real as those concrete things we have actually observed and tested. We must replace the limited reality of everyday life with a far greater and imposing reality. To make this larger reality available and concrete is the aim of a true and free philosophy.

It is very important that philosophy provisionally accept the following hypothesis: the Pentateuch is neither sublime poetry, nor an aberration of ideas, nor a moral allegory, but a true testimony, for that is what the scriptures claim to be. From this supposition, philosophy defines the precision of its own mission: it will only be correct if the document it considers authentic and whose integrity it absolutely respects can perfectly and clearly be shown to conform to reason without losing any of its sovereign dignity. . . . Goldberg constructed a precise, solid, and complete world in which the extraordinary and marvelous (biblical) account sounds different from the way it usually does. The Pentateuch, the Hebrews' mythic and nonmythic reality, acquires a veritable life, intense, more remote, but also more palpable than ever.

The "mystical rationalism" of this ontology (the science of being, in general), makes the principle of Judaism shine with a surprising light, and shows us our essential task. It draws for us the difficult road that leads to the theoretical and practical solution of the problem Judaism poses.[12]

And what is the problem? According to Katunal's reading of Goldberg, it is to help the Jewish people develop once again their authentic (magical) connection to God, to their biological center. Goldberg took the ancient texts literally, not as symbolic statements or allegories, and claimed he was able to demonstrate that the biblical Hebrews, themselves a biological entity, had an organic relationship to God, a relationship that flourished until the days of King Solomon.

Before Solomon built his temple, the God of the ancient Hebrews walked with His people and had His dwelling place among them. But during the time of this much heralded philosopher-king, God lost his welcome on earth and retreated to heaven. When God left this world, the Jews entered a period of decline from which they have never recovered.

Goldberg's "proof" involved a sophisticated philological approach to the text. By studying the etymology of almost every word in the Torah, he claimed to be able to determine the original context and meaning. Through this arduous task, Goldberg attempted to demonstrate that in the early days the Jews maintained their magical relationship to God by means of ritual. But when King Solomon built his central sanctuary and tried to confine God to His heavenly abode, he introduced abstract theological monotheism, which became the basis of postbiblical Judaism and Christianity. In the process, the Jews lost their magical connection to God. They stopped being a cultic community and became members of a state.

In the words of the late Jacob Taubes, one of the few Jewish philosophers of religion who found Goldberg's work important, "I see Goldberg's originality not so much in his interpretation of myth, later confirmed in rough outline by empirical anthropology and ethnology, as in the terrifying literalness with which he set out to translate myth into reality and in his uncompromising will to take the records of archaic cults and rituals seriously and not merely as a way of flirting with current fashions."[13]

This literalness fascinated Olga Katunal. A linguist and translator, she admired the philosopher's careful etymological research. Goldberg appreciated her interest and skills. Few people, he realized, were as capable as she to represent his work in other languages. In later years he asked Katunal to translate his books into French. Although she agreed to do *Die Wirklichkeit der Hebräer,* she never got very far with the project.

Goldberg's wife, Dora Hiller, died after the war, and the philosopher returned to France. In love with Olga and eager to leave his papers in competent hands, he asked his student to marry him, but she refused, for a number of reasons. Among others, she did not want the responsibility of publishing his complete works, particularly those manuscripts written in the United States, where Goldberg's ideas had developed in ways she could no longer defend.

In addition to his research on ancient Judaism, Goldberg had always been interested in primitive religions, in studying cultures that still had magical ties to their deities. He was fascinated, as well, by the highly complex mystical religions of Asia, which he claimed had also maintained this magical connection. At one point, perhaps before the First World War, perhaps in the early 1920s, he went to Tibet to live in a monastery. While Goldberg's detractors claimed the philosopher came under the influence of the Russian theosophist Madame Blavatsky,[14] Katunal denied it; his Far East experience did, however, reveal to him new possibilities beyond Judaism, and he began to experiment with these in the United States, where he changed dramatically. During his stay there, Goldberg stopped observing Jewish rituals and began to concentrate on parapsychological interpretations of religion.

Although she disapproved of the new work, Olga Katunal agreed to translate an article of Goldberg's for the esoteric journal *Initiation et science*.[15] In the piece, he described an event that took place in Millvale, Pennsylvania, near Pittsburg, in 1937: A Yugoslav, hired to paint the inside of a Croate church, saw a ghost blow out the sanctuary's everlasting light. Goldberg claimed that the ghost extinguished the religion in the church because the Croates there had stopped believing. The philosopher went on to discuss in general terms how restless spirits occasionally came back to life.

Oskar Goldberg died suddenly of a heart attack in Nice in 1952. He was sixty-seven years old and no longer on good terms with Olga Katunal. The last person to talk to the philosopher about his work was Simon Guttmann, and he inherited Goldberg's papers.

Simon Guttmann had nothing more than a philosophical interest in Goldberg's work. He had never considered observing the rituals, for example. And although he had studied Hebrew with Goldberg, he did not know the language well. As a result, he could do little more than authorize the editing of the notes for the second volume of *Die Wirklichkeit der Hebräer*. He could not undertake the task himself. Katunal was probably the last person left from the group who had the necessary skills and the proper orientation to bring out the long-awaited volume. But she and Guttmann had a disagreement soon after Goldberg died, and they never spoke again. They only heard about each other, from time to time, through go-betweens Katunal sent to London on her behalf. According to Guttmann, the problem had to do with timing. Madame Katunal, he claimed, was in too much of a rush to bring out Goldberg's unpublished manuscripts. While this may have been true in the 1950s, as the years went by, the two seemed to have reached similar conclusions about what should be done with Goldberg's work: (1) Nobody should publish any of Goldberg's writings that treat his post-World War II deviations. The public would misinterpret them and dismiss the importance of Goldberg's earlier contributions; (2) Any notes for a second volume of *Die Wirklichkeit der Hebräer* or for a treatise refuting the philosophy of Kant, if such notes exist, should be edited and prepared for publication.

As it happens, Guttmann claimed to have found nothing of importance in the many boxes of papers stored in his flat. The only manuscript of philosophical interest was an outline for a book Goldberg never wrote. In no way do these few pages suggest the great masterpiece Katunal and Guttmann had anticipated. Goldberg's last project seemed destined for a popular audience in the United States. Written in English and bearing the title, *The World Politics of the Gods: Philosophy of Life in the Era of Moses,* Goldberg promised that it would answer "all the questions people have about the Bible."

Although Goldberg did not fulfill his promise, he played a significant role in the philosophical debates going on in Berlin in the interwar years.[16] According to Taubes, Goldberg's interpretation of the Penteteuch was "the only Jewish magical resurgence" in modern times. While Goldberg was not alone in seeing the Five Books of Moses as myth, he set himself apart by accepting the reality of these accounts. In his early works, Martin Buber also expressed interest in the mythical elements of the Torah, Taubes suggested, but the latter's concern was "sheer phraseology." When confronted with someone who took the myths seriously, Buber rejected the man and the approach. Actually, Buber had no idea what Goldberg was talking about, Taubes continued, but Gershom Scholem understood all too well, for he could have gone in a similar direction.[17] As he refused the temptation, Scholem turned on Goldberg with venom, revealing his vulnerability through the passion of his epithets.

Other German Jewish scholars of religion criticized Goldberg for taking a stand against ethical Judaism. The philosopher had to go elsewhere to find support, and this he did. According to Taubes, whose opinion has been challenged,[18] Goldberg attracted a number of students of his "pagan counterpart," Alfred Schuller, the man who "invented" the swastika. Schuller, unlike Goldberg, claimed that magical ritual life culminated in the late Roman Empire, not among the ancient Hebrews. Goldberg received praise, as well, from the controversial paleontologist Edgar Dacqué.[19]

But Goldberg did not interest only protofascists. Much to Scholem's dismay, Walter Benjamin found aspects of Goldberg's philosophy intriguing and was deeply impressed by the work of Erich Unger. Benjamin even attended meetings of the circle on occasion, but never joined.[20]

Thomas Mann took an interest in Goldberg, as well. In preparation for writing *Joseph and His Brothers,* he studied the Five Books of Moses with Goldberg and then based the first volume of the novel on the philosopher's interpretations of Genesis.[21] In the 1930s Goldberg was also invited to contribute articles on mythology to Mann's journal *Mass und Wert*.[22] Despite their close association for many years, Mann turned around and ridiculed Goldberg in his post–World War II novel, *Dr. Faustus*.

In chapter 27, Mann introduces the reader to Chaim Breisacher, a character based entirely on Oskar Goldberg.[23] He describes Breisacher as "a racial and intellectual type in high, one might almost say reckless development and of a fascinating ugliness." This curious Jew represents a new kind of conservatism, which Mann, through his narrator, contrasts with that of the aristocratic Baron von Riedesel: "Here [for Breisacher] it was a matter not so much of 'still' as 'again'; for this was an after- and anti-revolutionary conservatism, a revolt against bourgeois liberal standards from the other end, not from the rear but from the front, not from the old but from the new."[24]

Presented as a philosopher of culture with anticultural views, Breisacher describes the history of culture as a process of degeneration; the very word *progress* is an anathema. Offering first a general critique of world civilization, Breisacher turns next to an analysis of the Old Testament, using many of Goldberg's actual words.[25] Like Goldberg himself, Breisacher blames King Solomon for destroying the special connection the Jewish people had to their God:

> The man [King Solomon] was an aesthete unnerved by erotic excesses and in a religious sense a progressivist blockhead, typical of the back-formation of the cult of the effectively present national god, the general concept of the metaphysical power of the folk, into the preaching of an abstract and generally human god in heaven; in other words, from the religion of the people to the religion of the world. To prove it we only need to read the scandalous speech which he made after the first temple was finished, where he asks: "But will God indeed dwell on the earth?" as though Israel's whole and unique task had not consisted therein, that it should build God a dwelling, a tent, and provide all means for His constant presence. But Solomon was so bold as to declaim:

"Behold, the heaven and heaven of heavens connot contain Thee; how much less this house that I have builded!" That is just twaddle and the beginning of the end, that is the degenerate conception of the poets of the Psalms; with whom God is already entirely exiled into the sky, and who constantly sing of God in heaven, whereas the Pentateuch does not even know it as the seat of the Godhead.[26]

The narrator ends the chapter by making a clear connection between Breisacher's (or Goldberg's) ideas and National Socialism. Returning to the contrast between the new conservatism and the old, he notes ironically:

> I really felt sorry for the Baron. Here was his aristocratic conservatism outbid by the frightfully clever playing of atavistic cards; by a radical conservatism that no longer had anything aristocratic about it, but rather something revolutionary; something more disrupting than any liberalism, and yet, as though in mockery, possessing a laudable conservative appeal. . . . One could easily have disputed him, . . . but a sensitive man does not like to disturb another; . . . Today we see, of course, that it was the mistake of our civilization to have practiced all too magnanimously this respect and forebearance. For we found after all that the opposite side met us with sheer impudence and the most determined intolerance.[27]

Gershom Scholem portrayed Oskar Goldberg in unflattering terms, as well. In *Walter Benjamin: The Story of a Friendship,* he described the philosopher as "a small, fat man who looked like a stuffed dummy, and [who] exerted an uncanny magnetic power over the group of Jewish intellectuals who gathered around him."[28] Adding that Goldberg's work had a "demonic dimension," Scholem objected in particular to the way the circle used their mentor's ideas to attack Zionism. In the early 1920s, for example, Unger wrote a book that in English translation would be called *The Stateless Formation of the Jewish People*.[29] Basing his argument on Goldberg's teachings, Unger claimed that the transformation of the Jews must come about by metaphysical means, not by establishing a nation-state.

Goldberg's disciples felt no more kindly toward Scholem than he did toward them. Olga Katunal, for one, rose to the occasion every time she heard his name mentioned. So did Simon Guttmann, who carrying forward the group's position on Israel, criticized Scholem for his Zionism, as well. Katunal, however, endorsed the existence of the Jewish state. Like many other Jews of her generation, the Second World War had forced her to agree that Jews needed a homeland. While she maintained a theoretical stand against all nation-states, she refused to single out Israel for special criticism.

Olga Katunal took her distance from Goldberg for philosophical reasons unrelated to the philosopher's anti-Zionism or his so-called fascist tendencies. Her objections concerned certain deviations that had crept into Goldberg's work during his stay in the United States. But Katunal's problems with Goldberg did not bring her closer to Scholem or Mann. Disagreeing with Taubes, she maintained that Scholem understood very little about Goldberg. He wrote out of ignorance and malice and did her mentor much harm. In the case of Thomas Mann, what could you expect? He was not above slandering members of his family—remember how he used incest in *Buddenbrooks!* Anyway, his brother Heinrich was the better novelist of the two.

In the end, while Katunal vigorously opposed Goldberg's new direction, she continued to see him as one of the most important voices in twentieth-century philosophy. But why? How could she be swayed by what some call Goldberg's radical conservatism when her own political choices and intellectual interests led her more naturally to social revolution and modernist culture?

But is it fair to characterize Goldberg as a radical conservative? Can his mystical rationalism be dismissed so simply as the ravings of a Jewish fascist? Are Goldberg's ideas about the biological center of the Jewish people truly reminiscent of theories of race supremacy? Can we reduce Goldberg and Unger's attack on the nation-state to a Jewish version of pan-Germanism and the idealized Volk, as the selections from Mann suggest? Perhaps someone in the generation of 1968 will study Goldberg's work seriously and make it possible for us to evaluate his contributions to Jewish scholarship and to the debates about nationalism and the nation-state going on at the time he was writing. Such a person would need excellent training in ancient Hebrew and Judaism, as well as in the European philosophical tradition.

In France, Michael Löwy has taken the first step, but he summarizes Goldberg's work in only a couple of sentences in *Rédemption et utopie*. Characterizing him as entirely marginal to the major currents of his day, Löwy suggests that Goldberg envisioned a new theocracy that responded to the concerns of social revolutionaries.[30] He then drops Goldberg and discusses the work of Erich Unger, the "metaphysical anarchist" whose work fascinated Walter Benjamin. As Löwy describes the reasons Benjamin found Unger's ideas significant, he presents the latter's views in terms that would probably interest members of the Yéchiva des Etudiants too. According to Benjamin, Unger made two important arguments, one against the utility of all existing political parties, in *Politik und Metaphysik,* and the other, as we have already noted, against the nation-state.[31] In *The Stateless Formation of the Jewish People,* Unger maintained that Jews gained strength from their religious traditions and from their unusual circumstances of being a people without a state.[32]

Unger's celebration of diaspora Jewry and Goldberg's call for the rigorous study of the Five Books of Moses echo the concerns of many in the generation of 1968, even beyond those involved with the Yéchiva des Etudiants. But Goldberg, if not Unger, would probably have angered many people as well. Even if we dismiss Scholem and Mann's explosive accusations about Goldberg's fascist tendencies, the philosopher would surely trouble students of Judaism with his attacks on the rabbinic tradition and his explorations of the magical relation Jews supposedly had with YHWH in the days before Solomon built the Temple. Still, even if they vehemently disagreed with his ideas, Goldberg's "mystical rationalism" and his approach to the Torah would probably interest members of the generation of 1968, the way it fascinated Olga Katunal and her friends in the 1920s. Both then and now, former activists turned to Jewish thought and Judaism for "metaphysical reasons."

This brief digression into the work of Oskar Goldberg has taken us away from Lite, but not from the concerns that have interested Lithuanian Jews and their disciples in France. As marginal as this philosopher might seem from the perspective of today, the debates surrounding his work raise the same questions that have been with us from the beginning, namely the problem of nationalism and the nation-state and the role of Jewish culture in the Diaspora. These issues were central to the intellectual life of German Jews at the time Goldberg was writing and therefore, understandably, to the Jews of Lite who studied in the Weimar Republic.

The Lithuanian Jews discussed in this book came of age intellectually through German philosophy and literature. In virtually every case, German thinkers and artists even influenced the way they eventually redefined their relationship to Judaism—influenced, but did not determine. As we have already seen, these children of maskilim grew up in a culturally rich and diverse world that combined Jewish and European traditions. In contrast with their peers in Germany, most of them received a serious education in Hebrew and Jewish culture. They were also exposed to a far more radical political and social climate, and this affected them deeply. When Jews such as these returned to Judaism, they had vast resources to draw on, the culmination of an extraordinary range of cultural and political experiences.

Conclusion

Some books come naturally to an end. Others merely stop, leaving the questions they raise open for further debate. As *Vilna on the Seine* now draws to a close, we find the people described here discussing many of the same issues that led them to reconsider the problem of being Jewish in France in the years following 1968. I am interrupting the story in 1989, during the celebration of the bicentennial of the French Revolution. For the occasion, several Jewish intellectuals have done further research on the history of the emancipation of Jews in France and have published their findings in honor of the festivities. Among the new works, there is *Libres et égaux*, written by Robert Badinter, the minister of justice during Mitterand's first term and a man who proudly claims he is Jewish.[1]

Defending those who supported the emancipation of Jews during the French Revolution, Bandinter challenges critics in the country today who portray Clermont-Tonnerre and the Abbé Grégoire as dubious friends of the Jewish people. Instead of condemning the efforts of these early pioneers, the former minister of justice praises the generosity of their project, endorsing their strategy to diffuse ethnic conflict by forging a single nation. Thanks to allies like them, Badinter argues, the French National Assembly in 1791 became the first sovereign body in all of Europe to proclaim that Jews were "free and equal."

Badinter dedicates *Libres et égaux* to his father, a Jewish immigrant from Eastern Europe, "who chose France because it was the country of the Rights of Man." In doing so, he draws attention once again to enlightened Jews born in czarist Russia at the turn of the century who enthusiastically embraced the universalistic ideals of the French Revolution. As I have argued throughout the pages of this book, people such as these have inspired intellectuals identified with 1968 in a number of different ways, often leading them back to the humanistic ideals they had come to question during the student revolt.

The four people from Lite I describe in detail were raised in families where they learned about Judaism and the cultures of Europe. While they all identified with their Lithuanian Jewish heritage, they were deeply attached to the cultural traditions of Europe as well, traditions their parents had introduced them to at home. Even Olga Katunal, the most radical of the four in her return to Judaism, maintained a keen interest in secular philosophy and literature, continuing to read widely in the many languages she knew.

Enlightened Jews from Russia had rich backgrounds to draw on in both the Jewish and European traditions. Few belonging to the generation of 1968 could claim the same. Nevertheless, they modeled themselves on those who did, not always realizing, at first, the full implications of what they had done. In the early days following the student revolt, minority nationalists turned to Eastern European Yiddishists as they looked for ways to make a break with their French heritage and define themselves culturally as Jews. But as they embraced the ideas of their mentors, members of the younger generation found themselves supporting Yiddish interpretations of French Enlightenment thinkers.

As people celebrate the traditions of secular Yiddishists in France today, they necessarily go back into French, for the Shoah destroyed the possibility of developing the ideals of the Enlightenment in the language of Eastern European Jews. Litvine acknowledges this sad fact and knows that he is at the end of the line. So does Rachel Ertel, who has chosen to preserve the contributions of Yiddish writers to European culture by translating their efforts into French.

Assimilationists in France have had fewer conflicts than minority nationalists about identifying with the French Enlightenment in the original. Their difficulty lies in living as Jews while remaining tied to a secular French culture. Some have tried to resolve the problem by following the teachings of Emmanuel Lévinas. In doing so, they have begun to study the sacred texts, hoping to learn to read them with authority, despite their poor preparation for the task.

Those who converted to Orthodox Judaism have trained themselves seriously to study Torah and Talmud. Unlike their peers in the other two groups, they continue to defy the Enlightenment with a vengeance. Rejecting models offered by Lévinas, Gordin, and Olga Katunal, they challenge those who believe in the possibility of living as Jews while identifying with the values of Europe.[2] But even members of this group have begun to work in institutions representing the universalistic ideals of the Enlightenment, among them Shmuel Trigano and his team of instructors who offer courses at the Alliance Israélite Universelle.

In doing this research, I have been struck by the ways Jewish intellectuals in France have looked to their elders, preferring to work within established traditions, rather than to invent, American style, something entirely new. Although many have challenged mainstream Judaism and rejected the French nation-state that produced it, they have often gained inspiration from people who believed in the universalistic values of the West. With the help of their mentors, many younger Jews have begun to reconsider the virtures of a culture they had vigorously opposed.

What the future will bring, I leave to the prophets. But I can say with confidence that the years ahead will continue to reflect the last two decades, during which time Jewish intellectuals of the generation of 1968 have turned to the East and into the past, as they looked for ways to enrich their lives as Jews in contemporary France.

Appendix

In this book I have focused on only a handful of people. Many others deserve our attention as well, some of whose contributions we turn to now. But even in an appendix, it is impossible to include every scholar and writer in the community who has helped redefine Jewish culture in France.[1] Although the following discussion remains incomplete, in it I hope to accomplish two objectives: first, to acknowledge the important roles played by a few more members of the generation of 1968 and by their mentors; and second, to give examples of other Jews whose positions have evolved over the years as they move back and forth, combining ideas and making places for themselves "betwixt and between" the three groups identified in the introduction: the minority nationalists, the reaffirmed assimilationists, and the ultra-Orthodox Jews.

Some of the people described below claim no spiritual ties to Lite. But many of them do. And even those who express little interest in Lithuanian Jewry raise questions about the nation-state and universal culture in terms similar to those that led others to study the works of Jews from Vilna and the surrounding towns.

I begin with Edmond Fleg, a distinguished member of the older generation, who was mentioned only in passing in previous chapters. Poet, playwright, and essayist, he was one of the founding fathers of Jewish studies in France. Fleg was born in Geneva in 1874, into a family of highly assimilated Alsatian Jews. He received a Jewish education in keeping with his class and background and continued to celebrate the ideals of the French universalistic tradition to the end of his life, demonstrating in the process the compatibility of the Enlightenment with the teachings of the Jewish law. During his long association with the French Jewish community, Fleg served as president of the Eclaireurs Israélites de France, was a member of the central committee of the Alliance Israélite Universelle, founded an organization to promote friendship between Jews and Christians (L'Amitié Judéo-

Chrétienne) after the Second World War, helped initiate the first Colloque des Intellectuels Juifs de Langue Francaise, and wrote voluminously on Jewish thought, culture, and politics. He died in 1963.

André Neher is also important to our story. He was born in Alsace in 1914 and went on to specialize in ancient and modern Jewish litera-ture. Neher taught at the University of Strasbourg after the Second World War, influencing many students both in the classroom and through his books. Over the years he wrote extensively on the prophets and on a wide range of philosophical questions concerning Jews in the contemporary world. Like Edmond Fleg, André Neher participated in the Colloque des Intellectuels Juifs from the beginning. He died in Israel during the autumn of 1988.[2]

Then, there is Vladimir Jankélévitch, the philosopher and musicologist of Russian Jewish origin who was born in Bourges (Cher) at the turn of the century. Writing in the universalistic tradition of an ethical Judaism, he spoke out regularly on a wide range of moral and political issues in his books and articles. In addition to publishing in established academic journals, Jankélévitch also contributed to some of the new periodicals founded by members of the generation of 1968. In 1978, his students paid tribute to him by collaborating on a book in his honor: *Ecrits pour Jankélévitch*.[3] Their teacher died in 1985.

The historian Léon Poliakov has influenced many, as well, both as a teacher and a scholar. He was born in Saint Petersburg in 1910 and has lived in France since 1920. In the post–World War II years, Poliakov gained international recognition for his multivolume study *The History of Antisemi-tism*. The historian has consistently given his enthusiastic support to mem-bers of the younger generation who have revived Jewish studies in France, first by signing the proclamation in 1967 that called for the creation of Le Cercle Gaston Crémieux, then by endorsing programs initiated by members of the generation of 1968. In the early 1980s former students of his published a collection of essays on racism in his honor, expressing in this way their gratitude for all his help and inspiration.[4]

Nahum Goldmann also influenced Jews of the generation of 1968 in France. Founder of the World Jewish Congress, Goldmann was born in Lithuania at the beginning of the century and raised in Germany. Although he was a resident of the United States for many years, then a citizen of Israel, Goldmann spent much of his time in France, and in later years he endorsed the efforts of Jewish minority nationalists, participating in activities spon-sored by them in Paris. When Goldmann died in 1982, Luc Rosenzweig wrote his obituary for *Le Monde,* characterizing the man as the "last of the giants of world politics."[5]

Among the active Yiddishists of the older generation, there is Kiwa Vaïsbrot. He was born in Poland in the early years of this century, and in 1989 he continues to serve as head librarian of the Bibliothèque Medem, the largest archive of Yiddish books in Europe. Named after the founder of the Bund, the Bibliothèque opened its doors in 1929 with a modest collection. Today it has more than twenty thousand volumes in Yiddish alone.

Since the Second World War, there is probably not a student in France doing research on Eastern European Jewish culture and history who does not know Monsieur Vaïsbrot. Anyone interested in the subject has visited the Bibliothèque Medem to find an obscure book that this man undoubtedly knew and could probably locate on the shelves of the library without referring to the card catalog.[6] Among the many students who have received help and encouragement from Monsieur Vaïsbrot is his son Bernard, who went on to receive, in the early 1980s, the first doctorate in Yiddish literature ever given in France.

Isaac Pougatch was another major figure in the French Yiddishist community. Born in Minsk in 1897, he lived to celebrate his ninetieth birthday, an event he shared with many of his students, but he died shortly thereafter. For the occasion, Anne Grynberg paid tribute to her teacher by publishing a special article on Pougatch in *Les Nouveaux cahiers,* the journal of the Alliance Israélite Universelle.[7] Pougatch devoted many years of his life to translating historical and literary works from the secular Diaspora tradition. In 1936 he published the French edition of Dubnow's *A Short History of the Jewish People.*[8] After the Second World War, he prepared French versions of fiction by Sholem Ash and Sholem Aleichem, the latter in collaboration with Joseph Gottfarstein.

While Pougatch contributed to furthering the secular tradition from Eastern Europe, he also remained an observant Jew and inspired students during the Second World War to bring Yiddishism and Judaism together. Recalling the efforts of her teacher, Lilly Scherr remembers how Pougatch gave frightened children in hiding the strength to maintain their Jewish tradition.[9]

Finally, let us end this list of members of the older generation with Raymond Aron. Sociologist, historian, philosopher, and journalist, Aron was born in Paris at the turn of the century into an old Jewish family originally from eastern France. Raised in a secular home, he thought little about his Jewish origins until the rise of National Socialism forced him to confront his family's heritage and the position of Jews in the modern world. In the 1930s he began writing about the threat of Nazism. After the War he turned to other related questions as well. Until his death in 1983 he published widely on subjects of concern to Jews both in the Diaspora and in Israel.

In later years Raymond Aron also assumed major responsibilities in the French Jewish community, holding important positions at the Alliance Israélite Universelle and at the CRIF and passing on to his daughter his deep commitment to the Jewish people. A sociologist like her father, Dominique (Aron) Schnapper went on to do a systematic study of Jews in contemporary France, and the resulting book, *Juifs et Israélites,* is recognized today as the major text on the subject.[10] Schnapper has also helped create a Jewish studies program at the Ecole des Hautes Etudes en Sciences Sociales, where she is directeur d'études en sociologie.

In the intermediate generation, those who were born in the 1920s, there is the philosopher Edmond Jabès, who comes originally from Egypt. Although he is not active in the French Jewish community, Jabès identifies himself as a Jew through "the Book" and has influenced members of the generation of 1968 to do the same. In 1981, for example, when the editors of *Traces* published the first issue of their journal, they pointed to Jabès as the inspiration for the name they chose. On the opening page, the editors quoted from *Le Livre des ressemblances,* reprinting the beautiful story Jabès tells about Reb Doubbah, who recalled the invisible, yet indelible traces Reb Samhob had left in the souls of those who had studied with him.[11]

The historian and sociologist Annie Kriegel, of French Jewish origin, has played a major role as well. A former Communist, she has written extensively in recent years against the party and for the state of Israel. As professor of political sociology at Nanterre, she has enthusiastically sponsored the research of Shmuel Trigano, among others, and has helped the young man establish a place for himself in the French Jewish community. In 1985, for example, Kriegel and Trigano founded a scholary journal, *Pardès.* Highly regarded for the quality of its articles, *Pardès* publishes the work of people in the generation of 1968 who represent a wide range of political and cultural tendencies.

Adolphe Steg has also been important in promoting Jewish studies in France and has helped bring together the tradition of Talmudic scholarship and the principles of French universalistic culture.[12] Steg was born in Ruthenia, near the Carpathian Mountains, in a part of the Ukraine that belonged to the Austro-Hungarian Empire in the early days of the twentieth century and then went to Czechoslovakia after the First World War. In 1938, the region changed hands again, going first to Hungary and finally to the Soviet Union after 1945.

Born in 1925 and raised in an observant home, Adolphe Steg has remained a practicing Jew who continues to value the kind of Jewish education provided by the small centers of learning that existed throughout Eastern Europe before the Second World War. Today, Steg is a distinguished professor of medicine in France and assumes major responsibilities in the Jewish community: in the 1970s he served as president of the CRIF, and in 1985 he became president of the Alliance Israélite Universelle.

Soon after Steg took office, Shmuel Trigano approached the new president with the idea of beginning a small school of Jewish studies at the Alliance Israélite. Enthusiastic about the proposal, the professor of medicine endorsed the project. In doing so, he, like Annie Kriegel, has helped bring one of France's most outspoken critics of nation-state Judaism back into the fold, permitting Trigano to open his Beit Hamidrach in the very institution that symbolizes the kind of assimilated Judaism the young man has vigorously opposed.

The school held its first classes in January 1986 with a series of courses aimed at making "Hebrew texts accessible to university-level students who may not be familiar with Jewish sources or with the Hebrew language." In a statement signed by both Steg and Trigano, the program also promised to "maintain the tension that exists between Jewish thought and contemporary thinking."[13] Among the instructors, we find Aaron Fraenckel and Charles Mopsik, as well as other representatives of the Yéchiva des Etudiants and the Verdier collective.

At the Alliance Israélite, we should also note the role played by the staff of the institution's excellent library and archives, in particular the librarian Yvonne Lévyne and the archivist Georges Weill. Madame Lévyne is a Lithuanian Jew and belongs to the older generation. Active in the intellectual Jewish community in Paris since before the Second World War, she remembers well how Oskar Goldberg caused great excitement among Eastern European immigrants in the 1930s.[14] Georges Weill belongs to the intermediate generation and has written extensively on French Jewish historiography and on the availability of archival material.

Jean Halpérin is another important figure in the intermediate generation.[15] He has held the position of chairman of the program committee of the Colloque des Intellectuels Juifs since 1967, a position he inherited from André Neher. Halpérin is the son of aristocratic Jews from Russia. On his mother's side, he is the direct descendant of the Gunzburgs from Saint Petersburg, of people who mixed regularly with Gentiles in prerevolutionary Russia, but who also maintained strong ties to Judaism, both in St. Petersburg and Paris. Recalling his childhood in France, Halpérin observed that his experiences at home resembled those described by Lévinas of his youth in Kovno. As a young boy, Halpérin said, his family "breathed Russian and Jewish [Hebrew] culture." In later years, when Halpérin became the organizer of the Colloque des Intellectuels, he tried to carry forward the rich blend of European and Jewish traditions that his parents had transmitted to him.

The idea of bringing Jewish intellectuals together began with Léo Algazi, the choral director of the consistorial synagogue on the rue de la Victoire. As Halpérin tells the story, in the mid-1950s, Algazi realized that a number of French Jews, teaching in universities throughout the nation, had become interested in their heritage. Given what had happened during the Second World War, people like Raymond Aron, for example, who had no background in Judaism, now felt a need to know something about it. Algazi decided to create a forum where secular intellectuals could meet with Edmond Fleg, André Neher, Léon Askenazi, and Emmanuel Lévinas, in other words with some of the country's most distinguished scholars of Jewish thought.

The first Colloque took place in Versailles in May 1957. Edmond Fleg gave the opening speech on the meaning of Jewish history.[16] Thirty people showed up. Two years later, Algazi organized a second meeting. As interest grew, the group moved to Paris and began running sessions annually on such topics as politics, history, religion, and Jewish consciousness in the modern world.

During the early years, the Colloque attracted between one- and two-hundred participants. Then, with the revival of Jewish studies in France in the late 1970s, the numbers grew dramatically. In the late 1980s, more than seven hundred people were attending these events, to hear, in particular, Emmanuel Lévinas give his annual talk on a Talmudic text. Under Jean Halpérin's direction, the meetings today also offer many sessions organized by members of the generation of 1968. Younger Jews now make keynote speeches as well, and some of them, like Alain Finkielkraut, have developed a large following.

In the Yiddishist community, perhaps the most important figure from the intermediate generation is Alexandre Derczansky.[17] Like Isaac Pougatch before him, Derczansky is a practicing Jew. Born in Strasbourg in 1924, his parents came from Vilna and identified with the secular traditions of the Jews from Lite—his mother was a Bundist and his father a member of the Po'alei Zion. Despite their political differences, his parents shared a deep attachment to the Yiddish language and culture, and this expressed itself in a variety of ways. At home, for example, the only picture that hung on the wall was a charcoal portrait of the writer I. L. Peretz.

For many years, Derczansky's parents were leading figures in the Strasbourg Yiddish community, particularly his mother, who ran an office to help Jewish immigrants find jobs. She also arranged to get working papers for people who had come to the country illegally. Both his parents gave courses in Yiddish, directed theatrical productions, and organized other cultural activities for Yiddish-speaking Jews.

By 1929, however, Jewish immigrants living in Strasbourg began abandoning the programs sponsored by Bundists and socialist Zionists. They joined the Communists instead. Even young Derczansky defected. In 1936, at the age of twelve, Alex became a member of the Red Pioneers, but the group expelled him shortly thereafter because he opposed the Moscow trials. Several years later, the teenager turned to religion, Catholicism, first, then Judaism.

At home Derczansky received little religious instruction. His father was trained in philosophy, he explained, and encouraged his son to read Spinoza's *Ethics* instead, the work of the seventeenth-century Jewish philosopher from Holland. The "heretical" Spinoza served as the religious inspiration for this maskil from Vilna.

Still, Derczansky was exposed to Judaism through school, for Strasbourg belonged to one of the three regions in France in which religious instruction was part of the curriculum. In the Bas-Rhin, Haut-Rhin, and Moselle, Protestant, Catholic, and Jewish children each attended special classes on Thursdays and Sundays. Since Derczansky's father did not want his son to be different from his classmates, he agreed to send Derczansky to a Talmud-Torah run by the French Jewish community, preferring this more assimilated program to the one conducted in Yiddish at the Orthodox Polish shul.

What Derczansky learned on Thursdays and Sundays was not compelling enough to convince him to embrace Judaism when he decided to turn to religion. Growing up in a Catholic neighborhood, he felt closer to the Christian faith than to his own and seriously considered converting in 1940, during the early days of the Second World War. But as the Germans moved forward and the French army retreated, Derczansky realized he would soon be segregated and discriminated against. If he wanted religion, he had better choose the one observed by his own people.

After the war, Derczansky specialized in the sociology of religion but remained closely tied to the Yiddishists as well. In 1964, he took over the direction of the Yiddish program at the Ecole Nationale des Langues Orientales (known today as L'Institut National des Langues et Civilisations Orientales, or INALCO), a responsibility he shared for a few years with Rachel Ertel, until the latter went to the University of Paris VII. The institute began offering courses in Yiddish for the first time in the 1930s and then again after the Second World War.

For many years now, Derczansky has also held a position at the Centre Nationale de la Recherche Scientifique. In this capacity, he has written monographs on the work of Max Weber, on Judaism and modernity, and on religious texts written in Yiddish. Derczansky has also contributed regularly to a wide range of journals, including the liberal Catholic magazine *Esprit*, and he serves on the editorial committee of *Les Nouveaux cahiers*.

Admired for his extraordinary breadth of knowledge, Derczansky lectures in universities and special programs overseas and throughout the country. Recently, he has also participated in the newly organized Beit Hamidrach at the Alliance Israélite Universelle and has run a seminar on the epistemology of Jewish studies at the Maison des Sciences de l'Homme.

Over the years, Derczansky has taken part in special events organized by the Yiddishists, even though he does not share their enthusiasm for the Bund's "worker intellectuals." According to Derczansky, many of these Bundists were bad workers and bad intellectuals. What is more, they have passed nothing down, because "they lived for the moment, not for eternity."

Derczansky has had a number of students who identify with the generation of 1968, among them, Jean Baumgarten who comes from an Alsatian Jewish family. Since the mid-1980s Baumgarten has held a post at the CNRS as the Yiddishist in Henri Meshonnic's laboratory of scholars involved in the analysis of literary texts.

One of the founding editors of *Traces*, Baumgarten began studying Yiddish seriously in the late 1970s. In the early 1980s, he became the librarian of the Yiddish collection at the Bibliothèque Nationale, a job Itzhok Niborski has subsequently taken over. He also completed a doctoral degree with Rachel Ertel, writing his thesis on a Polish-Jewish shtetl. Since then, Baumgarten has been studying popular Yiddish literature and culture from the Middle Ages to the eighteenth century, in Central and Eastern Europe, working closely with Meschonnic and Derczansky and consulting with Litvine, as well.

In 1987 Verdier published Baumgarten's French translation of the *Ze'enah u-Re'enah,* an exegetical reading in Yiddish of the Five Books of Moses and of the additional biblical texts taken from the Prophets and Haggiographa (Haftarot) that accompany the weekly portions of the Torah read in the synagogue. The volume was prepared in the seventeenth century by Jacob ben Isaac Ashkenazi, an itinerant preacher from a small town near Lublin. A man of the people, Jacob ben Issac wanted the sacred texts to be accessible to women and uneducated men and so he translated them, together with the commentaries, into the language the simple folk could read. Combining "literal exegesis" (*peshat*) with "free interpretation" (*derash*), he used Rashi's commentary on the Torah, among others, but depended most heavily on the Baḥiya, as he wove interpretations and legends together from the various commentaries and the Talmud. Jacob ben Isaac then organized his selections according to the liturgical calendar, so that Jews with no background in Hebrew could still go to synagogue and study the particular portions of the Torah and Haftarah assigned for every week of the year. What made the *Ze'enah u-Re'enah* interesting to Baumgarten and worthy of translation into French was the fascinating choice of commentaries and the way Jacob ben Isaac put the material together, creating, in the process, one of the most popular pieces of Yiddish literature of all times.[18]

Despite this recent work, Baumgarten has not become a practicing Jew. Still, the evolution of his interests in the last few years parallels that of other members of the generation of 1968 who have taken an interest in studying religious texts.

Other Yiddishists have become strictly observant Jews. Kiwa Vaisbrot's son Bernard is one example. So is the Argentinian-born Dvora Kosman.[19] Raised in Buenos Aires, Dvora Kosman's parents came from Poland, where her father had played an active role in the Bund in Lodz. After the Second World War, her parents moved to Argentina and joined the large Yiddish-speaking community in Buenos Aires. As a young girl, Dvora Kosman spoke Yiddish at home and attended a special Bundist school in the afternoon, together with the children of other refugees whose parents were eager to preserve the secular traditions of Eastern European Jews. Among her classmates was Itzhok Niborski.

After high school, Dvora Kosman went to Israel to study and to live on a kibbutz. There, she met and later married her husband, Joseph Kosman, a

Brazilian Jew from a similar background. By the late 1960s the couple had settled in Paris, and Dvora Kosman had begun taking courses in anthropology at the University of Paris VII. Soon, she switched to Yiddish, first at Paris VII, then at INALCO, where she eventually became the assistant of the Polish immigrant Itzhak Varsat-Warschawsky, the successful businessman who donated a great deal of money and time to building up Yiddish culture in France before he moved to Israel in the early 1980s.

In 1973, Dvora and Joseph Kosman became ultra-Orthodox Jews in the Lithuanian tradition. Still, they remained firmly identified with the left and kept many of their radical friends, some of whom made choices similar to theirs a few years later under the influence of Eliahou Abitbol. Committed to fulfilling the Commandments and having a large family—for a while a new baby arrived every two years—Dvora Kosman managed to keep teaching and studying all the same and had plans to write her doctoral thesis on the religious literature composed in Yiddish. Joseph did translations to help support their ever-growing family and gave as much time as he could to studying Talmud with other young Jews like himself who had recently made a teshuvah. In the early 1980s, the Kosmans left Paris for Me'ah Shearim in Jerusalem, where they could be sure their children would receive an Orthodox education.

Lilly Scherr is another Yiddishist who is also a practicing Jew. She, however, does not identify with the extreme Orthodox. As a child during the Second World War, she studied with Pougatch and embraced his more moderate mix of religion and Yiddishism. A teacher of Jewish Studies at INALCO, Lilly Scherr frequently participates in conferences about Jews that take place in France, giving talks on women and Judaism and on Jews in the American cinema.[20]

Other Yiddishists have remained purely secular Jews. In addition to those associated with Le Cercle Gaston Crémieux and L'Association pour l'Etude et la Diffusion de la Culture Yiddish, many have also been influenced by the socialist Zionist organization le Cercle Bernard Lazare and by the prominent socialist Zionist in Paris, Henri Bulawko, a Jew of Polish Jewish origins who was deported from France during the Second World War. Mr. Bulawko served for many years as the president of l'Amicale des Anciens Deportés Juifs de France. According to Luc Rosenzweig, those who have worked with *Traces* owe much to the support they received from Bulwako.

Among the secular Yiddishists, the filmmaker Robert Bober deserves our attention, as well. A contemporary of Marienstras, he has made several films for national television, among them a documentary in 1976 about his visit to Radom in Poland, where his parents were born. In the film he interviews the only Jew who still lives there who knew the city in 1939. With so little left, he then falls back on his imagination and creates a mythic image of life in Radom before the Second World War.[21]

In addition to the cultural Yiddishists, historians of Eastern Europe and political theorists of minority nationalism have also remained active. There is Annette Wieviorka, for example, the former editor-in-chief of *Traces,* who recently published a book about Jews who joined the Communist resistance in France.[22] Important as well is Claudie Weill, who has written extensively on questions concerned with minority nationalism. Then there is Nathan Weinstock, who published in the mid-1980s his three-volume study on the history of the Jewish workers' movement in Europe.[23]

In this context, I draw attention, as well, to the editors of a collection of oral histories of Sephardic and Ashkenazic Jews living in France, mentioned only in passing in chapter three. *Mémoires juives* was compiled by Lucette Valensi and Nathan Wachtel. Valensi is the social historian of North African Jewry who represents the Sephardic community on the National Council of Regional Languages and Cultures, established by Jacques Lang in 1986. Wachtel is a historian of colonial Peru, who decided to turn his attention, at least for a while, to the recent history of his own people, the Ashkenazic Jews.[24]

I end this list of scholars who have campaigned for and written about minority nationalism with Pierre Vidal-Naquet. A highly regarded classicist from an old Sephardic French family, he has enthusiastically supported the efforts of Le Cercle Gaston Crémieux from the beginning. His many acts of solidarity include being among the twelve who signed the original manifesto of the Cercle. He also wrote the preface to Richard Marienstras' *Etre un peuple en Diaspora.* Vidal-Naquet is known, as well, for being one of the most outspoken critics of Robert Faurisson and other revisionists.[25]

Next, let us turn to a group of Jewish intellectuals who have not participated in the activities of Le Cercle Gaston Crémieux or other Yiddishist groups, nor have they written about Eastern European Jews. Nevertheless, they have contributed to the debate about Jews and the nation-state as secular Jews. Although these individuals do not all share the same points of view, they have been concerned with similar questions about Judaism, anti-Semitism, and the state. In different ways, they have each influenced the direction Jewish studies has taken, both through their own work and through the promotion of the works of others. We turn briefly, then, to

Bernard-Henri Lévy, Jacques Tarnero, Pierre Birnbaum, and Blandine Barret-Kriegel.

Of the four, Bernard-Henri Lévy has provoked the most controversy. He arrived on the French intellectual scene in the mid-1970s as one of the "new philosophers," a group of former student radicals who now condemn Marxism with a vengeance (*La Barbarie à visage humain*). As he attacked political ideologies, Bernard-Henri Lévy, like many others, turned to the Old Testament and wrote a book about the meaning of monotheism for the modern world (*Le Teastament de Dieu*). This work, however, revealed his inadequate training in biblical studies and, many felt, a profound lack of judgment. Undaunted by the mixed reviews, Lévy kept writing and produced an equally controversial book on French fascism that challenged the Enlightenment and the ideals of French nationalism (*L'Ideólogie française*).[26]

During these same years Bernard-Henri Lévy became the director of a book series at Grasset, where he has continued to publish some of his own work and those of internationally famous writers—some of whom have made contributions as Jews (for example, Daniel Sibony and Elie Wiesel). A media personality who has enraged many, Bernard-Henri Lévy has nonetheless called attention to some of the same issues that have concerned other members of his generation. What is more, he, like many of his peers, identifies himself as a student of Emmanuel Lévinas.[27]

Jacques Tarnero has a position at the CNRS in philosophy. Together with Nelly Gutman, he ran the Centre d'Etudes et de Recherches sur l'Antisémitisme Contemporain (CERAC) discussed in chapter 2, which finally stopped all activities in 1987 for lack of funds. During that time, he issued reports regularly for CERAC and wrote in *Les Nouveaux cahiers,* where he served and continues to serve on the editorial board during the 1980s.

Pierre Birnbaum teaches sociology at the University of Paris I and has written extensively about the state, as well as about anti-Semitism and the participation of Jews in the politics of the state. Director of a book series at Editions Fayard, he has published some of his own work, most recently *Un Mythe politique: La République juive, de Léon Blum à Mendès France,* and that of historians who write about Jews in France, including translations of books by American scholars (for example, Nancy Green and Paula Hyman).[28]

Blandine Barret-Kriegel, the niece of Annie Kriegel, holds a research position in political science at the CNRS and teaches at the Institut d'Etudes Politiques de Paris. With her husband, the noted journalist Alexandre Adler, Barret-Kriegel has become highly visible in the French intellectual community in the late 1980s. Having written a great deal about the state, she was invited in 1988 to make some introductory remarks at the Colloque des Intellectuels Juifs, whose theme that year was on the relationship of Jews to the state. In 1988 alone, she brought out three separate volumes that treated historical questions relating to the state.[29]

Among those in the generation of 1968 who have played a central role in helping to plan the Colloque des Intellectuels Juifs is Elisabeth de Fontenay, professor of philosophy at the University of Paris I. On her mother's side of the family, she is the descendant of assimilated Russian Jews. Elisabeth de Fontenay has written on Marx and the Jewish question, but she is best known for her work on the eighteenth-century philosopher Denis Diderot, in particular her highly acclaimed book, *Diderot ou le matérialisme enchanté,* and for three plays she created out of the works of Diderot and Michelet.[30] Elisabeth de Fontenay began teaching at the University of Paris I in the late 1960s at the invitation of Vladimir Jankélévitch, with whom she maintained a close working relationship until her sponsor died.

Deeply committed to the principles of the Enlightenment, Elisabeth de Fontenay has participated in a number of Jewish organizations that maintain these values: the Colloque des Intellectuels Juifs, La Fondation du Judaisme, the socialist-Zionist organization Le Cercle Bernard Lazare and, together with Raymond Aron, Henri Atlan, Vladimir Jankélévitch, Adolphe Steg, and the historian Emmanuel Le Roy Ladurie, she was one of the founding members of the Association of Intellectuals and Researchers for Peace in the Middle East.[31] She has also served on the editorial board of *Les Nouveaux cahiers.*

Elisabeth de Fontenay has taught a number of students who have since chosen to work on questions that engage both European philosophy and Jewish thought. Among these are Catherine Chalier, who has gone on to specialize in the work of Lévinas, and Gilles Bernheim, who had Fontenay as a teacher when he was still a student in the lycée.[32]

Today, Bernheim is an ordained rabbi and a researcher in philosophy at the CNRS, where he studies the Talmud within the European philosophical tradition. In addition to his scholarly activities, Bernheim teaches Jewish thought to private groups, and in seminars organized by established Jewish studies programs in Paris. In the mid-1970s, Bernheim began meeting with a group of psychoanalysts who wanted to study the sacred texts. More recently he has been giving classes at the Centre Edmond Fleg, the Centre Rachi, and the Beit Hamidrach of the Alliance Israélite Universelle.

According to Jean-Jacques Wahl, educational director of the Alliance Israelite, one of the early "stars" on the faculty of the Beit Hamidrach is another young philosopher-rabbi, by the name of Marc-Alain Ouaknin.[33] The son of the chief rabbi of Metz, Ouaknin's father came from Morocco and his mother from Alsace. Despite his origin, Ouaknin firmly identifies with the Lithuanian Jewish tradition, the tradition in which he was educated.

Ouaknin started studying Judaism seriously at Chaim Chaikin's yeshiva in Aix-les-Bains. Next, he went to England, where he attended the Yeshiva Getsed and studied with Abraham Gurevitch, who was trained in the Slobodka Musar tradition. Finally, he went to Jerusalem, to the Yeshiva Merkaz Ha-Rav, and studied with Rav Kook, also of the Lithuanian tradition. In addition to his studies in Orthodox yeshivas, Ouaknin spent five years at the Séminaire Israélite de France, where he unenthusiastically endured the training required of all rabbis ordained in France. Graduating in 1980, Ouaknin has since finished a doctorate in philosophy as well.

Even though he is a strictly Orthodox Jew, Marc-Alain Ouaknin works mostly with students who have little background in Jewish studies, at such liberal institutions as the Alliance Israélite and the Centre Rachi. He also gives seminars for neighborhood groups in the sixteenth arrondissement and for the group of psychoanalysts whom he inherited from Gilles Bernheim. Ouaknin teaches the uninitiated, he explains, not because he is looking for converts, but because he wants to study Jewish texts with people trained seriously in the secular philosophic and psychoanalytic traditions. Discouraging naive questions from the floor about Orthodox rituals, Ouaknin offers his students the opportunity to address some of the central problems posed by Jewish thought that bear reflection for those living in the secular world.

Ouaknin says that he learned how to work with students from Gilles Bernheim. His earlier training in Lithuanian-style yeshivas taught him how to read the Five Books of Moses, together with the commentaries, but Bernheim was the one who showed him how to teach this material. Today, Ouaknin presents his students with a mix of classical interpretations of the Talmud and commentaries, together with theories he has developed by combining rabbinic scholarship with the ideas of European philosophy and psychoanalytic theory.

Like other rabbis and teachers who run study groups for people with little or no background, Ouaknin circulates a page from the Talmud, or perhaps from the Kabbalah. He then translates the text, interpreting the passage as he goes along. Aware that he is talking to people who do not have the education they need to discuss the material as peers, Ouaknin still defends his method: "C'est le marketing," he explains. The best way to reach intellectuals is through ideas. Those truly interested in the subject will go on by themselves to gain the skills they lack.

Amid the explosion of interest in Jewish studies, new programs have appeared since the early 1980s, and older ones have expanded throughout the university system in Paris and elsewhere in the country. Today a student can take courses in Yiddish at the University of Paris I, IV, VII, VIII (Vincennes), the Institut National des Langues et Civilisations Orientales (INALCO), and the University of Strasbourg. The Centre d'Etudes Judéo-Américaines at Paris VII is the most developed program at this point, with four levels of instruction. Directed by Rachel Ertel, it also offers seminars concerned with the history and culture of American and Eastern European Jews.

As Jewish studies started growing in France in the early 1980s, programs in Hebrew, Aramaic, Judeo-Spanish (Ladino), and Judeo-Arabic expanded, as well, at INALCO. Then in 1986, René Sirat, former chief rabbi of France, established a special Ecole des Hautes Etudes du Judaïsme at the Institute. A few years earlier the University of Paris IV set up its own Centre d'Etudes Juives and combined forces in 1984 with the Centre Rachi, the Jewish center funded by the Fonds Social Juif Unifié. Now, both the University of Paris I and IV offer undergraduate courses in Hebrew, Yiddish, and Judeo-Spanish, as well as in Jewish thought in conjunction with the Centre Rachi.[34]

Jewish studies in the social sciences have also expanded. Although I have not focused on the role of historians, we should note the important contributions made by such scholars as Bernhard Blumenkranz, Gérard Nahon, Solomon Schwarzfuchs, and Rita Thalmon, who, together with Léon Poliakov, laid the groundwork for studying Jewish history in France. We should also mention the *Revue des études juives,* which has been publishing articles on medieval and early modern French Jewry for decades.[35]

In sociology, Doris Bensimon, Freddy Raphaël, and Dominique Schnapper have made important contributions. By the late 1970s Bensimon-Donath at INALCO had organized a team of students and professors to study the various Jewish communities living in France. Among those who joined her efforts, we might note Martine Cohen, who has done extensive research on the mushrooming of study groups among Jewish and Catholic intellectuals.[36] The anthropologist Laurence Podselver (student of Dominique Schnapper), whom we mentioned briefly in chapter 2, participated in the meetings Bensimon called in the late 1970s, as well, as she prepared to work on a project concerned with Ḥasidim in Paris. More senior scholars (for example, Freddy Raphaël, Dominique Schnapper, Lucette Valensi, and Nathan Wachtel) also endorsed Bensimon's effort and coordinated their work with that of Bensimon and her students.

Finally, in 1981 La Fondation du Judaïsme offered to provide seed money to establish a program at the Ecole des Hautes Etudes en Sciences Sociales. The following year, the school began inviting distinguished foreign scholars like Saül Friedländer and Yosef Hayim Yerushalmi to Paris to offer month-long seminars on problems of Jewish history and sociology. As directeur d'études en sociologie, Dominique Schnapper looked after the program virtually alone, until 1985 when the Ecole hired the historian Nancy Green to help organize the program. Trained at the University of Chicago with the economic historian Arcadius Kahan, Green is the author of a book on Eastern European Jewish immigrants to Paris at the turn of the century.[37]

If we tried to include the programs available in secondary schools, yeshivas, Jewish centers, and in private groups, our list would go on indefinitely. Let us conclude, instead, by recalling the major journals of Jewish studies in France: *Combat pour la Diaspora, Revue des études juives, Yod, Pardès,* and *Les Nouveaux cahiers.* Of all these publications, *Les Nouveaux cahiers,* sponsored by the Alliance Israélite, offers the most complete record of the concerns of Jews of the generation of 1968. And, in the best universalistic tradition of this institution, the journal's editor-in-chief, Gérard Israël, has appointed an editorial committee with representation from many of the groups we have described in these pages. Born in Algeria, Israël has written about Sephardic and Ashkenazic Jews, including a highly praised work of oral history about Jews in France during the German occupation.[38]

Notes

INTRODUCTION

Note to epigraph: Edward W. Said, "Representing the Colonized: Anthropology's Interlocuters," *Critical Inquiry* 15 (Winter 1989), 225.

1. Judith Friedlander, *Being Indian in Hueyapan: A Study of Forced Identity in Contemporary Mexico* (N.Y.: St. Martin's, 1975).

CHAPTER ONE: VILNA ON THE SEINE

Note to epigraph: Richard Burgin, "Isaac Bashevis Singer Talks . . . About Everything," *New York Times Magazine,* November 26, 1978, 32.

1. The history of Lite is complicated. In the fourteenth and fifteenth centuries, it belonged to the Grand Duchy of Lithuania, which itself became part of Poland in 1386, but continued to enjoy political autonomy for nearly three hundred more years. Absorbed by Greater Poland in the middle of the seventeenth century, Lite then became Russian in the late eighteenth, when Poland lost a great deal of territory to the czarist empire. For twenty-two years after the First World War, an independent Republic of Lithuania came into being, but the new nation-state did not even include the grand duchy's old capital: Vilna went to Poland for those few years, then back to Russia during the Second World War. Assuming the Lithuanian form of its name, Vilna became Vilnius, the capital of the Soviet Republic of Lithuania, and the lands of Lite were divided among several republics of the USSR (see maps 1, 2, 3).

2. Laurence Podselver, "Le Mouvement lubavitch: Déracinement et réinsertion des Sépharades," *Pardès,* no. 3 (1986). In this article, Podselver points out that more than three-fourths of the Lubavich Hasidim in Paris are Sephardim (54).

3. According to the demographers Doris Bensimon and Sergio della Pergola, between 1950 and 1969, 220,000 North African Jews moved to France. *La Population juive de France: Socio-démographie et identité* (Paris: CNRS, 1986 [1984]), 36, 311–16 (hereafter cited as *La Population juive*).

Today, Jews of North African origin represent more than 50 percent of the French Jewish population. See references in note 26 of this chapter for the precise breakdown given in *La Population juive,* which is based on the 1980 census. Also, see figures given by Patrick Girard, *Les Juifs de France* (Paris: Index, 1983), 47, based on information gathered in the mid-1970s.

4. See, for example, Dominique Schnapper, *Juifs et Israélites* (Paris: Gallimard, 1980), trans. A. Goldhammer, under the title *Jewish Identities in France: An Analysis of Contemporary French Jewry* (Chicago: University of Chicago Press, 1983) (hereafter cited as *Juifs et Israélites*); and Girard, *Les Juifs de France.*

5. Jean-Paul Sartre, *Réflexions sur la question juive* (Paris: Paul Monihien, 1946; Gallimard, 1954). *Anti-Semite and Jew,* trans. George J. Becker (N.Y.: Schocken, 1948).

6. Schnapper, *Juifs et Israélites,* chap. 2.

7. I use the term *Jewish community* as a popular cultural category, the way the French press does when it talks about those who identify themselves as Jews. I do not mean to suggest that Jews in France have created a political lobby, as certain Jews in the United States have done, or that they all share the same ideals and goals. I do not imply either that the community in France resembles the Jewish *kehillot* that once existed in Eastern Europe.

8. Between 1944 and 1959, 5,000 French Jews emigrated to Palestine/Israel. Then, between 1960 and 1979, the number rose to 33,000 (Bensimon and della Pergola, *La Population juive,* 36).

9. Marek Halter, *Le Fou et les rois* (Paris: Albin Michel, 1976). Trans. Lowell Bair, under the title *The Jester and the Kings* (N.Y.: Arcade, 1989).

10. Halter, *La Mémoire d'Abraham* (Paris: Robert Laffont, 1983). Trans. L. Bair under the title *The Book of Abraham* (N.Y.: Henry Holt, 1986).

11. See, for example, comments made in *Libération,* January 31, 1986, 20.

12. See chapter two for a lengthy discussion of Robert Faurisson and for references.

13. Richard Marienstras, "Les Juifs de la Diaspora ou la vocation minoritaire," *Les Temps modernes* (August–September 1973), 455–91. Repr. R. Marienstras, *Etre un peuple en Diaspora* (Paris: François Maspéro, 1975), 61–112. Marienstras' main work on Shakespeare is *Le Proche et le lointain, sur Shakespeare, le drame élisabéthain, et l'idéologie anglaise aux XVIe et XVIIe siècles* (Paris: Editions de Minuit, 1981). Trans. J. Lloyd, under the title *New Perspectives on the Shakespearean World* (London: Cambridge University Press, 1985).

14. The summary of the Cercle's political positions comes from mimeographed handouts distributed by the group in the 1970s. See chapter three for a more detailed discussion of the Cercle's ideology and activities.

15. The brief sketches of Richard Marienstras and his wife Elise draw on information the Marienstrases shared with me during a formal interview in July 1986 and in several informal conversations over the years.

16. Among Elise Marienstras' works on Native Americans in the United States, she has written, *La Résistance indienne aux Etats-Unis: du XVe au XXe siècle* (Paris: Editions Gallimard-Julliard, 1980). She also wrote *C'est nous, le peuple, les origines du nationalisme américain* (Paris: Editions Gallimard, 1988).

17. Alain Finkielkraut, *Le Juif imaginaire* (Paris: Editions du Seuil, 1980), 51.

18. Eliahou Abitbol went to study with the "black hats," the ultra-Orthodox in Israel, most of whom happen to be of North African origin, but have adopted the Lithuanian Jewish tradition (see Avishai Margalit, "Israel: The Rise of the Ultra-Orthodox," *New York Review of Books* 36 (17): November 9, 1989, 38–44).

Information recorded here about Eliahou Abitbol's personal history comes from an interview he kindly gave me in June 1986. See chapter seven for more details about the rabbi's life and his yeshiva.

19. Jean-Paul Sartre, "L'Espoir, maintenant . . . ," *Le Nouvel observateur,* March 10–16, 1980, 18–19, 56–60; Sartre, "L'Espoir, maintenant . . . (II): Violence et fraternité," *Le Nouvel observateur,* March 17–23, 1980, 52–58; Sartre, "L'Espoir maintenant . . . (III)," *Le Nouvel observateur,* March 24–30, 1980, 55–60; transl. Adrienne Foulke, under the title "The Last Words of Jean-Paul Sartre," *Dissent,* Fall 1980, 397–422. See chapter seven for a lengthy discussion of the life and work of Benny Lévy.

20. Rabbi Hayyim de Volozhyn, *L'Ame de la vie,* trans. Benjamin Gross, (Lagrasse: Verdier, 1986).

21. To date nobody has offered a serious estimate of the number of Jews involved in these study groups. The best work on the subject is qualitative, rather than quantitative. See, for example, two articles by Martine Cohen, "Renouveaux religieux au sein du judaïsme et du catholicisme en France: premières observations," *Pardès,* no. 3 (1986), 132–48; and "Jalons pour une histoire socio-culturelle de la comunauté juive en France depuis 1945," *Yod,* no. 24 (1987), 65–81.

22. See chapter three for a brief sketch of the life and work of Rachel Ertel.

23. Schnapper, *Juifs et Israélites.*

24. Nancy Green, *Pletzl of Paris* (N.Y.: Holmes & Meier, 1985). Trans. Michel Courtois-Fourcy, under the title *Les Travailleurs immigrés juifs à la Belle Epoque* (Paris: Fayard, 1985).

25. See chapters three and seven for brief discussions of the work and life of Shmuel Trigano.

26. Although figures vary in the literature, at times approaching 700,000, scholars usually put the number of Jews living in France in the 1980s at around 535,000, accepting the conclusions reached by Bensimon and della Pergola on the basis of their work with the 1980 census (*La Population juive,* 35). By 1989, however, articles in popular magazines and newspapers were estimating that there were 600,000 Jews in the country, out of a general population of 56,000,000 people. *L'Express,* January 20–26, 1989, 58; and the *New York Times,* May 3, 1989, A3.

Bensimon and della Pergola confirm the impression commonly held that, of those born after 1905, the two main groups of Jews living in France in the 1980s were either born there or came from North Africa (Bensimon and della Pergola, *La Population juive,* 93, 107). In the Paris region alone, 53.9 percent of these Jews were of North African origin (ibid., 46).

Demographers estimate that, on the eve of the Second World War, there were anywhere from 250,000 to 320,000 Jews in France (ibid., 32), two thirds of whom were resident foreigners or refugees trying to escape persecution in Central and Eastern European countries (33). During the 1930s, there were about 150,000 Jews in the Paris region, 90,000 of whom were from Eastern Europe: 45,000 Poles (Vilna was a Polish city in this period [see map 3]), 16,000 Russians, 12,000 Hungarians, 11,000 Romanians, and 1,700 Lithuanians and Latvians (David Weinberg, *Les Juifs de Paris de 1933 à 1939,* trans. Micheline Pouteau (Paris: Calmann-Lévy, 1974), 20. (The American edition appeared later, Weinberg, *A Community on Trial: The Jews of Paris* in the 1930's (Chicago: University of Chicago Press, 1977).

Today, Jews who were born in Eastern Europe represent only 10 percent of the Jewish population in the Paris region and less elsewhere. However, 37.4 percent of French Jewish heads of household in the Paris region have at least one parent who is of Eastern European origin (Bensimon and della Pergola, *La Population juive,* 45).

CHAPTER TWO: REMEMBERING THE PAST IN THE PRESENT

Note to epigraph: Philippe Ganier Raymond's interview with Louis Darquier de Pellepoix, "L'Express Document," *L'Express,* October 28–November 4, 1978, 167 (hereafter cited as *L'Express* interview).

1. Philippe Ganier Raymond, *Une Certaine France* (Paris: Balland, 1975). A few days after the book appeared in bookstores, it temporarily disappeared by court order. When it came back on sale, fourteen pages had been excised. The censured material included compromising statements by the novelist Louis Ferdinand Céline.

2. *L'Express* interview, 167, 173.

3. Robert Faurisson, "'Le Problème des chambres à gaz' ou 'la rumeur d'Auschwitz,'" *Le Monde,* December 29, 1978, 8.

4. The mole is an allusion to an allusion to an allusion. Shakespeare used the image first in the ghost scene in Hamlet. Then Hegel borrowed it and Marx took the idea from Hegel, creating his now famous phrase: "Our old friend, our old mole, who knows how to work so well beneath the earth in order to appear unexpectedly as the Revolution."

The version of the quotation given here is a translation of what appears in books published by La Vieille Taupe.

5. Nadine Fresco, "Parcours du ressentiment," *Lignes,* no. 2 (February 1988), 38–40 (hereafter cited as "Parcours du ressentiment"). See also Fresco's earlier article on the revisionists in France: "Les Redresseurs de morts," *Les Temps modernes,* no. 407 (June 1980) 2150–2211. "The Denial of the Dead: On the Faurisson Affair," *Dissent,* Fall 1981, 467–83 (abridged version of the French).

6. Robert Faurisson, *Mémoire en défense* (Paris: La Vieille Taupe, 1980). In English, see Robert Faurisson, *Holocaust Debate: Revisionist Historians versus Six Million Jews* (Brooklyn, N.Y.: Revisionist Press, 1980); and *Is the Diary of Ann Frank Genuine?* (Torrence, Calif.: Institute for Historical Review, 1985).

7. Nicole Bernheim, "'Le Débat intellectuel français est marqué par le goût de l'irrationnel et le mépris pour les faits,' nous déclare M. Noam Chomsky," *Le Monde,* December 24, 1980, 10.

8. Serge Thion, *Des Courtisans aux partisans: Essai sur la crise cambodgienne* (Paris: Gallimard, 1971).

9. Serge Thion, *Vérité historique ou vérité politique* (Paris: La Vieille Taupe, 1980).

10. Fresco, "Parcours du ressentiment," 63.

11. Jean-Paul Cruse, "Chambres à gaz: zones d'ombre autour d'une thèse," *Libération,* July 31, 1986, 11.

12. In a lame attempt to include a specialist in the field, somebody added the name of an assistant professor of German history to the list of those who had judged

the thesis, identifying Thierry Buron as a "consultant." Known for siding with the extreme right, Buron was actually out of town on the day the defense took place (ibid., 10).

13. Philippe Bernard, "Un An après la soutenance de thèse de M. Roques: L'Université de Nantes sous le choc," *Le Monde,* July 2, 1986, 9.

14. Henri Roques, *Faut-il brûler Henri Roques?* (Paris: Ogmios, 1986). See Fresco, "Parcours du ressentiment," 66ff. for discussion of the book.

15. *Libération,* January 7, 1988. See chapter seven for a brief history of this highly influential daily newspaper, which represents the views of people on the left.

16. For Emmanuel Lévinas, see, for example: *En découvrant l'existence, avec Husserl et Heidegger* (Paris: Vrin, 1949), trans. A. Lingis, under the title *Existence and Existents* (The Hague: Nijhoff, 1978); *Totalité et Infini: Essai sur l'extériorité* (La Haye, M. Nijhoff, 1961), trans. A. Lingis, under the title *Totality and Infinity: An Essay on Exteriority* (Pittsburgh: Dusquesne University Press, 1979); *Ethique et Infini* (Paris: Artheme Fayard et Radio France, 1982), trans. Richard A. Cohen, under the title *Ethics and Infinity: Conversations with Philippe Nemo* (Pittsburgh: Dusquesne University Press, 1985); *Emmanuel Lévinas, qui êtes-vous,* avec François Poirié (Paris: La Manufacture, 1987).

For Jacques Derrida, see, for example: "Violence et métaphysique, essai sur la pensée d'Emmanuel Lévinas," *Revue de métaphysique et de morale,* nos. 3 and 4 (1964); repr. *L'Ecriture et la différence* (Paris: Editions du Seuil, 1967), 117–228, trans. A. Bass, under the title *Writing and Difference* (Chicago: University of Chicago Press, 1978); and *De l'Esprit, Heidegger et la question* (Paris: Galilee, 1987).

17. Victor Farias, *Heidegger et le Nazisme,* trans. M. Benarroch and J-B. Grasset (Lagrasse: Verdier, 1987); In English, under the title *Heidegger and Nazism,* trans. J. Margolis and T. Rockmore (Philadelphia: Temple University Press, 1989).

18. Elisabeth de Fontenay, "Fribourg-Prague-Paris, comme l'être, la détresse se dit de multiples manières," *Le Messager Européen,* no. 1 (1987), 75–122; and "'Quant à son essence la même chose,' écrit Heidegger," *Le Messager Européen,* no. 2 (1988), 159–78.

19. During the same period, a scandal broke out in the United States concerning the late Paul de Man, professor of comparative literature at Yale University. See Jacques Derrida, "Like the Sound of the Sea Deep within a Shell: Paul de Man's War," trans. Peggy Kamuf, *Critical Inquiry* 14, no. 3 (Spring 1988), 590–652; James Atlas, "The Case of Paul de Man," the *New York Times Magazine,* August 28, 1988, 36ff.; W. Hamacher, N. Hertz, and T. Keenan, eds., *Wartime Journalism, 1939–1943, by Paul de Man* (Lincoln: University of Nebraska Press, 1989); W. Hamacher, et. al., eds., *Responses: On Paul de Man's Wartime Journalism* (Lincoln: University of Nebraska Press, 1989).

20. Jacques Givet, "Jacques Vergès, avocat de Klaus Barbie," in *Archives d'un procès, Klaus Barbie,* ed. Bernard-Henri Lévy (Paris: Le Livre de Poche, 1986), 183–88 (hereafter cited as *Archives d'un procès*).

21. During the trial the press reported that many feared Vergès would implicate French collaborators. It also described how Vergès attacked Israel's treatment of Palestinians. Richard Bernstein, "'Crimes' by Israel are cited by Barbie's Lawyers," the *New York Times* (hereafter referred to as *N.Y. Times*), July 2, 1987, A3; Richard

Bernstein, "French Court Finds Barbie Guilty and Orders Him to Prison for Life," *N.Y. Times,* July 4, 1987, A1, A3. In addition to newspaper stories covering the trial, published in the United States and France, see Lévy, *Archives d'un procès;* Marcel Ophuls' film *Hôtel Terminus,* 1988; and Alain Finkielkraut's *La Mémoire vaine* (Paris: Gallimard, 1989).

22. James M. Markham, "Fugitive Nazi Collaborator Seized from a Catholic Priory in France," *N.Y. Times,* May 25, 1989, A1, A13.

23. Bruno Frappat, "M. Le Pen et l' 'effet détail,'" *Le Monde,* September 16, 1987, 1, 8.

24. The following spring, Le Pen won over fourteen percent of the votes in the first round, dividing the right and gaining the support of people who had voted Communist in previous elections (James Markham, "Mitterand Far Ahead in Round 1; Chirac is Second as Le Pen Gains," *N.Y. Times,* April 25, 1988, A1, A9). In the second round, however, he took a sound beating in the legislative elections. The results challenged those who associated his earlier success with a dangerous rise of xenophobic and racist sentiments in the country. Since then, Le Pen has continued making inflammatory remarks, like the pun he coined in 1989, referring to the politician Durafour as "Durafour Crématoire." In French "four" means oven, and the crematoria were called "fours crématoires."

25. Claude Lanzmann, *Shoah,* 1985. See also the book version of the interviews by the same title (Paris: Fayard, 1985). In English, under the title *Shoah: An Oral History of the Holocaust* (N.Y.: Pantheon, 1985).

26. Rachel Ertel, "Les Juifs d'Europe orientale en France," *Les Langues d'origine étrangère,* vol. 2 of *Par les langues de France,* ed. Gilles Verbunt (Paris: Editions du Centre Georges Pompidou, 1985), 88.

27. Michael Marrus and Robert Paxton, *Vichy France and the Jews* (N.Y.: Basic Books, 1981), 344, trans. M. Delmotte, under the title *Vichy et les Juifs* (Paris: Calmann-Lévy, 1981).

28. Serge Klarsfeld, *Le Mémorial de la déportation des Juifs de France* (Paris: Centre de Documentation Juive Contemporaine de Paris, 1979), transl. under the title *Memorial to the Jews Deported from France, 1942–1944* (N.Y.: Beate Klarsfeld Foundation, 1983). The pages are not numbered. Look for "Tableau des Nationalités des Déportés de France, III," presented on the page before "Convoi No. 1."

29. Maurice Rajsfus, *Des Juifs dans la Collaboration, l'U.G.I.F., 1941–1944* (Paris: Etudes et Documentation Internationale, 1980).

30. Yerachmiel (Richard) Cohen, "The Jewish Community of France in the Face of Vichy-German Persecution, 1940–1944," *The Jews of Modern France,* ed. F. Malino and B. Wasserstein (Hanover: Brandeis University Press, 1985), 181–204.

31. Jacques Adler, *The Jews of Paris and the Final Solution: Communal Response and Internal Conflicts, 1944–1944* (New York: Oxford University Press, 1987), 161, transl. under the title *Face à la persécution: les organisations juives à Paris de 1940–1944,* abridged ed. (Paris: Calmann-Lévy, 1985) (hereafter cited as *The Jews of Paris*).

32. In addition to Mosco's television film *Des Terroristes à la retraite* (Antenne 2, July 2, 1985), see Philippe Robrieux, *L'Affaire Manouchian: Vie et mort d'un héros communiste* (Paris: Fayard, 1986). In English, see Jane Kramer, "The Groupe Manouchian," in *Europeans* (New York: Farrar, Straus and Giroux, 1988), 345–53.

33. "La Recrudescence des actions antisémites en France depuis 1975," *Le Monde,* October 7, 1980, 11.

34. Claude Bonjean and Daniele Molho, "Les Erreurs et les blessures," *Le Point,* October 13–19, 1980, 65. This group grew out of a Zionist organization called Comité Juif d'Action, which had been founded in 1973, and it maintained close ties to the Jewish Agency. See Phyllis Albert, "French Jewry and the Centrality of Israel: The Public Debate," *From Ancient Israel to Modern Judaism:* Intellect in Quest of Understanding, vol. 4, ed. Ernest Frerichs and Jacob Neusner (Providence: Brown Judaic Studies Series, 1989), 214.

35. See, for example, Frank Prial, "Younger French Jews Are Assuming Militant Stance," *N.Y. Times,* April 29, 1980, A3, and "Thousands in Paris March to Protest Temple Bombing," *N.Y. Times,* October 8, 1980, A1, A3. A front page photo accompanies the second article, and it shows demonstrators marching behind a huge Renouveau Juif banner.

36. "Thousands in Paris March," *N.Y. Times,* October 8, 1980.

37. In 1986 Paris endured a new rash of bombings. Although some of the sites attacked belonged to Jews, this time France, not just French Jews, was the target, and the aggressors were pro-Iranian terrorists, for the most part, attacking the French government for siding with Iraq in the Iranian-Iraqi war, and not Palestinians lashing out against the so-called world Zionist conspiracy. See Annette Lévy-Willard, "Copernic, Goldenberg, Tati, Point Show . . ." *Libération,* May 2, 1989, 7.

38. Luc Rosenzweig, personal communication, 1986.

39. Handout distributed by CERAC.

40. André Wormser, "Comment la France 'ratifia' la Déclaration Balfour," *La Tribune juive,* January 29–February 4, 1988, 16–18. Unless otherwise noted, information about the Wormser family comes from personal interviews with André Wormser, 1979–89.

41. Adler, *The Jews of Paris,* 157.

42. André Wormser, quoted in interview by Léa Marcou, "Le Nouvel antisémitisme," *La Tribune juive,* June 29–July 5, 1979, 20 (hereafter cited as "Le Nouvel antisémitisme").

43. Among the many articles that appeared on the subject, see those in *France soir,* March 28, 1979, 3; *Le Monde,* March 29, 1979, 6; *La Tribune juive,* March 30–April 4, 1979, 11.

44. *France soir,* March 28, 1979, 3.

45. *La Tribune juive,* March 30–April 4, 1979, 11.

46. See, for example, "L'Attentat de la rue de Médicis à Paris," *Le Monde,* March 29, 1979, 6; Jean Daniel's editorial, "Le Sang, rue de Médicis," *Le Nouvel observateur,* April 2–8, 1979, 30; and the articles in *La Tribune juive,* April 6–12, 1979, 14ff., where there is also a brief historical sketch of the student restaurant.

47. Wormser, "Le Nouvel antisémitisme," 21.

48. Jean-Marie Pontaut, et al., "L'Attentat de la rue Copernic, plusieurs pistes pour le terrorisme noir," *Le Point,* October 13–19, 1980, 59.

49. See, for example, articles in *France soir,* October 4, 1980, 1ff.

50. "Une Mise au point de l'hôtel Matignon à propos d'une déclaration du premier ministre," *Le Monde,* October 7, 1980.

51. "M. Bonnet: l'oeuvre d'un petit groupe," *Le Monde,* September 30, 1980, 16.

52. Philippe Boggio, "La Polémique sur le rôle de la police," *Le Monde,* October 7, 1980.

53. "Les Manifestations de protestation s'amplifient," *Le Monde,* October 7, 1980.

54. "Thousands in Paris March to Protest Temple Bombing," *N.Y. Times,* October 7, 1980, A1, A3.

55. "L'Attentat de la rue Copernic," *France soir,* October 4, 1980, 3.

56. See articles in *Le Monde,* October 7, 1980, 12 and October 8, 1980, 13.

57. See articles cited in note 56 and those on the following day too.

58. Jacques Tarnero, "Un Eté 82: la communauté juive de France et son environnement politique et culturel" *Les Nouveaux cahiers,* no. 72 (Spring 1983), 15 (hereafter cited as "Un Eté 82").

59. Nelly Gutman and Jacques Tarnero, "Trois ans après Copernic—un an après la rue des Rosiers—l'antisémitisme en France—le point autonne 1983," pamphlet distributed by CERAC (Centre d'Etudes et de Recherches sur l'Antisémitisme Contemporain), 3.

60. See, for example, John Vinocur, "Six Killed in Attack on Jews in Paris," *N.Y. Times,* August 10, 1982, A1, A6; Flora Lewis, "France Takes a Firmer Hand with Terrorism," *N.Y. Times,* August 22, 1982, E3 (hereafter cited as "France Takes a Firmer Hand"); Bernard-Henri Lévy, "La Bête est revenue" and "Juifs et chrétiens, même combat," *Questions de principe* (Paris: Editions Denoël), 351–62.

61. Lévy, *Questions de principe,* 350–60.

62. Tarnero, "Un Eté 82," 15.

63. See, for example, Lewis, "France Takes a Firmer Hand" and the review article in *Libération,* May 2, 1989, 7. According to André Wormser, CERAC and others always knew that Palestinian factions had done the shooting in the rue des Rosiers massacre. Members of Action Directe, however, were involved in the plot, as well, for they provided housing and the necessary network for passing the arms along. Palestinians were also responsible for the bombing, on the rue Copernic, he claimed. Although unable to prove it conclusively, CERAC was fairly sure that Carlos, a Latin American terrorist with ties to the PLO, was responsible for the bombing at the rue de Médicis (personal communication, 1989).

64. See, for example, the heated controversy published in *Les Temps modernes,* October and November 1982.

65. Among the organizations that have played, and in some cases continue to play, an important role, let us note the following: L'Association des Intellectuels et Chercheurs pour la Paix au Moyen Orient; socialist Zionist groups like Le Cercle Bernard Lazare and L'Union Juive Internationale pour la Paix. In May 1989, for example, when many in the Jewish community vehemently opposed François Mitterand's decision to invite Yasir Arafat to France, groups such as these supported the President's initiative (*Libération,* May 2, 1989, 6 and *N.Y. Times,* April 30, 1989, 13).

66. J. Louis Péninou, "L'Assassinat de Pierre Goldman," *Libération,* September 21, 1979, 3.

67. Laurent Greilsamer et Bertrand Le Gendre, "Juif, militant, gangster, écrivain," *Le Monde,* September 22, 1979, 12 (hereafter cited as "Juif, militant").

68. Unless otherwise noted, the following summary of Pierre Goldman's life comes from his memoirs, *Souvenirs obscurs d'un Juif polonais né en France* (Paris: Editions du Seuil, 1975), trans. J. Pinkham, under the title *Dim Memories of a Polish Jew Born in France* (N.Y.: Viking, 1977) (hereafter cited as *Souvenirs obscurs*).

69. *Ibid.*, 33. English, 7.

70. *Ibid.*, 56. English, 28.

71. Greilsamer and Le Gendre, "Juif, militant."

72. Pierre Goldman, *L'Ordinaire mésaventure d'Archibald Rappaport* (Paris: Julliard, 1977).

73. "Entretien avec Pierre Goldman (October 1977)," reprinted in *Rouge,* September 28–October 4, 1979, 11.

74. Goldman, *Souvenirs obscurs,* 62.

75. Catherine Chaine, "Une Interview inédite: Goldman l'étranger," *Le Monde,* September 30, 1979.

76. Laurence Podselver, personal letter, October 1979.

77. Luc Rosenzweig, "Kaddish pour Pierre," *Libération,* September 21, 1979, 4.

78. Luc Rosenzweig et Bernard Cohen, *Le Mystère Waldheim* (Paris: Editions Gallimard, 1986), trans. Josephine Bacon, under the title *Waldheim* (N.Y.: Adama, 1987).

79. Daniel Lindenberg, quoted in an interview conducted by Jacques Tarnero, "Dérapage de la gauche?" *Les Nouveaux cahiers,* no. 71 (Winter 1982–83), 19.

The Occitans are speakers of the Provençal language Oc. They, like the Bretons and the Corsicans, became active cultural nationalists in the late sixties and early seventies.

CHAPTER THREE: THE RIGHT TO BE DIFFERENT

Note to epigraph: Richard Marienstras, "Les Juifs de la Diaspora ou la vocation minoritaire," *Les Temps modernes* (August-September 1973) reprinted in Richard Marienstras, *Etre un peuple en Diaspora* (Paris: François Maspéro, 1975), 72 (hereafter this article will be cited as "La Vocation minoritaire"; when referring to other articles in this volume, I cite as *Etre un peuple,* frequently mentioning only the book and appropriate page numbers).

1. "Le Manifeste," flier circulated by Le Cercle Gaston Crémieux and published in several journals (personal communication, Richard Marienstras).

The founding members of Le Cercle Gaston Crémieux are Joseph Huppert, E. Isotti-Rosowsky, Claude Lanzmann, Philippe Lazar, Jacques Lebar, Richard Marienstras, Léon Poliakov, Oscar Rosowsky, Bernard Sarel, Rita Thalman, Pierre Vidal-Naquet, Raphael Visocékas.

2. Mimeographed sheet distributed by Le Cercle Gaston Crémieux in the 1970s.

3. Marienstras, "La Vocation minoritaire," 72.

4. Mimeographed sheet distributed by Le Cercle Gaston Crémieux in the 1970s.

5. Marienstras, "Les Grandes lignes d'une politique culturelle de la Diaspora," *Etre un peuple,* 201.

6. Albert Memmi, *Portrait d'un Juif* (Paris: Gallimard, 1962), trans. Elisabeth Abbott under the title *Portrait of a Jew* (N.Y.: Viking, 1971); *La Libération du Juif* (Paris: Gallimard, 1966), trans. J. Hyun under the title *The Liberation of the Jew* (N.Y.: Orion, 1966). See also Marienstras' article, "Albert Memmi et 'La Libération du Juif,'" reprinted in *Etre un peuple*, 144–70.

7. Albert Memmi, comments made during a round-table debate on Jewish identity at "Les Journées de la culture yiddish," Le Centre Georges Pompidou, Paris, November 23, 1978.

8. Shmuel Trigano, *La Nouvelle question juive, l'avenir d'un espoir* (Paris: Gallimard, 1979) and *La République et les Juifs après Copernic* (Paris: Les Presses d'Aujourd'hui, 1982) (hereafter cited as *La République et les Juifs*).

9. Aḥad Ha-Am (Asher Ginzburg) was born in the Ukraine in 1856 and died in Palestine in 1929. See Lucy Dawidowicz, *The Golden Tradition: Jewish Life and Thought in Eastern Europe* (Boston: Beacon, 1967) (hereafter cited as *The Golden Tradition*) and *Selected Essays by Aḥad Ha-Am*, trans. Leon Simon (Philadelphia: Jewish Publication Society of America, 1912).

Simon Dubnow was born in Byelorussia in 1860. Committed to life in the Diaspora, even after the rise of National Socialism, the historian chose to remain in Europe. The Nazis caught up with him in Latvia in 1941 and murdered him in Riga, during a routine roundup of old and sick Jews. See Lucy Dawidowicz, *The Golden Tradition*; Aaron Steinberg, ed., *Simon Dubnow: The Man and His Work* (Paris: French Section of the World Jewish Congress, 1963), especially Sophie Erlich-Dubnov's biographical sketch of her father, 1–25; Simon Dubnow, *Nationalism and History: Essays on Old and New Judaism*, ed. K. S. Pinson (N.Y.: Atheneum: 1970); and references made below in chap. 4, note 4, and chap. 5, note 83.

For a comparison of the two, see Josef Fraenkel, *Dubnow, Herzl and Aḥad Ha-Am* (London: Ararat Publications Society, 1963).

10. Arnold Toynbee, *The World after the Peace Conference: Being an Epilogue to the History of the Peace Conference to Paris and a Prologue to the Survey of International Affairs, 1920–23* (London: Oxford University Press, 1926), 4–5.

11. Jean-Jacques Rousseau, *Treatise on the Government of Poland*, chap. 4, "Education," excerpted in *Emile, Julie and Other Writings* (Woodbury, N.Y.: Barron's Educational Series, 1964), 65.

12. Count Stanislas de Clermont-Tonnerre, cited in Léon Poliakov, *Histoire de l'antisémitisme* (Paris: Calmann-Lévy, 1968), vol. 3, *De Voltaire à Wagner*, 234, note 2, trans. under the title *The History of Anti-Semitism* (N.Y.: Vanguard, 1975), vol. 3, *From Voltaire to Wagner* (henceforth cited as *Histoire de l'antisémitisme*, vol. 3).

In recent years, the literature on the subject has grown a great deal, much of it focusing on another friend of the Jews, the Abbé Grégoire. See, for example, Shmuel Trigano, *La République et les Juifs;* and Pierre Birnbaum, "Sur l'étatisation révolutionnaire: L'Abbé Grégoire et le destin de l'identité juive," *Le Débat,* no. 53, Jan.–Feb., 1989, 157–73.

Then, in honor of the bicentennial, several new books have appeared in 1989, among them, Patrick Girard, *La Révolution française et les Juifs* (Paris: Robert Laffont, 1989), and Robert Badinter, *Libres et Egaux . . . L'Emancipation des Juifs* (Paris: Fayard, 1989). See conclusion for more references.

13. Poliakov, *Histoire de l'antisémitisme,* vol. 3, 235.

14. For excellent discussions of the Bund, see, H. J. Tobias, *The Jewish Bund in Russia from Its Origins to 1905* (Stanford: Stanford University Press, 1972); Jonathan Frankel, *Prophecy and Politics* (Cambridge: Cambridge University Press, 1981); Rachel Ertel, *Le Shtetl* (Paris: Payot, 1982); Nathan Weinstock, *Le Pain de misère: histoire du movement ouvrier juif en Europe,* 3 vols. (Paris: Editions la Découverte, 1984, 1986).

15. For a fascinating account of YIVO in Vilna on the eve of the war, see Lucy S. Dawidowicz, *From That Place and Time* (New York: W. W. Norton, 1989).

The *New York Times* reports that hundreds of thousands of publications belonging to YIVO have just been identified in warehouses in Vilnius. Some of the material will be duplicated and the copies sent to New York, but most of the documents will remain in Lithuania and become part of a Jewish museum that the city of Vilnius is talking about establishing in the near future. Richard Shepard, "Rejoining the Chapters of Yiddish Life's Story," *New York Times,* August 30, 1989, C15, C21.

16. See, for example, J. L. Cahan, ed., *Jewish Folklore,* Philological Series, vol. 5 (Vilna: Publication of the Yiddish Scientific Institute, 1938); and *YIVO's Bibliographical Listings for 1925–1941* (N.Y.: YIVO, 1943).

17. S. Ansky, *The Dybbuk,* trans. H. Alsberg and W. Katzin (N.Y.: Liveright, 1971 [1926]). See also Joseph C. Landis' introduction to the play in *The Great Jewish Plays,* ed. and trans. J. C. Landis (N.Y.: Bard, 1980 [1966]).

18. Benjamin Harshav, *The Meaning of Yiddish* (Berkeley: University of California Press, 1990).

In 1989, Yiddishists in Paris published a French translation of two volumes of the modernist Yiddish journal *Khaliastra* (The Band), which had originally appeared in Warsaw and Paris during the interwar years: Rachel Ertel, ed. *Khaliastra: Revue littéraire, Varsovie 1922, Paris 1924* (Paris: Lachenal et Ritter, 1989).

19. Harold W. V. Temperly, *A History of the Peace Conference of Paris* (London: Henry Frownde & Holder & Stoughton, 1921), vol. 5, *Economic Reconstruction and Protection of Minorities,* 134–35 (henceforth cited as *Peace Conference of Paris,* vol. 5).

20. Ibid., 136.

21. Woodrow Wilson, *The Hope of the World: Messages and Addresses by the President, July 10, 1919–December 9, 1919* (N.Y.: Harper and Brothers, 1920), 76.

22. Temperly, *Peace Conference of Paris,* 141–42.

23. See, for example, Celia Heller, *On the Edge of Destruction: Jews in Poland between the Two World Wars* (N.Y.: Columbia University Press, 1977) and Ertel, *Le Shtetl.*

24. Marienstras, *Etre un peuple,* 154.

25. F. M. Barnard, "National Culture and Political Legitimacy: Herder and Rousseau," *Journal of the History of Ideas* 44, 2 (April–June 1983): 251.

26. François Mitterand, cited by Henri Giordan, *Démocratie culturelle et droit à la différence* (Paris: Collection des rapports officiels, La Documentation Française, 1982), 7.

27. Ibid., 19.

28. Giles Verbunt, ed., *Par les langues de France,* vol. 2, *Les Langues d'origine étrangère* (Paris: Edition du Centre Georges Pompidou, 1985).

29. Rachel Ertel, personal communication, 1986.

30. Among other works, Lucette Valensi has published *Juifs en terre d'Islam: Les Communautés de Djerba,* with Abraham Udovich (Paris: Editions de archives, 1984), trans. under the title *The Last of Arab Jews: The Communities of Jerba* (N.Y.: Harwood Academic Press, 1984); and *Mémoires juives* with Nathan Wachtel (Paris: Collection Archives, 1986).

31. The festivals took place at la place du marché Sainte Catherine in 1983 and 1984 and at le marché du Temple in 1985 and 1986 (Itzhok Niborski, personal communication, 1986). I attended the fair in 1986.

32. Henri Minczeles, personal communication, 1986.

33. Jacques Hassoun, personal communication, 1988.

34. Jacques Hassoun, "Mon cher hakham Schleymen Adler," *Combat pour la Diaspora,* no. 13, 1983, 12 (hereafter cited as *Combat*).

35. Haïm Vidal Sephiha, "Vie et mort des Judéo-Espagnols," *Les Temps modernes,* numéro spécial, *Le Second Israël,* May 1979, 123. Sephiha has written a number of major works on the Judeo-Spanish culture and history, including *L'Agonie des Judéo-Espagnols* (Paris: Editions Entente, 1977).

36. Shmuel Trigano, "Les Fenêtres du temple," *Les Temps modernes,* May 1979, 473–74, n. 14.

37. Jacques Hassoun, personal communication, 1988.

38. "Israël, le Liban, et les Juifs de France," *Traces,* no. 5, Fall 1982, 23.

39. Luc Rosenzweig, ed., *Catalogue pour des Juifs de maintenant, Recherches,* no. 38, September 1979 (hereafter cited as *Catalogue*).

40. Luc Rosenzweig, *La Jeune France juive: Conversations avec des Juifs d'aujourd'hui* (Paris: Editions Libres-Hallier, 1980). Edouard Drumont, *La France juive: Essai d'histoire contemporaine* (Paris: C. Marpon & E. Flammarion, 1886).

41. Unless otherwise noted, the sketch of Wladimir Rabi is based on an interview I conducted with his sister, Sonia Rabinowitch Grinberg, in 1979.

42. Wladimir Rabi, *Anatomie du judaïsme français* (Paris: Les Editions de Minuit, 1962) and *Un Peuple de trop sur la terre* (Paris: Les Presses d'aujourd'hui, 1979). Rabi also published the highly regarded *L'Homme qui est entré dans la loi: Pierre Goldman* (Grenoble: Editions de la pensée sauvage, 1976).

43. Ibid., "Z comme Zede," in Rosenzweig, *Catalogue,* 24 n.

44. See obituary note by Luc Rosenzweig in *Traces,* no. 1, 1981, 113.

45. See French translation of Zalcman's memoirs, *Histoire véridique de Moshé: ouvrier juif et communiste au temps de Staline,* trans. Halina Edelstein (Paris: Encres-Recherches, 1977).

46. Luc Rosenzweig, personal communication, 1989.

47. In addition to Dajez and Rosenzweig, the other editors were Philippe Gumplowicz, Youval Micenmacher, and Isy Morgensztern. At the time they were involved in this endeavor, Morgensztern was also an active member of Le Cercle Gaston Crémieux.

48. Nat Lilenstein's *Les Révolutionnaires du Yiddishland* appeared on Antenne 2 in three sections, on March 4, 11, and 18, 1984.

49. Ertel, *Le Shtetl.*

50. Menuha Ram, *Le Vent qui passe,* trans. Rachel Ertel (Paris: Julliard, 1974).

The historical sketch that follows comes from interviews I had with Rachel Ertel over a ten-year period, from 1974–89, during which time she also helped me to understand a great deal about Yiddish culture and the Yiddishists in France. For a brief period of time, I also studied Yiddish with Madame Waldman (Menuha Ram), at the University of Paris VII.

51. Ertel, *Le Shtetl,* dedication page.

52. Ertel, *Le Roman juif américain* (Paris: Payot, 1980).

53. Abraham Sutzkever, *Où gîtent les étoiles: Oeuvres en vers et en prose,* trans. Charles Dobzynski, Rachel Ertel, et le collectif de traducteurs de l'Université de Paris-VII (Paris: Editions du Seuil, 1988). Among the ten translations Ertel has published in the 1980s, there are two works by Moshe Kulbak, another famous writer of Vilna (*Lundi* and *Les Zélminiens*).

54. Michael Löwy, *Rédemption et utopie* (Paris: PUF, 1988), 58–59. Among other publications, Löwy has collaborated on a book concerned with minority nationalism: Georges Haupt, Michael Löwy, et Claudie Weill, *Les Marxistes et la question nationale* (*Paris: Maspéro, 1974*).

CHAPTER FOUR: THE EUROPEAN ENLIGHTENMENT IN YIDDISH TRANSLATION

1. Unless otherwise noted, the biographical information presented in this chapter comes from personal interviews conducted with Mordecai Litvine between 1979 and 1989. My discussions with Litvine over the years have been invaluable, and I am deeply grateful to him and to Bella Chefkej for their warm hospitality.

2. For excellent brief sketches of the Gaon of Vilna, Chaim of Volozhin, and the Soloveichik family, see C. Roth and G. Wigoder, eds., *Encyclopaedia Judaica* (Jerusalem: Keter, 1971). The encyclopedia's genealogical chart of the Soloveichiks only traces the lines of male members of the family. Since Litvine is related to this distinguished lineage through his maternal grandmother, his branch of the family disappears from the chart in his grandmother's generation. His great uncles, however, are there (vol. 15, 127–28), two of whom figure in Litvine's telling of his family's history (Joseph Baer and Chaim-Simḥah). With the exception of the name *Chaim,* all other names follow the *Encyclopaedia Judaica's* spelling. For Joseph Baer Soloveichik, see Hillel Goldberg, *Between Berlin and Slobodka* (Hoboken, N.J.: Ktav, 1989), chap. 5.

For additional information on the Gaon of Vilna and Chaim of Volozhin, see the work of Emmanuel Lévinas, "'A l'image de Dieu' d'après Rabbi Haïm Voloziner," in *L'Au-delà du verset: Lectures et discours talmudiques* (Paris: Les Editions de Minuit, 1982), 182–200; "De la Prière sans demande," *Les Etudes philosophiques,* no. 2, 1984, 157–63; "Judaïsme et Kenose," *Archivo di filosofia,* no. 2–3, 1985, 13–28; and Rabbi Hayyim de Volozhyn, *L'Ame de la vie,* trans. Benjamin Gross (Lagrasse: Verdier, 1986), preface by Emmanuel Lévinas, introduction by Benjamin Gross.

3. On Purim, Jews traditionally read the Book of Esther, one of the five *Megillahs* (scrolls) of the Bible. For a discussion of "Second Purims," see, Yosef Hayim Yerushalmi, *Zakhor: Jewish History and Jewish Memory* (Seattle: University of Washington Press, 1982), 46ff.

4. Simon Dubnow, *History of the Jews in Russia and Poland: From the Earliest Times Until the Present Day,* vol. 2, *From the Death of Alexander I until the Death of Alexander III (1825–1894),* trans. I. Friedlander (Philadelphia: Jewish Publication Society of America, 1916–1920 [1914]), 58–59. The book was reissued by the Jewish Publication Society in 1975 with a new introduction by Leon Shapiro.

5. Ibid., 176 n.

6. See, Franco Venturi, *Roots of Revolution: A History of the Populist and Socialist Movements in the Nineteenth Century,* trans. F. Haskell (London: Weidenfield and Nicolson, 1960), 683; Barbara Engel, *Mothers and Daughters: Women of the Intelligentsia in Nineteenth-Century Russia,* (Cambridge: Cambridge University Press, 1983), 184; and "Hartmann's Revelations," *New York Herald,* July 30, 1881. According to the contemporary newspaper article, Hartmann was a "nihilist."

7. Solomon Buirski, *Mayn Lite* (Johannesburg: Kayor, 1976), 24; and Nora Levin, *While the Messiah Tarried* (N.Y.: Schocken, 1977), 33.

8. Traditionally, the woman of the house lights the Sabbath candles. When Litvine's mother died, his father took over the responsibility.

9. A Gentile woman who is allowed to work in a Jewish household, even on the Sabbath. A Gentile man is a *Shabbes Goy.*

10. Rosh Hashanah literally means the head of the year. I leave any reference to jokes about tails to the reader's imagination.

11. Mordecai Ze'ev Feierberg, "Whither?" in *Whither? and Other Stories,* trans. Hillel Halkin (Philadelphia: Jewish Publication Society of America, 1972), 128.

Feierberg represented the voice of maskilim Jews at the end of the nineteenth century. Born in 1874 in the Ukraine into a religious, Hasidic family, he died of tuberculosis at the age of twenty-five, soon after making the final corrections on "Whither?" which was his most famous piece of fiction.

See Meyer Waxman, *A History of Jewish Literature: From the Close of the Bible to Our Own Days,* vol. 4, 2d ed. (N.Y.: Bloch, 1947 [1941]), 54ff., for an analysis of Feierberg's contributions to literature by a celebrated scholar from Lite. Born in Slutsk (Byelorussia) in 1884, Waxman received rabbinical training in the Orthodox tradition of Lite and schooled himself in the growing secular Hebrew and Yiddish literary movements of the period. When he was nineteen or twenty, he came to the United States and settled in New York, where he prepared for the American rabbinate at the Jewish Theological Seminary and for a Ph.D. in philosophy at Columbia University. In 1917 Waxman helped found the Teachers Institute (Bet Midrash Le-Morim) and became its first director. Dedicated to teaching Hebrew as a national language, the school became the secular branch of Yeshiva University. Waxman taught at New York University, as well, and wrote extensively on Jewish theology, philosophy, and literature until he died in 1969 (personal communication, Rabbi Mordecai Waxman, 1989).

12. Michael Marrus and Robert Paxton, *Vichy France and the Jews* (N.Y.: Basic, 1981), 65. *Vichy et les Juifs,* trans. Marguerite Delmotte (Paris: Calmann-Lévy, 1981).

13. Marrus and Paxton, *Vichy France and the Jews,* 260; Serge Klarsfeld, cited in *New York Times,* September 17, 1989, 11.

14. *Poètes français,* trans. M. Litvine, 2 vols. (Paris: Editions Polyglottes, 1968, 1986).

15. Isaac Bashevis Singer, Nobel Prize Speech, delivered in Stockholm in November 1978 and again in Paris, at the Sorbonne, December 17, 1978.

16. Itzhok Niborski, letter, February 1988. See A. Wieviorka and I. Niborski, *Les Livres du souvenir: Mémoriaux Juifs de Pologne* (Paris: Gallimard/Julliard, 1983).

CHAPTER FIVE: THE LITHUANIAN JEWISH ENLIGHTENMENT
IN FRENCH TRANSLATION

Note to epigraph: Emmanuel Lévinas, interviewed by François Poirié, *Emmanuel Lévinas, qui êtes-vous?* (Lyon: La Manufacture, 1987), 65 (henceforth cited as Lévinas/Poirié).

Emmanuel Lévinas kindly received me in his home in July 1986. However, since several interviews with him had already been published, or were about to be published, he did not review his life story for me, but answered questions about matters not covered in the other interviews. What follows, then, is my own telling of Lévinas' life and work, based on several published interviews and on his philosophical and religious texts, all of which I cite. When I quote or paraphrase from the interviews, I use Lévinas' observations only. Lévinas' comments made directly to me are clearly noted as well.

1. Emmanuel Lévinas, interviewed by Myriam Anissimov, "Emmanuel Lévinas se souvient . . ." *Les Nouveaux cahiers,* no. 82, Fall 1985, 32 (henceforth cited as Lévinas/Anissimov).

2. Lévinas/Poirié, 67.

3. Ibid.

4. Ibid., 68.

5. Ibid.

6. Lévinas/Anissimov, 31.

7. Ibid.

8. Lévinas/Poirié, 69.

9. Ibid., 72.

10. Lévinas/Anissimov, 33.

11. Lévinas/Poirié, 69.

12. Ibid., 70.

13. Ibid., 72.

14. Ibid., 75–76.

15. Emmanuel Lévinas, *Théorie de l'intuition dans la phénoménologie de Husserl* (Paris: Alcan, 1930), trans. A. Oriane, under the title *Theory of Intuition in Husserl's Phenomenology* (Evanston, Ill.: Northwestern University Press, 1973).

16. Simone de Beauvoir, *La Force de l'âge* (Paris: Gallimard, 1960), 141–42, trans. P. Green, under the title *The Prime of Life* (N.Y.: Lancer, 1973 [1962]), 162.

17. Annie Cohen-Solal, *Sartre, 1905–1980* (Paris: Gallimard, 1983), 139ff., trans. A. Cancogni, under the title *Sartre: A Life* (N.Y.: Pantheon, 1987) (henceforth cited as *Sartre*).

18. Jean-Paul Sartre, *Les Carnets de la drôle de guerre* (Paris: Gallimard, 1983), 225, cited in Cohen-Solal, *Sartre,* 151.

19. Francis Jeanson, *Le Problème moral et la pensée de Sartre* (Paris: Editions du Seuil, 1965), 107, trans. Robert Stone, under the title *Sartre and the Problem of Morality* (Bloomington: Indiana University Press, 1980), 78.

20. Salomon Malka, *Lire Lévinas* (Paris: Les Editions du Cerf, 1984), 30 (hereafter cited as *Lire Lévinas*).

21. Martin Buber, *I and Thou,* trans. R. G. Smith (N.Y.: Scribner's Sons, 1937 [1923]). Lévinas/Poirié, 123–125.

22. Jean-Paul Sartre *L'Etre et le Néant* (Paris: Gallimard, 1943), trans. Hazel Barnes, under the title *Being and Nothingness* (N.Y.: Washington Square Press, 1966).

23. Emmanuel Lévinas, *Difficile liberté* (Paris: Albin Michel, 1976 [1963]), 190.

24. Ibid, 192.

25. Lévinas/Poirié, 110–11.

26. Ibid., 121.

27. Emmanuel Lévinas, "Entretien avec Emmanuel Lévinas," with Salomon Malka, in *Lire Lévinas,* 105–6 (hereafter cited as Lévinas/Malka).

28. Ibid. See Lévinas *Difficile liberté,* 235–60, for Lévinas' "spiritual biography" of Franz Rosensweig. He gave this paper at the second Collqoue des Intellectuels Juifs de Langue Française in 1959.

29. Lévinas/Poirié, 85–86.

30. Lévinas/Anissimov, 9.

31. Lévinas/Malka, 106.

32. Elie Wiesel, *Le Chant des morts, nouvelles* (Paris: Editions du Seuil, 1966), chap. 10, "Le Juif errant," 119–44; *Paroles d'étranger* (Paris: Editions du Seuil, 1982), chap. 9, "La Mort d'un Juif errant," 108–13.

33. Wiesel, *Paroles d'étranger,* 108.

34. Malka, *Lire Lévinas,* 54.

35. Lévinas/Anissimov, 32.

36. Alexandre Derczansky, personal communication, 1986.

37. Wiesel, "Juif errant," 113.

38. Lévinas/Poirié, 127.

39. Wiesel, "Juif errant," 111.

40. Lévinas/Anissimov, 32.

41. Lévinas/Poirié, 127–28.

42. Ibid., 130.

43. Emmanuel Lévinas, *L'Au-delà du verset, lectures et discours talmudiques* (Paris: Editions de Minuit, 1982), 231–34.

44. Yosef Hayim Yerushalmi, *Zakhor: Jewish History and Jewish Memory* (Seattle: University of Washington Press, 1982), 85–86.

45. Lévinas, *Difficile liberté,* 230.

46. Ibid., 192.

47. Jacques Derrida, "Violence et métaphysique: Essai sur la pensée d'Emmanuel Lévinas," *Revue de métaphysique et de morale,* nos. 3 and 4, 1964; reprinted in *L'Ecriture et la différence* (Paris: Editions du Seuil, 1967), 117–228, trans. A. Bass, under the title *Writing and Difference* (Chicago: University of Chicago Press, 1978).

48. Emmanuel Lévinas, personal communication, 1986.

49. Ibid.

50. Emmanuel Lévinas, *Les Nouveaux cahiers,* no. 85, Summer 1986, 28.

51. Unless otherwise noted, the following biographical sketch comes from interviews with Alain Finkielkraut between the years 1986 and 1989.

52. Alain Finkielkraut, *Le Juif imaginaire* (Paris: Les Editions du Seuil, 1980), 19.

53. Ibid., 22.

54. Ibid., 209–10.

55. Ibid., 215.

56. Ibid., 17 n.

57. Ibid., 16.

58. Ibid., 30.

59. Finkielkraut divides the group in two, distinguishing between those old enough to have taken an active part in opposing the Algerian War, and those, like himself, who were too young (Ibid., 27). The division he makes is comparable to the one I proposed in chapter 1.

60. Ibid.

61. Ibid., 121.

62. Ibid., 122–23.

63. Ibid., 123.

64. Ibid., *L'Avenir d'une négation: Réflexion sur la question du génocide* (Paris: Editions du Seuil, 1982), 55.

65. Ibid., 135. For references to the work of Nelly Gutman and Jacques Tarnero, Nadine Fresco, and Pierre Vidal-Naquet, see chapter 2 and Appendix.

66. Ibid., 178–79.

67. Emmanuel Lévinas, *Difficile liberté,* 170.

68. Alain Finkielkraut, *La Réprobation d'Israel* (Paris: Denoël, 1983), 166.

69. *Ibid., La Sagesse de l'amour* (Paris: Editions Gallimard, 1984), 152 (hereafter cited as *La Sagesse*).

70. Finkielkraut first raises the problem in chapter 5 of *La Sagesse* and then develops it further in *La Défaite de la pensée* (Paris: Gallimard, 1987), part 2 (hereafter cited as *La Défaite*).

71. Claude Lévi-Strauss, *Race et histoire* (Paris: Denoël, 1987 [1952]), 53, trans. under the title *Race and History* (Paris: UNESCO, 1952).

72. Finkielkraut, *La Sagesse,* 151.

73. Lévinas, *Difficile liberté,* 259.

74. Finkielkraut, *La Défaite* 136ff.

75. Ibid., 19.

76. Ibid., 47–48.

77. Ibid., 58–59.

78. See, for example, George Stocking, *Race, Culture and Evolution* (Chicago: University of Chicago Press, 1982 [1968]), chap. 9.

79. Finkielkraut, *La Défaite,* 66–67.

80. Ibid., 72.

81. Ibid., 131.

82. Jonathan Boyarin also mentions the warm reception Alain Finkielkraut's work has received in the Yiddish-speaking community, *Landslayt: Polish Jews in Paris,*

Ph.D. dissertation in anthropology at The New School for Social Research, May 1985, 278 (forthcoming, Indiana University Press).

83. Simon Dubnow, *Jewish History: An Essay in the Philosophy of History,* trans. Israel Friedlander (Philadelphia: Jewish Publications Society of America, 1927 [1903]), 187. It was first published in Russian in 1896–97.

84. Lévinas, *Difficile liberté,* 216.

85. Alain Finkielkraut, "Universalisme et liberté de l'esprit," *Les Nouveaux cahiers,* no. 85, Summer 1986, 30.

86. Lévinas, "Jacob Gordin," in *Difficile liberté,* 222.

CHAPTER 6: THE LITHUANIAN JEWISH ENLIGHTENMENT IN FRENCH TRANSLATION, CONTINUED

Note to epigraph: Wladimir Rabi, "Les Chemins de fuite (Engagement et non-engagement)," *La Conscience juive: Données et débats,* ed. A. Lévy-Valensi and J. Halpérin (Paris: PUF, 1963), 299. This volume includes the proceedings of the first three Colloques des Intellectuels Juifs de Langue Française (1957, 1959, 1960).

Rabi must have been alluding to comments made by Gordin that were recorded and published by an unidentified student three years after Gordin had died: "La Galouth d'après Jacob Gordin," *Les Cahiers du sud,* 1950, 114.

1. Unless otherwise noted, the following biographical information about Jacob Gordin and his wife Rachel Zaber Gordin comes from interviews conducted with the philosopher's widow in 1979. Madame Gordin agreed to have her interview taped, and I have therefore been able to quote her directly.

2. Georges Hertz, "Jacob Gordin," *Bulletin de nos communautes,* 3d year, no. 21, October 10, 1947, 2. This bulletin became *La Tribune juive* a few years later.

3. Lévinas, "Jacob Gordin," *Difficile liberté,* 219.

4. Hertz, "Jacob Gordin," 2.

5. Frederic C. Hammel, *Souviens-toi d'Amalek: Témoignage sur la lutte des Juifs en France* (Paris: C.L.K.H., 1982), 360–61 (hereafter cited as *Souviens-toi*).

6. Lévinas, *Difficile liberté,* 219.

7. Hammel, *Souviens-toi,* 361.

8. David Biale, *Gershom Scholem: Kabbalah and Counter-History* (Cambridge: Harvard University Press, 1979), 36.

9. Jacob Gordin, *Untersuchungen zur Theorie des unendlichen Urteils* (Berlin: Akademie-Verlag, 1929).

10. Lévinas, *Difficile liberté,* 220.

11. Maxime Piha published one of the lectures Gordin delivered at the Ecole Rabbinique de France in his journal *Cahiers juifs,* "Actualité de Maïmonide," *Cahiers juifs,* no. 10, 1934 (hereafter cited as "Actualité Maïmonide"), and Emmanuel Lévinas arranged to have a second one published a few years after Gordin's death, "Yehouda Halévy et l'hellénisme," *Evidences,* no. 21, 1951.

12. In addition to "Actualité de Maïmonide," Piha published the following other articles by Gordin, "Simon Doubnov et sa philosophie de l'histoire," nos. 11/12, 1934; "Benedictus ou maledictus (le cas Spinoza), no. 14, 1935; and "Maïmonide dans la pensée du XIXe siècle," nos. 16/17, 1935.

13. See chapter 8 for Olga Katunal's story.

14. Alain Michel, *Les Eclaireurs Israélites de France pendant la Seconde Guerre mondiale* (Paris: Edition des E.I.F., 1984), 221 (hereafter cited as *Les Eclaireurs*).

15. Ibid., 193.

16. Ibid., 182.

17. Hammel, *Souviens-toi,* 151.

18. Georges Hertz, "Jacob Gordin, le mystique venu d'octobre," *La Tribune juive,* September 16, 1977, 21.

19. Hammel, *Souviens-toi,* 374 and Michel, *Les Eclaireurs,* 182.

20. Hammel, Ibid., 390.

21. Ibid., 358.

22. Ibid., 341.

23. Lévinas, *Difficile liberté,* 222.

24. Ibid., 220.

25. See chapter 8 for a discussion of one of the outstanding exceptions to this rule: the German Jewish philosopher Oskar Goldberg, whose work caused quite a scandal in Berlin between the two wars, even though it has been virtually forgotten today. Goldberg considered himself to be a rationalist, a "mystical rationalist," but he, too, vigorously opposed the ideas of Kant and those of the neo-Kantians.

26. Michael Löwy *Rédemption et utopie* (Paris: PUF, 1988), 81.

27. Meyer Waxman, *A History of Jewish Literature: From the Close of the Bible to Our Own Days,* vol. 4, (N.Y.: Bloch, 1947 [1941]), 916. See chapter 4, n. 11 for a brief description of Meyer Waxman.

28. "La Galouth d'après Jacob Gordin," 124.

29. Gordin, "Actualité de Maïmonide," 17–18, cited by Hertz (without page numbers) in "Jacob Gordin," 3.

30. Jacob Gordin, quoted in Hammel, *Souviens-toi,* 363 (no reference given).

31. But Cohen, like Gordin, may be having a comeback. In 1987, *Pardès* devoted an entire issue (no. 5), to "Judéité et Germanité" and included a French translation of Hermann Cohen's essay, "Germanité et Judéité," published originally in 1915. Marc Lavnay translated and introduced the article.

32. See, for example, Jean Zacklad, *Pour une éthique, De Dieu* (book 1), *L'Etre au féminin* (book 2) (Lagrasse: Verdier, 1979 & 1981); *L'Alliance* (book 3) (Paris: Textes et Travaux, 1985); and with Claude Birman and Charles Mopsik, *Caïn et Abel* (Paris: Editions Grasset, 1980).

33. Biographical information about Jean Zacklad comes from an interview Professor Zacklad kindly gave me in his home in June 1986.

CHAPTER 7: FROM MAO TO MOSES (VIA LITHUANIA)

Note to epigraph: Benny Lévy, quoted by Alain Garric, "Une Génération de Mao à Moïse," *Libération,* December 22–23, 1984, 29 (henceforth quoted as "De Mao à Moïse").

1. Benny Lévy kindly received me in his home in Strasbourg in June 1986. Since he had already given lengthy interviews about himself to others, which had been, or were about to be, published, I did not ask him to review his life history again

for me. We discussed instead the possibility of Verdier publishing the work of the German-Jewish philosopher Oskar Goldberg (see chapter 8 for a discussion of Goldberg). What follows, then, is my own telling of Lévy's life and work, based on published interviews and on his own writings, all of which I cite.

2. During the 1988–89 academic year, Lévy tried unsuccessfully to get a full-time appointment in philosophy at the University of Paris VII.

3. Hervé Hamon and Patrick Rotman, *Génération* (Paris: Editions du Seuil, 1987), vol. 1, *Les Anneés de rêve*, 272. (hereafter cited as H&R, *Génération,* vol. 1).

4. The Union of Workers, Peasants, and Students broke off from a group called Iskra (personal communication, Jacques Hassoun).

5. H&R, *Génération,* vol. 1, 274.

6. Maurice Clavel, quoted by Alain Garric, "De Mao à Moïse," 28.

7. H&R, *Génération,* vol. 1, 275. Hamon and Rotman tell their story in the present tense. For stylistic reasons, I frequently translate selections from their volumes in the past tense.

8. Pierre Goldman, *Souvenirs obscurs d'un Juif polonais né en France* (Paris: Editions du Seuil, 1975), 99–100, trans. J. Pinkham, under the title *Dim Memories of a Polish Jew Born in France* (N.Y.: Viking, 1977).

9. H&R, *Génération,* vol. 1, 328.

10. Ibid., 468.

11. Ibid., 518.

12. Ibid., 514–15.

13. Ibid., 585.

14. Ibid., 590.

15. Hervé Hamon and Patrick Rotman, *Génération* (Paris: Les Editions du Seuil, 1988), vol. 2, *Les Années de poudre,* 24–25 (hereafter cited as H&R, *Génération,* vol. 2).

16. *La Cause du peuple* was named after the newspaper Marat founded during the French Revolution.

17. *La Cause du peuple,* as cited in H&R, *Génération,* vol. 2, 26 (their emphasis).

18. H&R, *Génération,* vol. 2, 121.

19. Ibid., 458.

20. Jacques Hassoun, personal communication, 1988.

21. H&R, *Génération,* vol. 2, 90.

22. Ibid., 91.

23. Ibid., 93.

24. Ibid.

25. Edward Said, quoted by Cohen-Solal, *Sartre, 1905–1980,* 651, or *Sartre: A Life,* trans. Cancogni, 512–13.

26. Cohen-Solal, *Sartre,* 606.

27. Ibid., 607.

28. Jean-Paul Sarte, quoted by ibid., 617. English, 484–85.

29. H&R, *Génération,* vol. 2, 462–63.

30. Ibid., 582.

31. Cohen-Solal, *Sartre,* 620.

32. Ronald Fraser, ed., *1968: A Student Generation in Revolt* (N.Y.: Pantheon, 1988), 331–32.

33. H&R, *Génération,* vol. 2, 480–91.

34. Benny Lévy, quoted by ibid., 529.

35. Jean-Paul Sartre, quoted by Cohen-Solal, *Sartre,* 629. English, 495.

36. Valéry Giscard-d'Estaing, quoted by ibid., 631. English, 496.

37. Jean-Paul Sartre, Philippe Gavi, and Pierre Victor, *On a raison de se révolter* (Paris: Gallimard, 1974).

38. Benny Lévy, quoted by Cohen-Solal, *Sartre,* 631–32. English, 497.

39. Jean-Paul Sartre, quoted by ibid., 632.

40. *Ibid.,* 635.

41. Simone de Beauvoir, *La Cérémonie des adieux* (Paris: Gallimard, 1981), 141, trans. P. O'Brien, under the title *Adieux: A farewell to Sartre* (NY: Pantheon, 1984) (hereafter cited as *La Cérémonie*).

42. H&R *Génération,* vol. 2, 592ff.

43. Beauvoir, *La Cérémonie,* 107.

44. Ibid., 139.

45. Jacques-Laurent Bost, quoted by ibid., 140. English, 110.

46. Beauvoir, ibid., 140.

47. Ibid., 125.

48. Ibid., 140.

49. Ibid., 140–41. English, 111.

50. Stuart L. Charmé, "From Maoism to the Talmud (With Sartre Along the Way): An Interview With Benny Lévy" (hereafter cited as Lévy/Charmé), *Commentary* 78, no. 6 (December 1984): 49.

51. Ibid.

52. Ibid., 50.

53. Benny Lévy, quoted in H&R *Génération,* vol. 2, 646–47.

54. *Les Temps modernes,* numéro spécial, *Le Second Israël,* May 1979.

55. Shmuel Trigano, *La Nouvelle question juive* (Paris: Gallimard, 1979).

56. The biographical information on Shmuel Trigano comes from my interviews with him between 1986 and 1989.

57. Shmuel Trigano, *Le Récit de la disparue* (Paris: Gallimard, 1977).

58. Shmuel Trigano *La Demeure oubliée* (Paris: Lieu Commun, 1984).

59. See appendix.

60. Jacob/Eïn Yaakov, *Aggadoth du Talmud de Babylone,* trans. Arlette Elkaïm-Sartre, Introduction de Marc-Alain Ouaknin (Lagrasse: Verdier, 1987).

61. I met Francis Gribe in 1976 at Le Cercle Gaston Crémieux. Over the years we kept in touch sporadically. When we met again in 1986, he was married, had two children, and was making a living in advertising. Although his wife is not Jewish, Gribe still buys kosher meat; but he is no longer observant. Laughing at himself, he added that he washes the plates off between the meat and cheese courses.

62. Benny Lévy, quoted in H&R *Génération,* vol. 2, 647.

63. Saolo Baron, *The Social and Religious History of the Jews,* 15 vols. 2d ed., rev. and enl. (NY: Columbia University Press, 1952).

64. See note 19 of chapter 1 for full citation of Sartre/Lévy interviews. Hereafter cited as Sartre/Lévy.

65. Simone de Beauvoir, *La Cérémonie,* 150.

66. Sartre/Lévy, 57; English, 418.

67. Sartre/Lévy, 58; English, 419.

68. Ibid., 58; English, 420.

69. Jean-Paul Sartre, quoted by Cohen-Solal, *Sartre,* 647.

70. Lévy/Charmé, 51.

71. Benny Lévy, *Le Nom de l'homme* (Lagrasse: Verdier, 1984).

72. Benny Lévy, *Le Logos et la lettre* (Lagrasse: Verdier, 1988).

73. Jean Zacklad, *Pour une éthique* (Lagrasse: Verdier, 1981), *L'Etre au féminin* (book 2), 14.

74. Ibid.

75. Emmanuel Lévinas, "'A l'image de Dieu' d'après Rabbi Haïm Voloziner," in *L'Au-delà du verset: Lectures et discours talmudiques,* 182–200; "De la Prière sans demande," *Les Etudes philosophiques,* no. 2, 1984, 157–63; "Judaïsme et Kenose," *Archivo di filosofia,* no. 2–3, 1985, 13–28; and Rabbi Hayyim de Volozhyn, *L'Ame de la vie,* trans. Benjamin Gross (Lagrasse: Verdier, 1986), preface by Emmanuel Lévinas, introduction by Benjamin Gross.

76. I spent a weekend in the Yéchiva des Etudiants community in June 1986.

77. I first met Jean-Michel Tolédano at gatherings of Le Cercle Gaston Crémieux in 1976.

78. I interviewed Alain Lévy and his wife Claudine in May 1986 and attended Rav Lévy's class for adults at the Collège Ozar Hatorah.

79. The following biographical information comes from an interview I conducted with Monique-Lise Cohen in Toulouse in May 1986.

80. Monique-Lise Cohen published a brief excerpt from her thesis in the issue of *Les Nouveaux cahiers* devoted to the question of the emancipation of the Jews in the French Revolution: "Les Juifs ont-ils du coeur?" *Les Nouveaux cahiers,* no. 97, Summer 1989, 73–75.

81. Trigano, *La République et les Juifs.*

82. As noted in chapter 1, I interviewed Rabbi Eliahou Abitbol in Strasbourg, in June 1986. Thinking that I was a journalist, Rav Abitbol did not want to talk to me. But when he learned that I was interested in tracing the influence of Lithuanian forms of Judaism in France, he warmed up to the project and agreed to meet with me.

83. Chochana Boukhobza, "La Yéchiva d'Aix-les-Bains," *Communauté nouvelle,* no. 25, June–July 1986, 74–75.

84. I interviewed Freddy Raphaël in Strasbourg in June 1986. Among his many publications, see two works he wrote with Robert Weyl: *Juifs en Alsace: Culture, société, histoire,* (Toulouse: Privat, 1977) and *Regards nouveaux sur les Juifs d'Alsace* (Strasbourg: Istra, 1980).

85. Lévy/Charmé, op. cit., 51.

86. Aaron Fraenckel kindly received me in his home in June 1986.

87. I interviewed Joseph Gottfarstein in his home on the outskirts of Paris in 1979 and his son Samuel in Strasbourg in 1986.

88. Joseph Gottfarstein, *L'Ecole du meurtre* (Paris: La Presse Française et Etrangère, 1946).

89. *Le Bahir: Le livre de la clarté*, trans. Joseph Gottfarstein (Lagrasse: Verdier, 1983). For a discussion of *The Bahir*, see Gershom Scholem, *On the Kabbalah and Its Symbolism*, trans. Ralph Manheim (N.Y.: Schocken, 1965 [1960]).

90. Richard Marienstras, personal communication, 1986.

91. Richard Marienstras, "Le Golem," *Max pauvre Max* (Paris: Denoël, 1964), 184.

92. Founded in the midnineteenth century by Israel Salanter (Lipkin), the Musar movement combined Torah learning with the study of Musar (ethical literature). A major center of the Musar movement was located at the Keneset Yisrael Yeshiva in Slobodka. For an interesting portrait of Israel Salanter and the Musar movement, see Goldberg, *Between Berlin and Slobodka*, chap. 2.

93. Edmond Fleg, *Anthologie juive: Des origines à nos jours* (Paris: Flammarion, 1951), 455.

94. Oskar Goldberg, *Die Wirklichkeit der Hebräer* (The Reality of the Hebrews) (Berlin: Verlag David, 1925).

CHAPTER 8: FROM TROTSKY TO MOSES

1. I met Olga Katunal in 1977 and visited her regularly thereafter on my annual trips to Paris, until she died in April 1988. Over the years, she shared a great deal with me about her extraordinary life. She also introduced me to the work of Oskar Goldberg and led me to think about the history and religion of the Jewish people in ways I had never imagined possible. I dedicate this chapter to Olga Katunal's memory.

I want to thank the painter Alain Kleinmann for introducing me to his cousin Olga Katunal. Over the years we have kept in touch, and he has been a generous and helpful friend. Some of the material reported in this chapter comes from discussions I have had with him.

Alain Kleinmann belongs to the generation of 1968 and was raised as a secular Jew. While still a young boy, he began to visit Olga Katunal regularly and to study Hebrew and the Torah with her. Deeply influenced by her, he decided to make a return to Judaism. As a university student in Paris, he started taking classes with Rav Charles Rottenberg, at the Polish-Lithuanian synagogue Agoudah Hakehilos, rue Pavée in the Marais. An ultra-Orthodox Jew from Belgium, Rav Rottenberg has been defying the French consistoire for years and attracting young Jews interested in making a return to the Lithuanian Jewish tradition.

I am grateful to Alain Kleinmann for alerting me to the fact that a friend of Olga Katunal wrote an obituary for her in a Yiddish anarchist paper published in Tel Aviv: Azka Zwi, "Olga Katunal," *Problemen*, August 1988, 30–31.

I want to thank Dr. Manfred Voigts in Berlin for reviewing the section on Oskar Goldberg and Dr. Walter Einhorn in Purchase, New York, for translating *Die Wirklichkeit der Hebräer* into English for me.

2. See map 3. This Subocz is not to be confused with an outlying district of Vilna that bears the same name.

3. The Ponevezh Yeshiva left Lithuania at the outbreak of the Second World War and moved to Palestine. Located today in the Bene Berak district of Tel Aviv, the yeshiva continues to teach in the Lithuanian tradition.

4. There was a large Polish-speaking population in Lithuania.

5. The Cafe des Westens still exists in West Berlin at the same address.

6. Gershom Scholem, *Walter Benjamin: The Story of a Friendship,* trans. H. Zohn (Philadelphia: Jewish Publication Society of America, 1981 [1975]), 18, 82, 95–96 (hereafter cited as *Walter Benjamin*).

7. Nicholas Jacob and Simon Guttmann, personal communications over the years 1983–89. Unless otherwise noted, when I refer to the life and opinions of Simon Guttmann, they come from interviews I conducted with him in London. Simon Guttmann kindly received me on several occasions between 1983 and 1989. He died in January 1990 at the age of 98.

8. A. Salmonoff, *Secrets et sagesse du corps: Médecine des profondeurs* (Paris: Editions de la Table Ronde, 1958).

9. André Schwarz-Bart, *Le Dernier des justes* (Paris: Editions du Seuil, 1959), trans. Stephen Becker, under the title *The Last of the Just* (Cambridge: Bently, 1960).

According to Olga Katunal, after she read the novel she told Schwarz-Bart what she thought of his interpretation of the legend of the thirty-six Just Ones and of his rendition of Jewish history. They never spoke again. Over the years, she kept in touch with Richard Marienstras, even though they saw each other rarely. Elise Marienstras said playfully, but only half in jest, that when she and Richard were dating in the 1950s, she knew her future husband had become serious about her when he took her to meet Olga Katunal (personal communication, 1979).

10. Erich Unger, *The Imagination of Reason: Two Philosophical Essays* (London: Routledge & Kegan Paul, 1952), 116–17.

11. The introductory essay by Unger is *Das Problem der mythischen Realität* (Berlin: Verlag David, 1926). Unger enjoyed the respect of many scholars in Berlin in the 1920s. Even Gershom Scholem, who criticized Goldberg and his group vigorously, grudgingly admitted that Unger had "considerable philosophical gifts," *Walter Benjamin,* 97.

In chapter 6 I refer to a contribution Jacob Gordin made to a special issue of the *Cahiers juifs* devoted to Maimonides. Erich Unger and Gershom Scholem also wrote articles for the same issue (nos. 16/17, 1935). Singularly missing, however, was Oskar Goldberg, who was publishing his book on Maimonides that very same year.

12. Olga Katunal, "Vers la solution du problème du judaïsme," *Le Rayon,* Organe de L'Union Libérale Israélite, 16th year, no. 2 (March–April–May 1935), 20–22.

13. Jacob Taubes, "From Cult to Culture," *Partisan Review* 21 no. 4 (July–August 1954), 400.

14. Gershom Scholem, *From Berlin to Jerusalem: Memories of my Youth,* trans. H. Zohn (N.Y.: Schocken, 1980 [1977]), 148.

15. Oskar Goldberg, "Le Fantôme de Millvale: Une Analyse psychologique et ontologique," trans. German by O. Katunal, *Initiation et science et bibliographie esotérique,* vol. 15, Jan. 1951.

16. In addition to *Die Wirklichkeit der Hebräer* (Berlin: Verlag David, 1925), Goldberg's best known works are: *Die fünf Bücher Moses: ein Zahlengebäude*

(Berlin: 1908), an excerpt from which has been published in French, "L'Edifice des nombres du Pentateuque," *La Revue juive de Genève,* nos. 94–95, Juin/Juillet 1947, 240–49; and *Maimonides: Kritik der Jüdischen Glaubenslehre* (Vienna: H. Glanz, 1935), in which he argued that the medieval philosopher Maimonides was responsible for diluting Jewish thought with the ideas of Aristotle.

17. Jacob Taubes, personal communication in Berlin, 1984.

18. Manfred Voigts, personal communication in Berlin, 1989.

19. Jacob Taubes, personal communication in Berlin, 1984.

20. Scholem, *Walter Benjamin,* 98.

The German scholar Manfred Voigts republished excerpts from letters and memoirs from a number of people in the Berlin intellectual community who were interested in Oskar Goldberg, including two letters to Gershom Scholem from Walter Benjamin and two selections by Franz Rosenzweig ("Oskar Goldberg— Texte," *Akzente: Zeitschrift für Literatur*), no. 2, April 1989, 168–91 (hereafter cited as *Akzente).*

21. Thomas Mann, *Joseph and His Brothers,* trans. H. T. Lowe (N.Y.: Alfred A. Knopf, 1934 [1933]).

22. See, for example, Goldberg's articles on Greek mythology in *Mass und Wert,* no. 3 (January–February 1938), and no. 5 (May–June 1938).

23. Scholem, *Walter Benjamin,* 98.

24. Thomas Mann, *Doctor Faustus: The Life of the German Composer Adrian Leverkuhn, as Told by a Friend,* trans. H.T. Lowe-Porter (N.Y.: Alfred A. Knopf, 1965 [1948]), 278–79 (hereafter cited as *Doctor Faustus*).

25. Scholem, *Walter Benjamin,* 98.

Olga Katunal and Jacob Taubes agreed that Mann had captured the way Goldberg expressed himself. The unflattering portrait was recognizably Goldberg, but the caricature presented the philosopher's ideas out of context and in an irresponsible way (personal communications, 1984). On Thomas Mann and Goldberg, see also Stéphane Mosès, "Thomas Mann et Oskar Goldberg: Un exemple de 'montage' dans le 'Doktor Faustus.'" *Etudes germaniques* (January–March 1976); and Taubes, "From Cult to Culture."

26. Mann, *Doctor Faustus,* 282.

27. Ibid., 284.

28. Scholem, *Walter Benjamin,* 96.

29. Erich Unger, *Die Staatslose Bildung eines Jüdischen Volkes* (Berlin: Verlag David, 1922) (hereafter cited as *Die Staatslose*).

30. Michael Loẅy, *Rédemption et utopie* (Paris: PUF, 1988), 127.

The Israeli-based Stéphane Mosès has written on Goldberg in French. Most of the new work on Goldberg, however, is taking place in Germany, where the philosopher has recently been rediscovered by members of the postwar generation of scholars, most importantly, by Manfred Voigts. Voigts wrote and produced a radio program on Goldberg for Sender Freies Berlin, December 27, 1988, and has been writing extensively on the philosopher for several years. See, for example, "Oskar Goldberg, Eingeleitet und Zusammengestellt," *Akzente,* 158–67.

31. Erich Unger, *Politik und Metaphysik* (Verlag, David, 1921).

32. Unger *Die Staatslose.*

CONCLUSION

1. Robert Badinter, *Libres et égaux* (Paris: Fayard, 1989). See also Patrick Girard, *La Révolution française et les Juifs* (Paris: Robert Laffont, 1989); Michael Graetz, *Les Juifs en France au dix-neuvième siècle: De la Révolution française à l'Alliance Israélite Universelle,* trans. S. Malka (Paris: Le Seuil, 1989); Pierre Birnbaum, "Sur l'étatisation révolutionnaire: L'abbé Grégoire et l'identité juive," *Le Débat,* no. 53, Jan.–Feb. 1989, 157–73; Gérard Israël ed., *Le Juif citoyen: Une révolution,* title of the summer 1989 issue of *Les Nouveaux cahiers,* no. 97, Summer 1989; Jean Halpérin and Georges Lévitte, eds., *La Question de l'état,* Données et débats, Acts du XXIX Colloque des Intellectuels Juifs de Langue Française (Paris: Editions Denoël, 1989).

2. The last major conflict in 1989 concerned the limits of separation between church (in this case mosque) and state, a conflict that has provoked impassioned discussions throughout France. Within the Jewish community, a wide range of individuals and groups took stands, from the chief rabbi of France to Alain Finkielkraut to the Cercle Gaston Crémieux. The issue at hand was whether Moslem girls should be allowed to enter a school dressed in the Islamic "scarf," which covers the head, but not the face. When the principal of a school located in a working-class neighborhood in Creil (Oise) refused to let three girls attend classes in religious attire, he set off a national debate that resulted in a decision by Lionel Jospin, the minister of education, to require the school to admit the girls in the scarves, if their families refused to comply with the secular traditions of France.

Those concerned with le droit à la différence and with the problems of immigrant workers in France have joined forces, albeit uncomfortably so, with those who are calling for greater freedom of religious expression. The left is divided on the question. So are the feminists, some of whom find themselves supporting the right of Moslem parents to continue a custom that discriminates against women in the name of respecting cultural differences.

To get a sense of the debate among Jewish intellectuals, see Alain Finkielkraut, "Voiles, la sainte alliance des clergés," *Le Monde,* October 25, 1989, 2; Elisabeth Badinter, Régis Debray, Alain Finkielkraut, Elisabeth de Fontenay, and Catherine Kintzler, "Profs, ne capitulons pas!" *Le Nouvel observateur,* November 2–8, 1989, 58–59; Shmuel Trigano, "Carrefour du judaïsme: Les Juifs illusoires," *L'Arche* (December 1989), 38; and Pierre Birnbaum, "L'Etat et les églises," *L'Arche* (December 1989), 63.

APPENDIX

1. The appendix does not provide bibliographic material for everybody mentioned but highlights the intellectual, political, and spiritual interests of the individuals discussed, as they relate to the concerns of this book. Included, however, are references to some of the articles and books written by members of the generation of 1968 and to volumes published by these younger Jews in honor of their mentors.

2. See R. Goetschel, et. al. "André Neher, l'homme et l'oeuvre," *Les Nouveaux cahiers,* no. 95, hiver 1988–89, 4–13.

3. Monique Basset, et. al., *Ecrits pour Jankélévitch* (Paris: Flammarion, 1978).

4. Maurice Oldender, ed., *Pour Léon Poliakov: Le Racisme, mythes et sciences* (Paris: Editions Complexe, 1981).

5. Luc Rosenzweig, "Nahum Goldmann est mort," *Le Monde,* August 31, 1982, 1, 5.

6. Henri Raczymow, "La Bibliothèque Medem, notre mémoire," *Arche,* no. 274, January 1980, 35–37. I too owe a great deal to Monsieur Vaisbrot.

7. Anne Grynberg, "Le Don de Poug," *Les Nouveaux cahiers,* no. 89, Summer 1987, 47–48.

8. Simon Dubnow, *Précis d'histoire juive,* trans. Isaac Pougatch (Paris: Editions Kyoum, 1936 [1933]).

9. Lilly Scherr, "Poug mon maître," *Les Nouveaux cahiers,* no. 62, Fall 1980, 55–57 (henceforth cited as "Poug").

10. Dominique Schnapper, *Juifs et Israélites* (Paris: Gallimard, 1980), trans. A. Goldhammer, under the title *Jewish Identities in France: An Analysis of Contemporary French Jewry* (Chicago: University of Chicago Press, 1983).

11. Edmond Jabès, quoted in *Traces,* no. 1, Spring 1981, 3, from *Le Livre des ressemblances,* vol. 3, *L'Inéffaçable, l'inapperçu* (Paris: Gallimard, 1980).

12. I first met Adolphe (Ady) Steg in 1976. Unless otherwise noted, what follows about his personal history and about his involvement with the Beit Hamidrach comes from discussions I have had with him, his wife Dr. Gilberte Steg, and with Shmuel Trigano. See also the brief biographical sketch of Professor Steg in *Les Nouveaux cahiers,* no. 81, Summer 1985, 4.

13. Ady Steg and Shmuel Trigano, flier distributed by the Alliance Israélite Universelle, announcing the Beit Hamidrach's program for the year 5747 (1986–87).

14. Yvonne Lévyne, personal communication, 1986.

15. Jean Halpérin kindly received me in his home in Geneva in June 1986, at a particularly difficult time for him and his family, when his mother was gravely ill. I deeply appreciated his willingness to see me. Unless otherwise noted, what follows about his own life and the history of the Colloque des Intellectuels Juifs de la Langue Française, comes from that interview.

16. Edmond Fleg, "Sens de l'histoire juive," *La Conscience juive* (Paris: PUF, 1963), 5–21.

17. I met Alexandre Derczansky in 1979 and interviewed him formally during that year. Since then, we have kept in touch and he has generously helped me think through certain aspects of this project.

18. *Le Tsenah urenah,* trans. Jean Baumgarten (Lagrasse: Verdier, 1987). For a brief description of the *Ze'enah u-Renah* in English, see the *Encyclopaedia Judaica* (Jerusalem: Macmillan & Keter, 1971), vol. 16, 968–69.

I first met Jean Baumgarten when he came to New York in the summer of 1978 to study Yiddish at the Columbia University/YIVO program. Over the years we have kept in touch. The biographical information recorded here comes from our many conversations.

19. I met Dvora Kosman in 1976, thanks to Francis Gribe, the ex-Maoist I described in chapter 7 who had been a member of Le Cercle Gaston Crémieux, a founder of *Traces* and a student of Hebrew with Shmuel Trigano and Benny Lévy. At the time he introduced us, he was still a member of Le Cercle Gaston Crémieux but was already looking elsewhere for inspiration.

In 1978–79, when I spent a year in Paris, I was a guest several times in Dvora and

Joseph Kosman's home, for Sabbath and the Jewish holidays. The biographical information included here comes mostly from conversations we had at that time.

20. In the late 1970s, I attended several lectures by Lilly Scherr, where she spoke autobiographically. Most spectacularly, she participated in a round-table at the Centre Georges Pompidou during Les Journées de la culture yiddish on the meaning of being a Jew (see n. 7 in chapter 3). Yiddishist, feminist, and a practicing Jew, Scherr began her speech in Yiddish, making reference to the title of a play based on a novel by Sholem Aleichem: "*Shver tsu zayn a Yid? Iz shverer tsu zayn a Yidene!* [As difficult as it is to be a Jewish man, it's even harder to be a Jewish woman]." In this secular crowd, however, few people were sympathetic to the complaints of a woman who wanted her feminist ideals to be accepted by observant Jews. For more biographical information, see Scherr's article "Pougatch."

21. Robert Bober, *Réfugié: provenant d'Allemagne apatride d'origine poloniase,* TF 1, September 26, 1976. That fall, Le Cercle Gaston Crémieux had a special showing of the film and a discussion afterward with Bober.

22. Annette Wieviorka, *Ils étaient Juifs, résistants, communistes* (Paris: Denoël, 1986).

23. Georges Haupt, Michael Löwy, and Claudie Weill, *Les Marxistes et la question nationale* (Paris: Maspéro, 1974); Claudie Weill, *L'Internationale et l'autre* (Paris: Editions de l'Arcantère, 1987); and Nathan Weinstock, *Le Pain de misère: histoire du mouvement ouvrier juif en Europe,* 3 vols. (Paris: Editions la Découverte, 1984, 1986). Weinstock is actually Belgian, but since he publishes regularly in France, I have included him as well.

24. Lucette Valensi and Nathan Wachtel, *Mémoires juives* (Paris: Gallimard, 1986).

25. See Pierre Vidal-Naquet, "Un Eichmann du papier: Réponse à Faurisson et à quelques autres," *Espirit,* Sept. 1980, 8–52; and *Les Assassins de la mémoire* (Paris: Editions, la Découverte, 1986). Faurisson has responded to Vidal-Naquet in print: Robert Faurisson, *Réponse à Pierre Vidal-Naquet/Robert Faurisson* (Paris: Vieille Taupe, 1982).

26. Bernard-Henri Lévy, *La Barbarie à visage humain* (Paris: Grasset, 1977), trans. G. Holoch, under the title *Barbarism with a Human Face* (N.Y.: Harper and Row, 1979); *Le Testament de Dieu* (Paris: Grasset, 1979), trans. G. Holoch, under the title *The Testament of God* (N.Y.: Harper and Row, 1980); *L'Idéologie française* (Paris: Grasset, 1981).

27. Bernard-Henri Lévy, *Questions de principe* (Paris: Denoël, 1983), 21.

28. Pierre Birnbaum, *La Logique de l'état* (Paris: Fayard, 1982), *Un Mythe politique: La République juive, de Léon Blum à Mendez-France* (Paris: Fayard, 1988). Nancy Green, *Les Travailleurs immigrés juifs à la Belle Epoque, trans. M. Courtois-Fourcy* (Paris: Fayard, 1985), English title *Pletzl of Paris* (N.Y.: Holmes and Meir, 1985). Paula Hyman, *De Dreyfus à Vichy, trans. S. Boulonge* (Paris: Fayard, 1985), English title *From Dreyfus to Vichy: The Remaking of French Jewry, 1906–1939* (N.Y.: Columbia University Press, 1979).

29. Blandine Barret-Kriegel, *Les Historiens et la monarchie,* 3 vols. (Paris: Presses Universitaires de France, 1988). See also her contribution to the Colloque des

Intellectuels Juifs: *La Question de l'état,* ed. J. Halpérin and G. Lévitte (Paris: Denoël, 1989), 15–23.

30. Elisabeth de Fontenay, *Les Figures juives de Marx* (Paris: Editions Galilée, 1973), *Diderot ou le matérialisme enchanté* (Paris: Grasset, 1981), trans. J. Mehlman, under the title *Diderot: Reason and Resonance* (N.Y.: G. Braziller, 1982). Her plays include *Diderot à corps perdu,* directed by Jean-Louis Barrault (1979) and *Michelet ou le don des larmes,* directed by Simone Benmussa (1989).

I met Elisabeth de Fontenay in 1976, and since then she has helped me a great deal to think through many of the ideas in this book, for which I am deeply grateful. The biographical information provided here comes from our discussions over the years.

31. Jacques Tarnero, "Dérapage de la gauche," *Les Nouveaux cahiers,* no. 71, Winter 1982–83, 9.

32. I met Gilles Bernheim in 1979 at the home of Dvora and Joseph Kosman. Bernheim has published widely. In 1988 he analyzed the relationship between the state and the nation in biblical texts at the Colloque des Intellectuels Juifs: Halpérin and Lévitte, *La Question de l'état,* 24–37.

33. Jacques Wahl received me in his office at the Alliance Israélite Universelle in June 1986.

I interviewed Marc-Alain Ouaknin in his home in July 1986 and attended one of the seminars he was giving that year to a group of psychoanalysts. See his book, *Le Livre brûlé: Lire le Talmud* (Paris: Lieu Commun, 1986) which offers the reader a glimpse at his pedagogical style. Ouaknin provides an introduction to the reading of the Talmud and then engages the ideas of the Ḥasidic master Rabbi Nahman of Bratslav. In 1989 he brought out a second book concerned with the ideas of Nahman of Bratslav, entitled *Lire aux éclats: Eloge de la caresse* (Paris, Lieu Commun, 1989).

34. *Le Monde,* March 8, 1988.

35. Nancy Green, "Jewish Studies in France", ms., 1986. Published in German.

36. See chapter 1, n. 21.

37. As noted in the introduction, Arcadius Kahan was originally from Vilna and wrote a great deal about the economic history of Eastern European Jews. Green's book, *Pletzl of Paris* came out in English and French in the same year.

38. Gérard Israël, *Heureux comme Dieu en France* (Paris: Robert Laffont, 1975).

Glossary

Aggadah   The nonlegal part of the Talmud and Midrash. It consists of folklore and legends.

Aramaic   A Semitic language spoken by the Hebrews and other peoples in the Middle East during late biblical and Talmudic times. Much of the Babylonian Talmud was written in Aramaic.

Arbete Ring   Workmen's Circle. Social groups bearing this Yiddish name were organized by the Bund throughout the Yiddish-speaking Diaspora.

Ashkenazic Jew (pl. noun *Ashkenazim*)   A Jew whose ancestors came from Rhineland (including Alsace and Lorraine), as well as from others parts of Germany or Central and Eastern Europe. Ashkenazic Jews are often contrasted with Sephardic Jews.

Beit Hamidrach   French spelling of a Hebrew term (*bet ha-midrash* or *besmedresh*). A school for studying Torah, Talmud, and the commentaries. Traditionally, a bet ha-midrash was also a house of prayer.

Blintz (pl. *blintzes*)   A thin pancake usually filled with cream or a fresh white cheese, like farmer's cheese. Blintzes are traditionally eaten on Shavuot, the holiday commemorating the giving of the Ten Commandments.

Breton   A native of Brittany (Bretagne, see map 4). The people of the region speak Breton, a Celtic language. Since the mid-1970s, Breton activists have joined other minority nationalists in France in demanding their cultural autonomy.

Bund   The General Jewish Workers Union of Lithuania, Poland, and Russia. The party was founded in Vilna in 1897 by socialist intellectuals and workers, and it became a major political force among Jews living in Poland during the interwar years.

CERAC (La Centre d'Etudes et de Recherches sur l'Antisémitisme Contemporain)   A research center founded in France in 1979 to study contemporary anti-Semitism. It closed in 1986 for lack of funds.

Cholent (also spelled *tcholent*)   A stew prepared with potatoes, groats, and animal fat, traditionally served for lunch on the Sabbath by Jews of Eastern European origin. Some varieties of the dish also have carrots and other root vegetables, beans, and chunks of meat.

CNRS (Le Centre National de la Recherche Scientifique)   A national research center with branches throughout France. The CNRS provides academics with full-time research positions outside the university. Scholars at the CNRS often organize themselves into teams and work on collective projects. Although they have no obligation to do so, many people at the CNRS give occasional courses at the university as well.

Corsicans   Natives of Corsica (Corse), an island in the Mediterannean Sea, 170 kilometers from Nice. Corsicans are considered members of the French nation, and Corsican activists have had a strong independence movement since 1976. In 1982 the inhabitants of the island gained some autonomy when the French government agreed to reclassify Corsica and give it the status of a "collective territory." Corsicans speak an Italian dialect called Corse.

Courland (Kurland)   A region in Latvia, located between the Baltic Sea and the Western Dvina River. While the Pale of Settlement did not include Courland, the area still had a sizable Jewish population by the turn of the century, particularly in such prosperous cities as Libau (Liepaja). Over the centuries the Courland region has changed hands many times, belonging at different periods to Poland, Prussia, Denmark, and Russia. In the interwar years it was part of the independent Republic of Latvia.

CRIF (Conseil Représentatif des Institutions Juives de France)   An umbrella organization for a wide range of Jewish groups in France, representing both immigrant and native-born Jews and religious and nonreligious Jews. It was founded during the Second World War.

Dacha   a Russian country home.

Diaspora   A Greek word referring to the dispersion of Jews from the land of Israel after the destruction of the Second Temple in the year 70 of the common era. Today, the majority of the world's Jews have chosen to remain in the Diaspora, even though their people have a homeland once again.

"Droit à la différence"   The right to be different. The slogan used by those who support the right of minority peoples in France to develop their own cultures.

Dybbuk   The spirit of a dead person that enters the body of somebody still living and possesses it.

Ecole   French word for school.

Essenes   A sect of Jews who lived in Palestine from the second century before the common era to the end of the first century of the common era. The

Essenes often lived in monastic communities that excluded women. With the recent discovery of the Dead Sea Scrolls, scholars have gained new insight about the sect or about people quite like them.

Etudiant   French word for student.

Existentialist   A member of a philosophical movement which argues that a person's existence comes before his or her essence, thereby leaving the individual with the freedom and responsibility to choose what he or she will do. Jean-Paul Sartre founded the French existentialist movement.

Gaon of Vilna   The Hebrew term *gaon* (genius) was used to refer to all heads of the Babylonian Jewish academy in the first centuries of the common era. It was also used in Lithuania in the eighteenth century to identify the brilliant rabbinic scholar Elijah ben Solomon.

Gauchistes   Term applied to leftists associated with the French student uprising of 1968.

Gefilte fish   Stewed or baked fish (usually pike or white fish in Lithuania), stuffed with a mixture of the flesh of the fish, bread or matzah meal, eggs, salt, and pepper. Instead of stuffing the skin of a fish, gefilte fish is often prepared as balls and stewed in fish stock.

Gemara   Part of the Talmud that offers interpretations of the law.

Gnostics   Members of a philosophical movement (Gnosticism). Gnostics claimed to be able to reconcile the differences that existed among religions by means of an all encompassing explanation of the sacred realm. The movement presented a serious threat to the teachings of Judaism and Christianity in the first centuries of the common era.

Goldene Keyt (The Golden Chain)   The title of the journal the Vilna poet Abraham Sutzkever founded in Tel Aviv in 1947.

Golem   According to Jewish legend, a golem is a man brought to life by artificial and magical means.

GP   La Gauche Prolétarienne. A Maoist faction of the French student movement. Founded by Benny Lévy (alias Pierre Victor) in 1968, the GP broke away from the Marxist-Leninist UJC(ml).

Gymnasium   Greek term used in Germany, czarist Russia, and other countries in Europe to refer to a secondary school that prepares students for the university.

Ḥakham   Hebrew word meaning a wise man. It is also the title used for rabbis of Sephardic congregations.

Halakhah   Jewish law.

Ha-Shomer Ha-Ẓa'ir (often spelled *Hashomer Hatsair* or *Hashomer Hatzair*)   A socialist Zionist youth movement associated with Israel's Labour party.

Ḥasidim   Hebrew word for the followers of the teachings of the Baal Shem Tov (the Master of the Good Name), the Ukrainean Jew who founded a movement within Judaism in the eighteenth century that emphasized spiritualism, prayer, and faith.

Haskalah   See *Jewish Enlightenment*.

Ḥeder   A primary school for young boys of Orthodox Jewish families for the study of Torah and the commentaries.

Hypokhâgne and khâgne   A two-year college-level program for French students who have successfully passed high school (lycée), received their baccalaureate degree, and now want to prepare for the highly competitive exam used to select students for the "Grandes Ecoles," like the Ecole Normale Supérieure. If a student gets admitted to a Grande Ecole, he or she receives a salary plus room and board and has the privilege of studying in one of the best universities in France.

INALCO   Institut National des Langues et Civilisations Orientales. A university-level institute in Paris where one can study Middle Eastern languages and cultures.

Ile de la Réunion   Island in the Indian ocean, east of Madagascar. Occupied by the French since the eighteenth century, it became an overseas department in 1946.

Israélites   Term used for assimilated French Jews. Many activist Jews in contemporary France reject the term and insist on calling themselves "Juifs."

Jewish Enlightenment   Based on the philosophical movement that dominated Western Europe in the eighteenth century. Seeking rational explanations for the nature of things, the European Enlightenment led the way for the secularization of society and the establishment of democracies, a process that also led to the emancipation and assimilation of the Jews. Those within the Jewish community who embraced the ideals of the Enlightenment redefined what it meant to be a Jew in the modern world, creating a Jewish Enlightenment within the wider European movement. About a hundred years later, the Western European Enlightenment moved East and inspired a second Jewish Enlightenment. Instead of assimilating into the wider society as Russians, many enlightened Jews in the czarist empire developed a secular Jewish culture in Hebrew and Yiddish, the national languages of Jews. People frequently refer to the Jewish Enlightenment, in both its Western and Eastern European forms, by the Hebrew term *Haskalah*.

Juif   Jew, in French.

Judeo-Spanish   See *Ladino*.

Judenrat   A council made up of prominent members of a Jewish community. Established by the Nazis, the Judenrat was forced to help control the Jewish population in the occupied territories.

Kabbalah   The mystical Jewish tradition.

Kehillah (pl. *kehillot*)   The town council in communities of Eastern European Jews.

Kosher (the laws of kashrut)   Jewish dietary laws.

Ladino   The language spoken by Sephardic Jews. It is primarily a mixture of fifteenth-century Spanish and Hebrew.

Landsmanschaft (pl. *landsmanschaftn*)   Social groups of Eastern European Jewish immigrants who come from the same town or region. In France and in other countries landsmanschftn frequently buy large plots of land in a cemetery so that their members can be buried together.

Lite (pronounced *Leetah*)   The Yiddish term for Jewish Lithuania, an area presently found in the Soviet Republics of Lithuania, Byelorussia, and parts of Latvia and Russia. Those living in the region were called Litvaks, and they spoke their own dialect of Yiddish, had special culinary customs, and studied Talmud in a style that distinguished them from Jews who had settled in other parts of Eastern Europe.

Lycée   French secondary school that prepares a student to go on to the university.

Manitou   French spelling of an Algonquian Indian word, meaning an important person, or leader.

Maquis   A French term meaning scrub or underbrush; it is used metaphorically to refer to underground movements. During World War II, the term identified those fighting the Germans in the French Resistance.

Maskil (pl. *maskilim*)   Hebrew term for a follower of the Jewish Enlightenment.

Megillah   Technically, the word means scroll in Hebrew. As a proper noun, the Megillah refers to the Book of Esther in the Bible.

La Métropole   A term used by people living in the French colonies to refer to the mainland of France.

Midrash (spelled *Midrach* in French)   A method of interpreting the Jewish Bible by explaining the legal aspects of the text with stories or homiletics. The term also refers to some of the earliest rabbinic interpretations of the Holy Scripture.

Mikveh   The Hebrew term for a ritual bath. Observant Jewish women must cleanse themselves in a mikveh one week after they have finished menstruating. Upon doing so, they can resume having sexual relations with their husbands.

Mitnaggedim (Mitnagdim)   Hebrew term for those who opposed the Ḥasidic movement. The followers of the Gaon of Vilna were Mitnaggedim.

Narodniks   Members of the Narodnaya Volya (The People's Will), the Russian populist party responsible for assasinating Czar Alexander II in 1881.

Neo-Kantian   A member of a movement calling for the return to Criticism, the doctrine proposed by the eighteenth-century German philosopher Immanuel Kant to examine the nature and limits of knowledge. The neo-Kantian movement was founded around 1860 and enjoyed considerable influence in the early years of the twentieth century. The German Jewish philosopher Hermann Cohen was a highly regarded member of the movement.

New Philosophers (les nouveaux philosophes)   A term assigned to a number of philosophers in France of the generation of 1968 who caused a great deal of controversy in the 1970s. Their work vigorously challenges the Marxist tradition.

Normalien   A student who attends the Ecole Normale Superieure.

Numerus clausus   A discriminatory law passed in 1887 in czarist Russia to limit the number of Jews allowed to attend schools sponsored by the government.

Occitans   Those who live in the Languedoc, a region in the south of France, and who speak the old Provençal language known as Oc (see map 4). The language belongs to the Romance family. Since the mid-1970s, Occitan activists have joined other minority nationalists in France in demanding their cultural autonomy.

Occupied France   The part of France known as the Occupied Zone (Zone Occupée), where the Germans ran the government during the Second World War. The other part of France was called the Zone Libre or Free Zone (see *Zone Libre* below and see maps).

Orientalists   When used in this book, the term refers to those who study the culture of Middle Eastern Jews.

Pale of Settlement   Those provinces in the western part of czarist Russia where Jews were allowed to live.

Pentateuch   The Greek term for the Five Books of Moses.

Phenomenology   A philosophical movement founded by the German thinker Edmund Husserl in the early years of the twentieth century. Phenomenology offers a way to analyze the form and content of experience and the relationship that exists between subjects and objects. Husserl's call for a return to the "things themselves" had a profound influence on Martin Heidegger, Emmanuel Lévinas, and Jean-Paul Sartre.

Po'alei Zion   Workers of Zion. A socialist Zionist party founded in czarist Russia at the turn of the century. The first group to use the name organized themselves in Minsk (Byelorussia) in 1897.

PLO   The Palestine Liberation Organization. The initials in French are OLP.

Rav   Hebrew word for teacher or rabbi.

Reb   The same as *rav.* In Yiddish *reb* was also used as a term of address meaning mister.

Sephardic Jew (pl. noun *Sephardim*)   A Jew whose ancestors lived in Spain and Portugal before the Inquisition in the late fifteenth century. Expelled from the Iberian Peninsula, some moved north into parts of Western Europe; others went east into the Levant. Most of the Jews who moved to France from North Africa and the Middle East in the 1950s and 1960s are of Sephardic origin.

Shalom   Hebrew word meaning peace. *Shalom* is also a term of greeting.

Shoah   Hebrew word meaning annihilation. This term is preferred by many to the word Holocaust for describing the fate of European Jews during the Second World War.

Shtetl   Yiddish word meaning little town, used to identify small Jewish communities in Eastern Europe.

Shtibl   A Yiddish word meaning a little house. It is used to refer to a small house of prayer.

Shtrayml   A Yiddish term for the fur-trimmed hat worn by Ḥasidic Jewish men.

Shul   A Yiddish term meaning synagogue or school.

Talmud   Hebrew word for the collection of writings that makes up the Jewish religious and civil law (see *Gemara*). The Talmud also contains legends and folklore (see *Aggadah*). There is a Jerusalem and a Babylonian Talmud. Both were written in the early centuries of the common era.

Tanaḥ   Hebrew acronym for the various parts of the Old Testament (Torah, Prophets, Haggiographa).

Teffilin (also spelled *tephillin*)   Hebrew word for the phylacteries worn by observant Jewish men in prayer.

Teshuvah   Hebrew term for the act of making a return to Judaism. One who makes a return is called a *baal teshuvah*.

Torah   The name given to the Five Books of Moses. Torah means law in Hebrew.

UEC   Union des Etudiants Communistes.

L'UGIF   L' Union Générale des Israélites de France. The French equivalent of the Judenrat established by Vicy during the Second World War to control Jews in both the occupied and free zones.

UJC(ml)   Union des Jeunesses Communistes (marxistes-léninistes). A group of Communist students founded in 1966 by Robert Linhart. It broke away from the Stalinist UEC in solidarity with Mao's Cultural Revolution.

Ukaz   Czarist decree.

Voyou   A French word for hoodlum or thief.

Wirklichkeit   German word meaning reality. Oskar Goldberg's book, *Die Wirklichkeit der Hebräer,* means the reality of the Hebrews.

Yarmulke   Yiddish term for the skullcap worn by Jewish males.

Yeshiva (spelled *Yéchiva* in French)   The Hebrew term for a Jewish religious school of higher learning.

YHWH   The Tetragrammaton, or the four Hebrew consonants that create God's name.

Yiddish   The language spoken by Eastern European Jews. Yiddish is based on middle high German with lexical, morphological, semantic, and syntactic elements from Hebrew, Aramaic, old French, old Italian, and Slavic tongues.

Yiddishkayt   A Yiddish term used originally to refer to Judaism and to the traditions observed by a practicing Jew. Today, secular Yiddishists have taken over the term to identify what they call Jewishness, or the folk culture of Jews. For them, Yiddishkayt does not necessarily have anything to do with the Jewish religion.

Yiddishists   Those who promote secular Yiddish culture.

YIVO   The Yiddish acronym stands today for the Institute for Jewish Research, located in New York City. Originally founded in Vilna in 1925, the acronym used to stand for the Jewish Scientific Institute.

Zone Libre (Free Zone)   The part of France during World War II that was controlled by Vichy, the French puppet government that agreed to collaborate with the Germans (see map 5).

Index